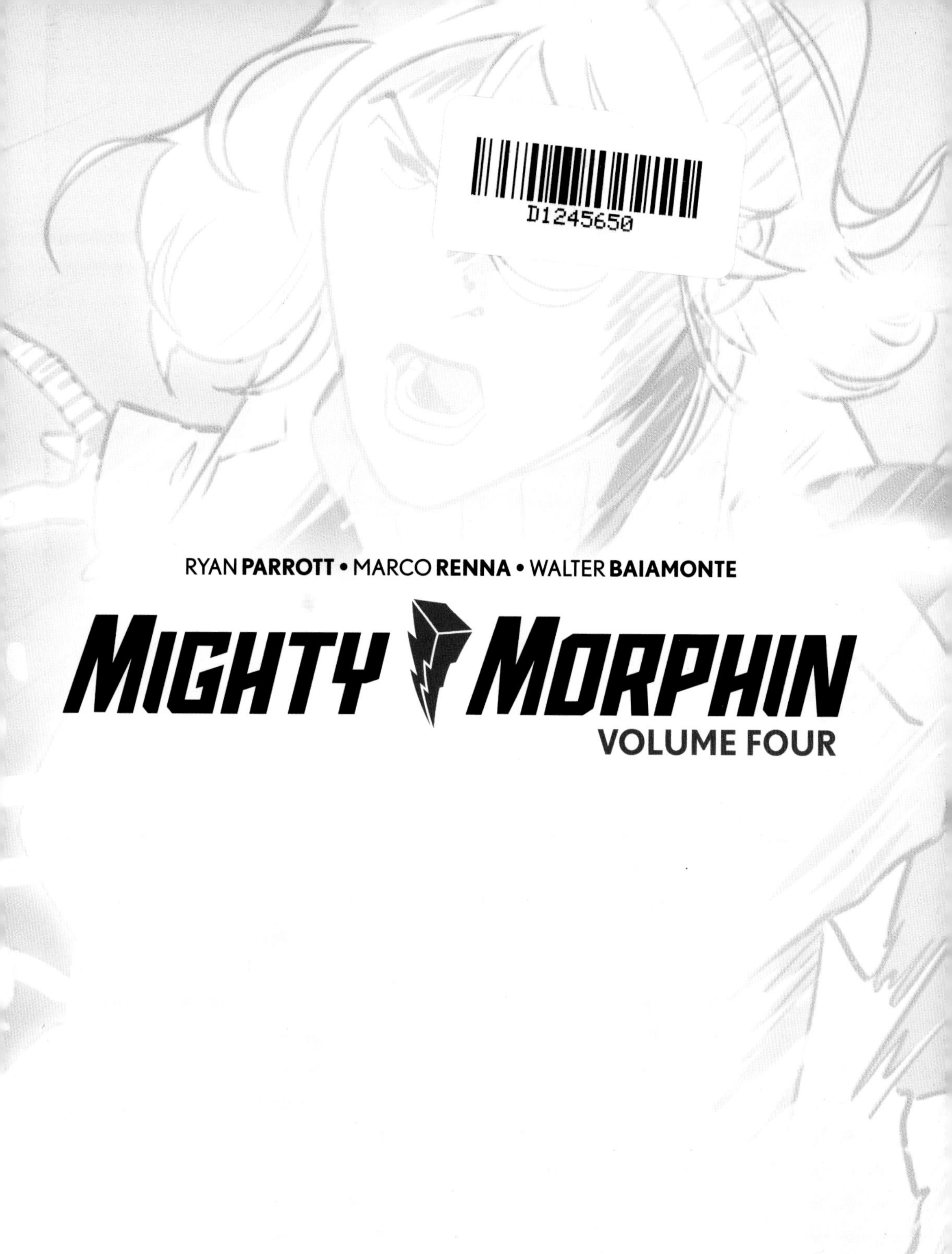

RYAN **PARROTT** • MARCO **RENNA** • WALTER **BAIAMONTE**

MIGHTY MORPHIN
VOLUME FOUR

Published by
BOOM! STUDIOS

SERIES DESIGNER
MICHELLE ANKLEY

COLLECTION DESIGNER
VERONICA GUTIERREZ

ASSISTANT EDITOR
GWEN WALLER

EDITOR
DAFNA PLEBAN

HASBRO SPECIAL THANKS
ED LANE, **TAYLA REO** ,
AND **MICHAEL KELLY**

Ross Richie Chairman & Founder
Jen Harned CFO
Matt Gagnon Editor-in-Chief
Filip Sablik President, Publishing & Marketing
Stephen Christy President, Development
Lance Kreiter Vice President, Licensing & Merchandising
Bryce Carlson Vice President, Editorial & Creative Strategy
Hunter Gorinson Vice President, Business Development
Josh Hayes Vice President, Sales
Ryan Matsunaga Director, Marketing
Stephanie Lazarski Director, Operations
Elyse Strandberg Manager, Finance
Michelle Ankley Manager, Production Design
Cheryl Parker Manager, Human Resources
Sierra Hahn Executive Editor
Eric Harburn Executive Editor
Dafna Pleban Senior Editor
Elizabeth Brei Editor
Kathleen Wisneski Editor
Sophie Philips-Roberts Editor
Allyson Gronowitz Associate Editor
Gavin Gronenthal Assistant Editor
Gwen Waller Assistant Editor
Ramiro Portnoy Assistant Editor
Kenzie Rzonca Assistant Editor
Rey Netschke Editorial Assistant
Marie Krupina Design Lead
Crystal White Design Lead
Grace Park Design Coordinator
Madison Goyette Production Designer
Veronica Gutierrez Production Designer
Jessy Gould Production Designer
Nancy Mojica Production Designer
Samantha Knapp Production Design Assistant
Esther Kim Marketing Lead
Breanna Sarpy Marketing Lead, Digital
Amanda Lawson Marketing Coordinator
Alex Lorenzen Marketing Coordinator, Copywriter
Grecia Martinez Marketing Assistant, Digital
José Meza Consumer Sales Lead
Ashley Troub Consumer Sales Coordinator
Morgan Perry Retail Sales Lead
Harley Salbacka Sales Coordinator
Megan Christopher Operations Lead
Rodrigo Hernandez Operations Coordinator
Jason Lee Senior Accountant
Sabrina Lesin Accounting Assistant

Licensed by:

WRITTEN BY
RYAN PARROTT

ILLUSTRATED BY
MARCO RENNA

COLORS BY
WALTER BAIAMONTE
WITH ASSISTANCE BY **KATIA RANALLI & SARA ANTONELLINI
& SHARON MARINO** (CHAPTERS 15-16)

LETTERS BY
ED DUKESHIRE

EMPYREALS, MECH SUIT ZORDON & ELTARIAN
CHARACTER DESIGNS BY
DAN MORA

COVER BY
INHYUK LEE

CHAPTER THIRTEEN

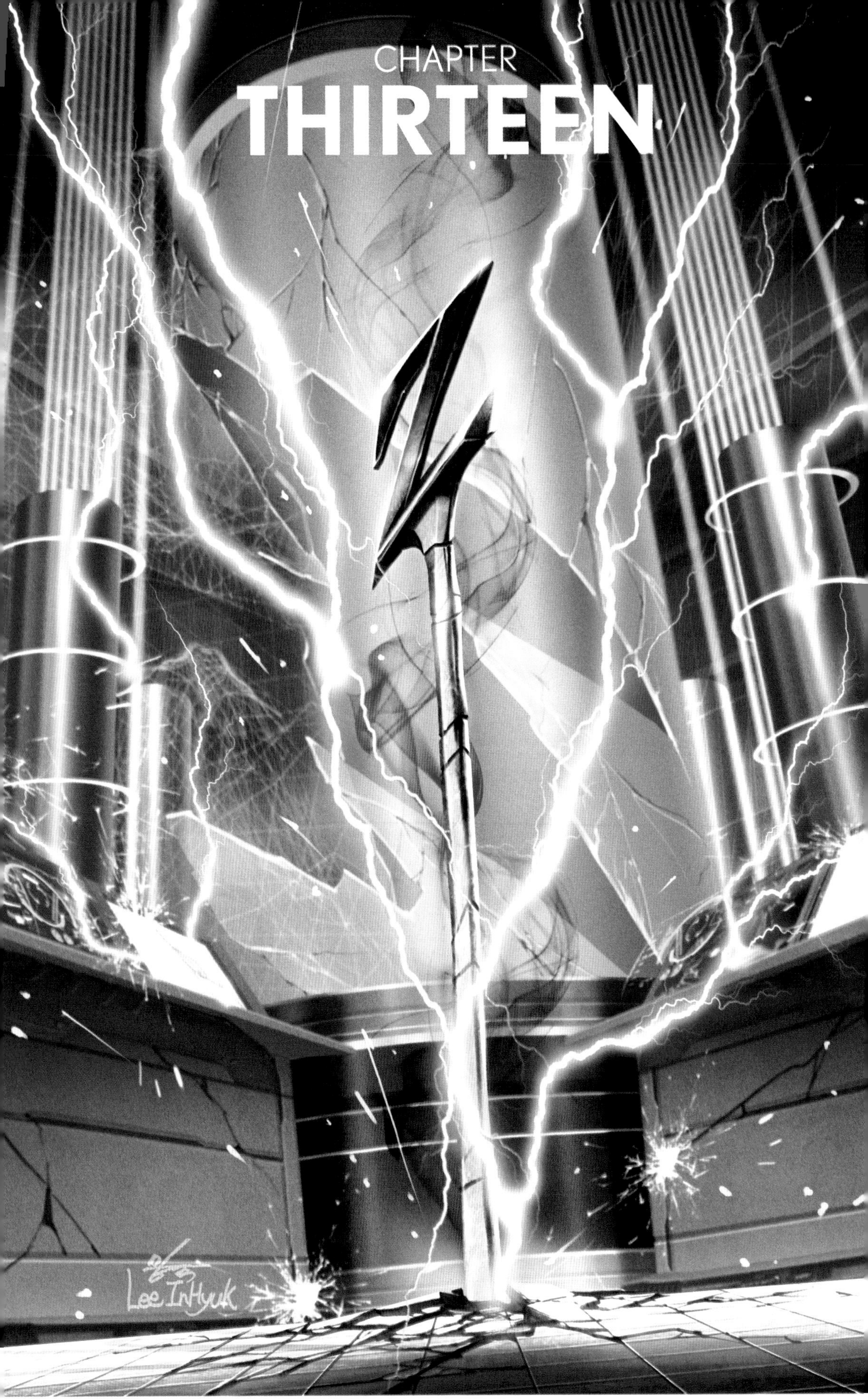
Lee InHyuk

INHYUK LEE ISSUE THIRTEEN COVER

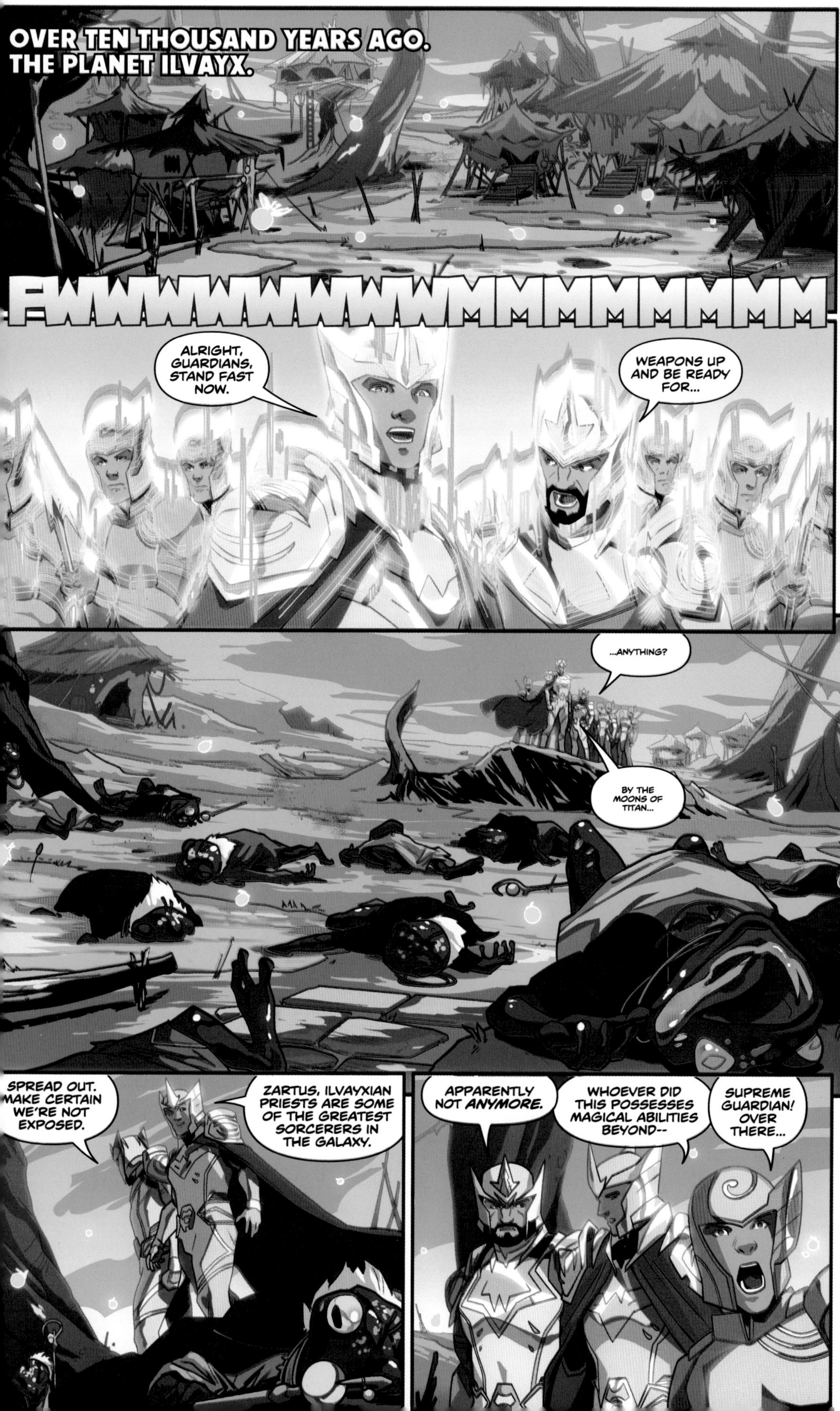
OVER TEN THOUSAND YEARS AGO.
THE PLANET ILVAYX.
FWWWWWWWWMMMMMMMMMMM
ALRIGHT, GUARDIANS, STAND FAST NOW.
WEAPONS UP AND BE READY FOR...
...ANYTHING?
BY THE MOONS OF TITAN...
SPREAD OUT. MAKE CERTAIN WE'RE NOT EXPOSED.
ZARTUS, ILVAYXIAN PRIESTS ARE SOME OF THE GREATEST SORCERERS IN THE GALAXY.
APPARENTLY NOT *ANYMORE.*
WHOEVER DID THIS POSSESSES MAGICAL ABILITIES BEYOND--
SUPREME GUARDIAN! OVER THERE...

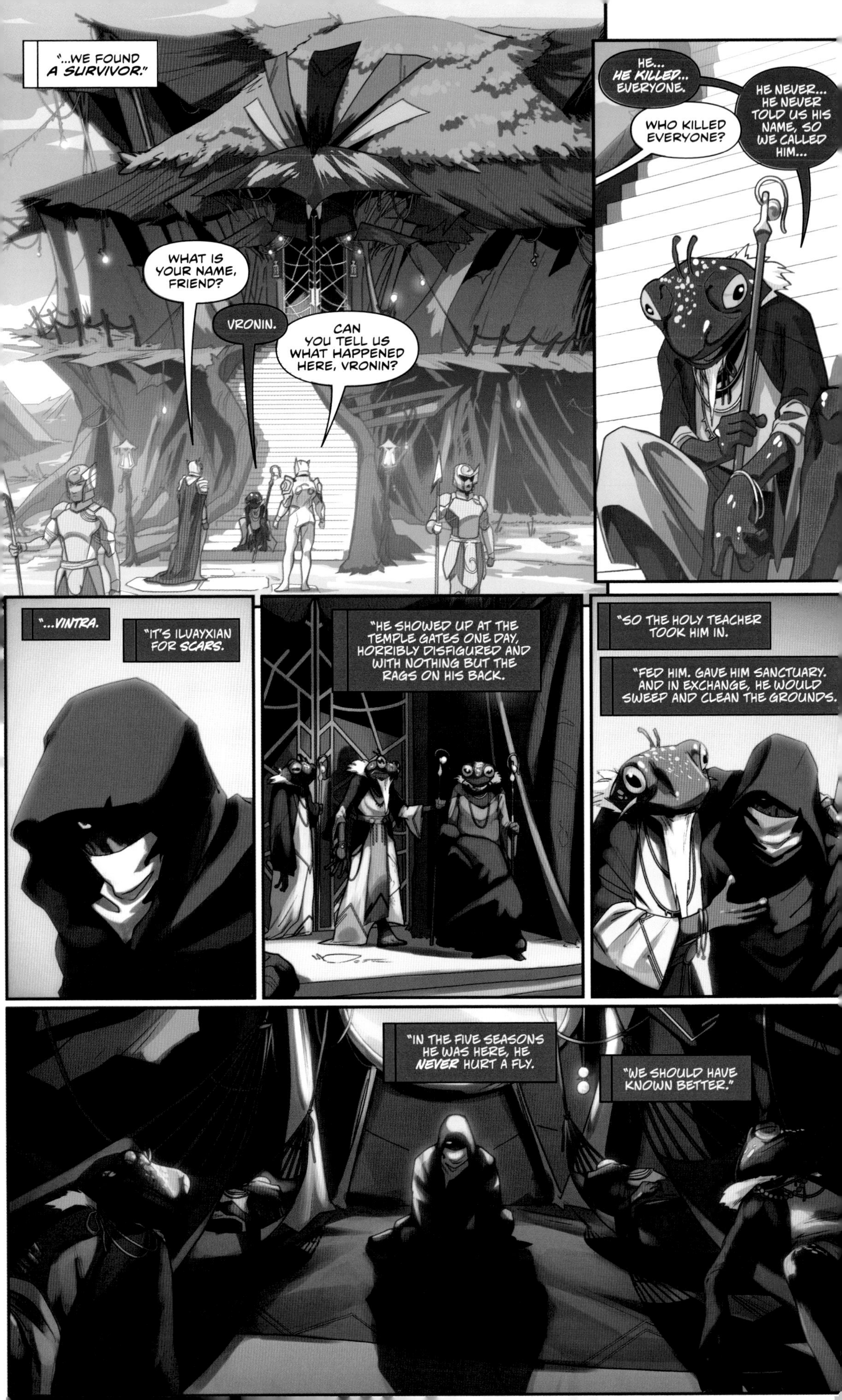
"...WE FOUND A SURVIVOR."
WHAT IS YOUR NAME, FRIEND?
VRONIN.
CAN YOU TELL US WHAT HAPPENED HERE, VRONIN?
HE... HE KILLED... EVERYONE.
WHO KILLED EVERYONE?
HE NEVER... HE NEVER TOLD US HIS NAME, SO WE CALLED HIM...
"...VINTRA.
"IT'S ILUAYXIAN FOR SCARS.
"HE SHOWED UP AT THE TEMPLE GATES ONE DAY, HORRIBLY DISFIGURED AND WITH NOTHING BUT THE RAGS ON HIS BACK.
"SO THE HOLY TEACHER TOOK HIM IN.
"FED HIM. GAVE HIM SANCTUARY. AND IN EXCHANGE, HE WOULD SWEEP AND CLEAN THE GROUNDS.
"IN THE FIVE SEASONS HE WAS HERE, HE NEVER HURT A FLY.
"WE SHOULD HAVE KNOWN BETTER."

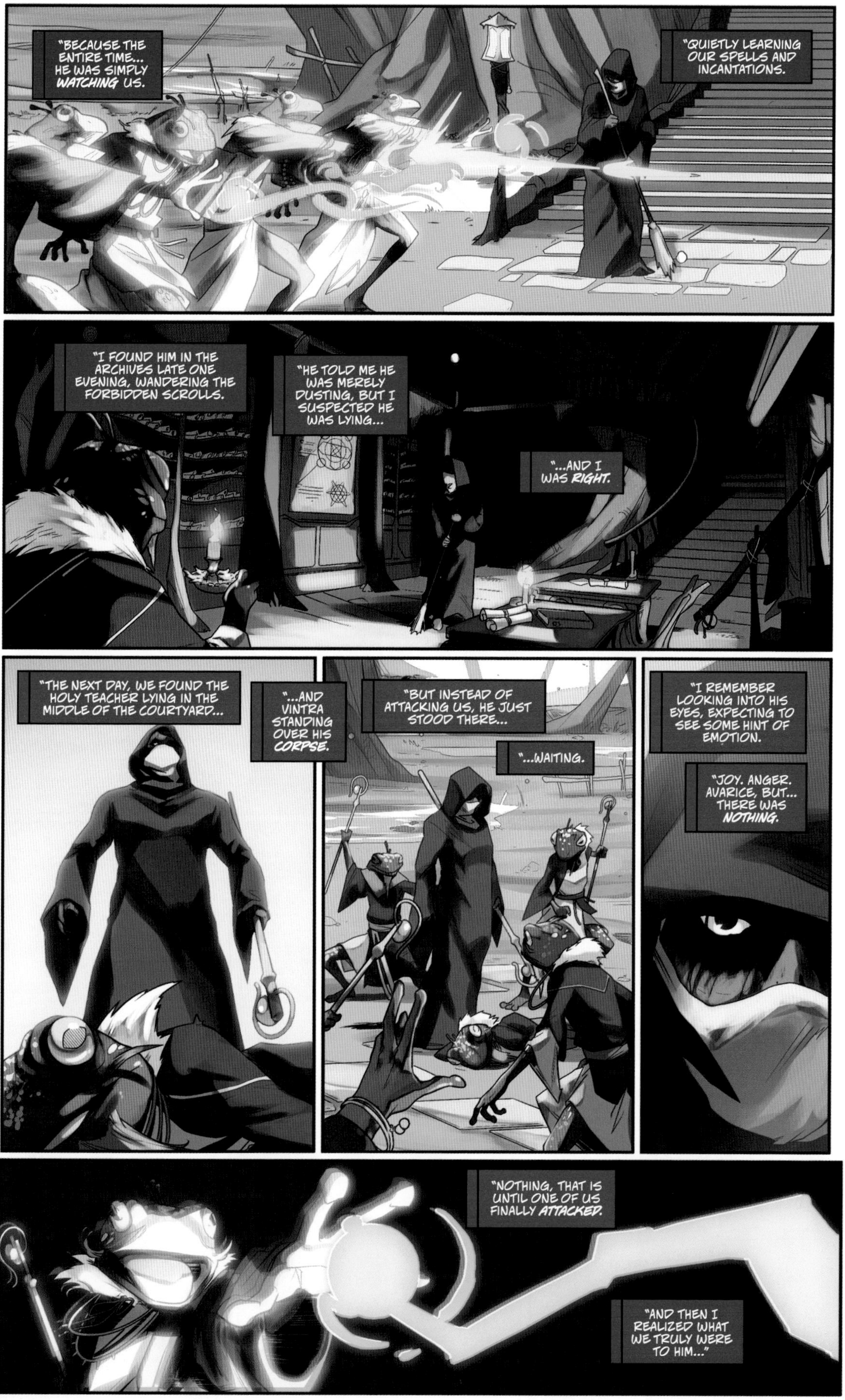
"BECAUSE THE ENTIRE TIME... HE WAS SIMPLY *WATCHING* US.
"QUIETLY LEARNING OUR SPELLS AND INCANTATIONS.
"I FOUND HIM IN THE ARCHIVES LATE ONE EVENING, WANDERING THE FORBIDDEN SCROLLS.
"HE TOLD ME HE WAS MERELY DUSTING, BUT I SUSPECTED HE WAS LYING...
"...AND I WAS *RIGHT*.
"THE NEXT DAY, WE FOUND THE HOLY TEACHER LYING IN THE MIDDLE OF THE COURTYARD...
"...AND VINTRA STANDING OVER HIS *CORPSE*.
"BUT INSTEAD OF ATTACKING US, HE JUST STOOD THERE...
"...WAITING.
"I REMEMBER LOOKING INTO HIS EYES, EXPECTING TO SEE SOME HINT OF EMOTION.
"JOY. ANGER. AVARICE, BUT... THERE WAS *NOTHING*.
"NOTHING, THAT IS UNTIL ONE OF US FINALLY *ATTACKED*.
"AND THEN I REALIZED WHAT WE TRULY WERE TO HIM..."

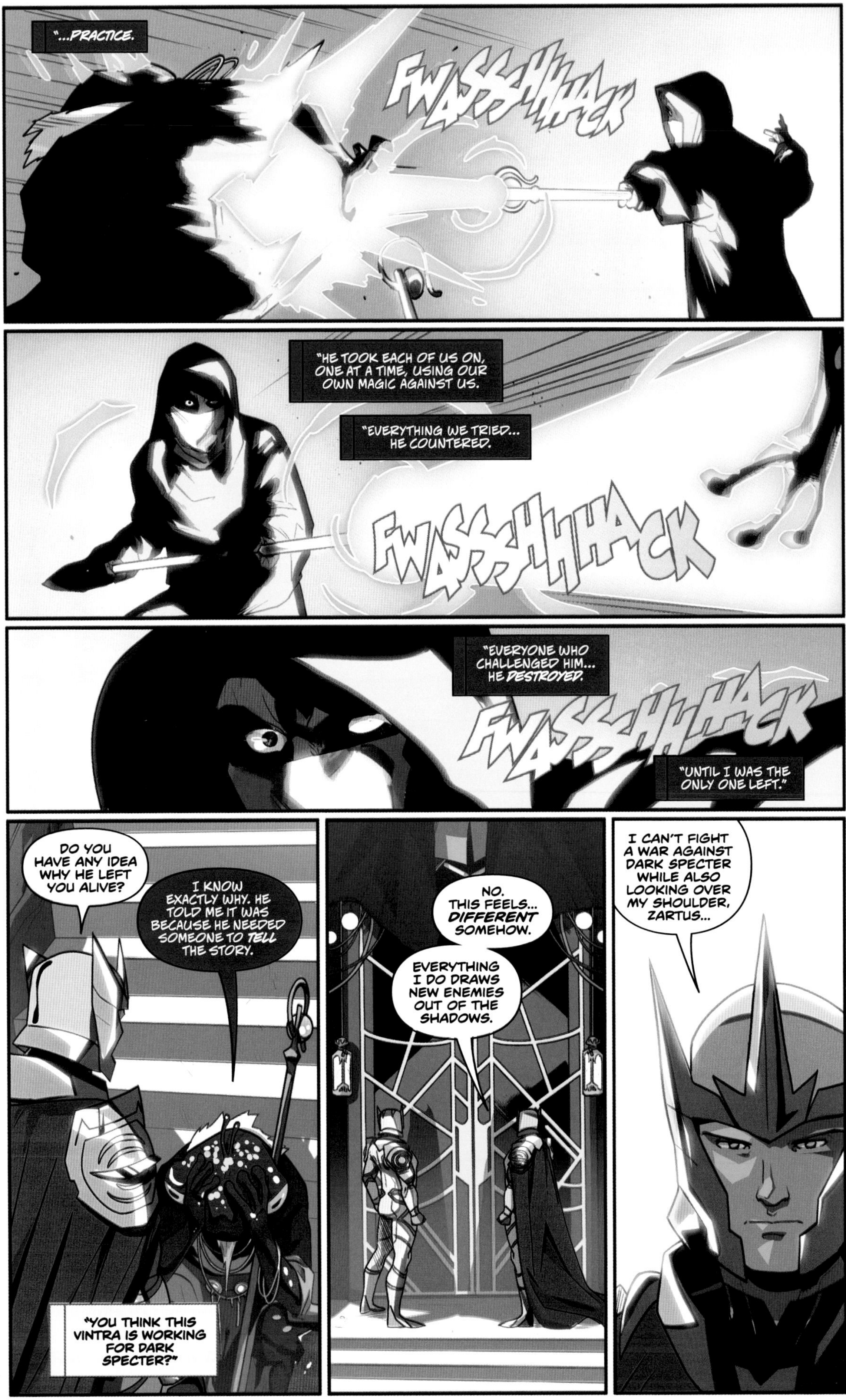
"...PRACTICE.
FWASSHHHACK
"HE TOOK EACH OF US ON, ONE AT A TIME, USING OUR OWN MAGIC AGAINST US.
"EVERYTHING WE TRIED... HE COUNTERED.
FWASSHHHACK
"EVERYONE WHO CHALLENGED HIM... HE DESTROYED.
FWASSHHHACK
"UNTIL I WAS THE ONLY ONE LEFT."
DO YOU HAVE ANY IDEA WHY HE LEFT YOU ALIVE?
I KNOW EXACTLY WHY. HE TOLD ME IT WAS BECAUSE HE NEEDED SOMEONE TO TELL THE STORY.
"YOU THINK THIS VINTRA IS WORKING FOR DARK SPECTER?"
NO. THIS FEELS... DIFFERENT SOMEHOW.
EVERYTHING I DO DRAWS NEW ENEMIES OUT OF THE SHADOWS.
I CAN'T FIGHT A WAR AGAINST DARK SPECTER WHILE ALSO LOOKING OVER MY SHOULDER, ZARTUS...

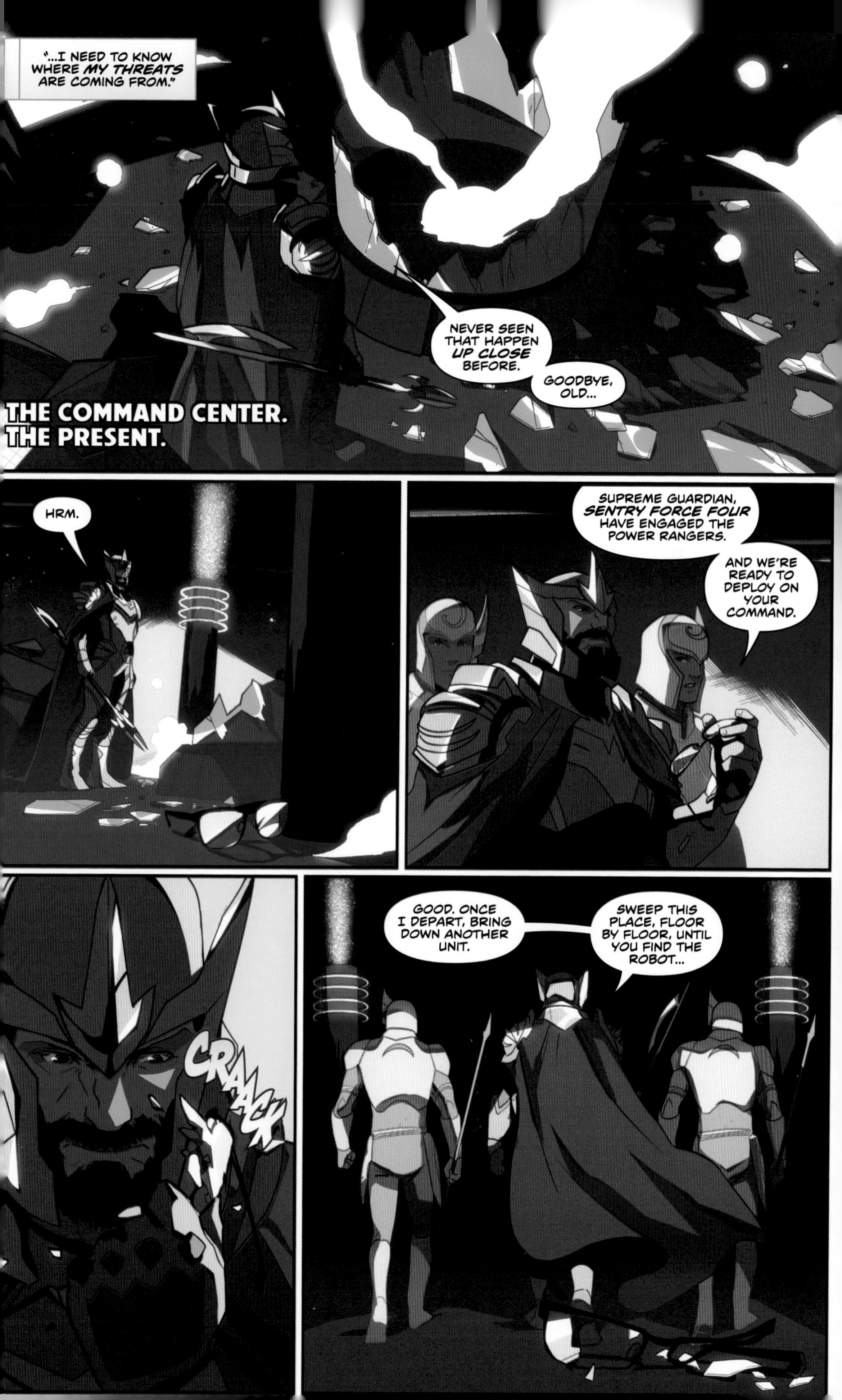
"...I NEED TO KNOW WHERE MY THREATS ARE COMING FROM."
NEVER SEEN THAT HAPPEN UP CLOSE BEFORE.
GOODBYE, OLD...
THE COMMAND CENTER. THE PRESENT.
HRM.
SUPREME GUARDIAN, SENTRY FORCE FOUR HAVE ENGAGED THE POWER RANGERS.
AND WE'RE READY TO DEPLOY ON YOUR COMMAND.
CRAACK
GOOD. ONCE I DEPART, BRING DOWN ANOTHER UNIT.
SWEEP THIS PLACE, FLOOR BY FLOOR, UNTIL YOU FIND THE ROBOT...

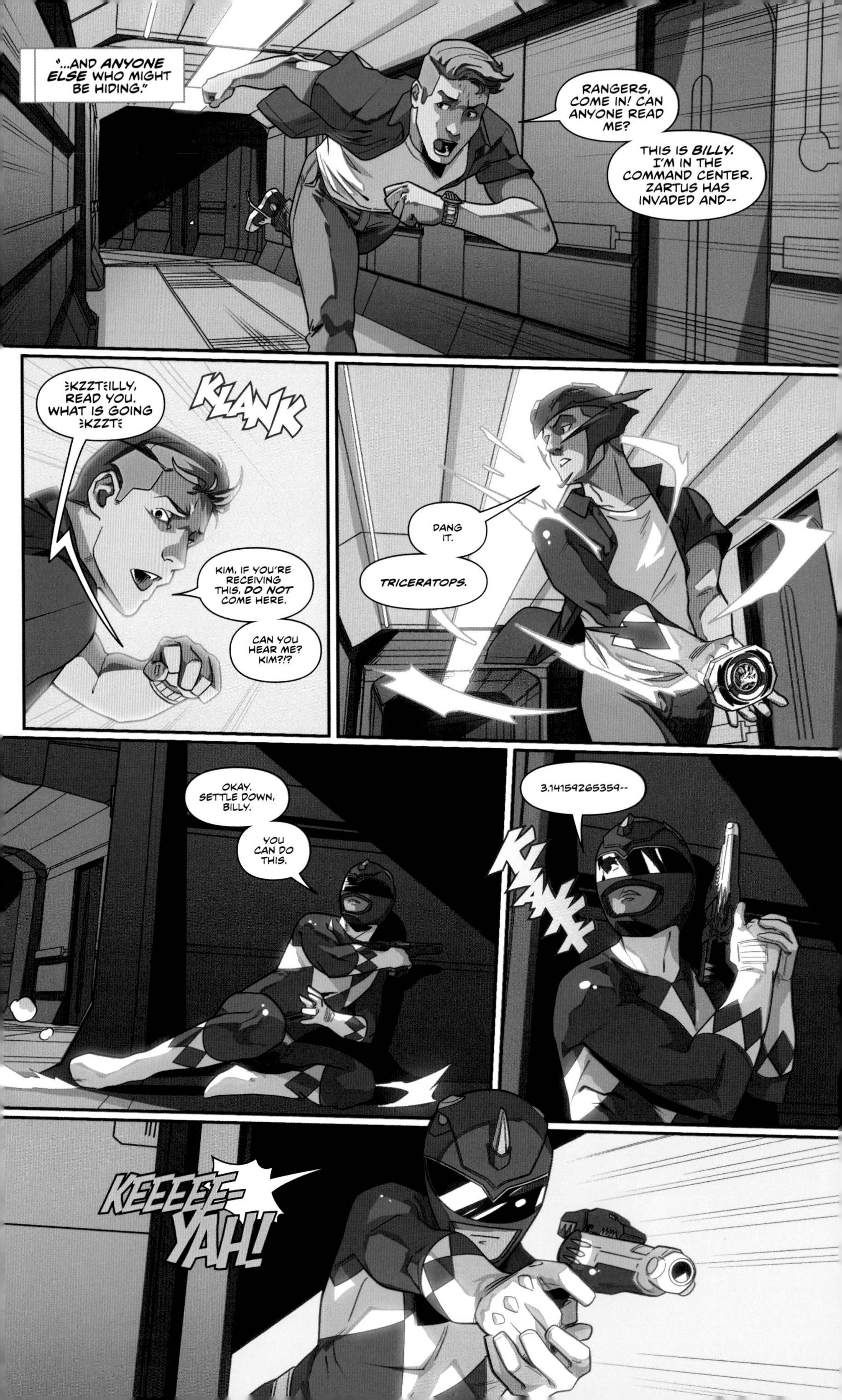
"...AND ANYONE ELSE WHO MIGHT BE HIDING."
RANGERS, COME IN! CAN ANYONE READ ME?
THIS IS BILLY. I'M IN THE COMMAND CENTER. ZARTUS HAS INVADED AND--
KZZT ILLY, READ YOU. WHAT IS GOING KZZT
KLANK
KIM, IF YOU'RE RECEIVING THIS, DO NOT COME HERE.
CAN YOU HEAR ME? KIM?!?
DANG IT.
TRICERATOPS.
OKAY. SETTLE DOWN, BILLY.
YOU CAN DO THIS.
3.14159265359--
KLANK
KEEEEEE-YAH!

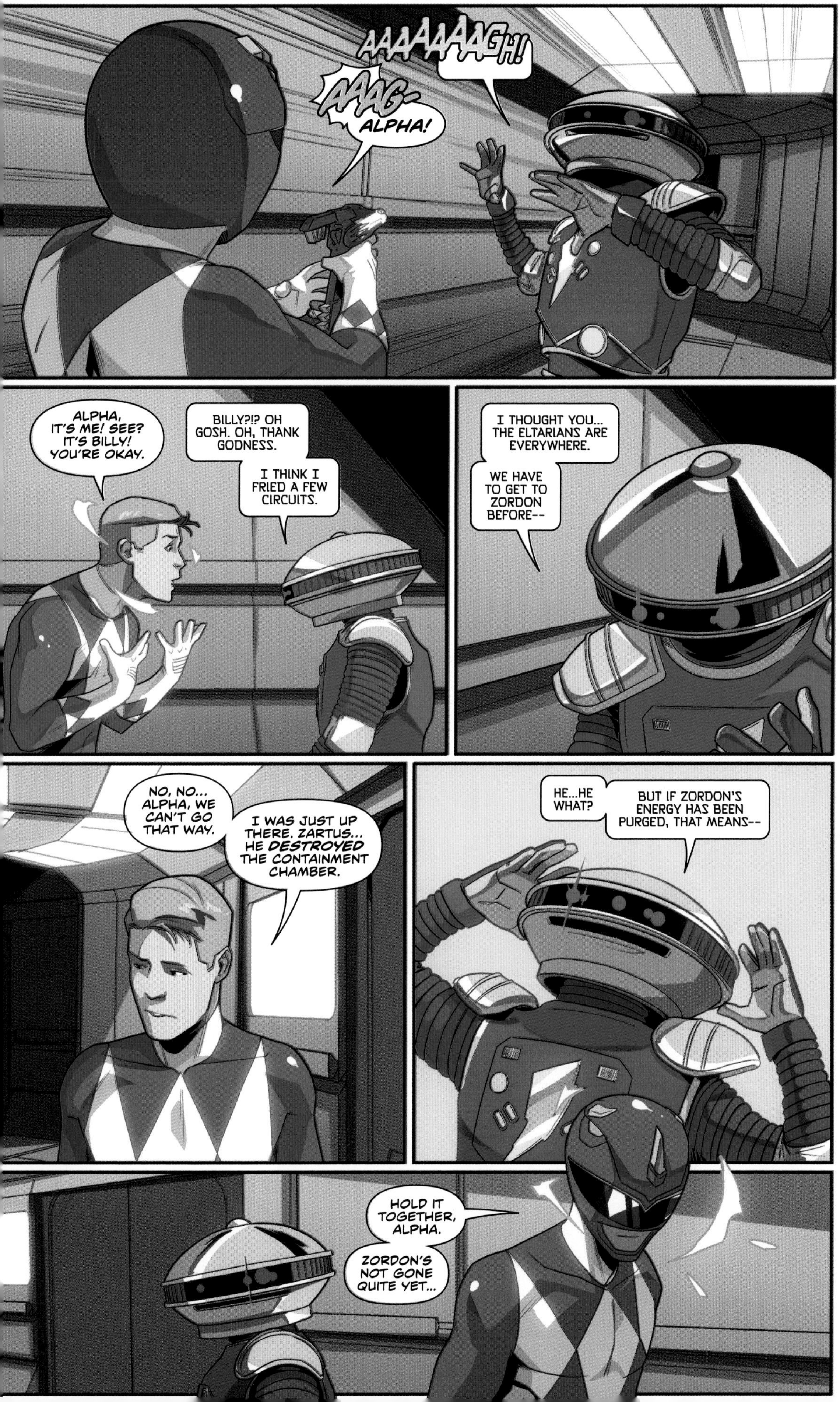
AAAAAAAGH!
AAAG-
ALPHA!
ALPHA, IT'S ME! SEE? IT'S BILLY! YOU'RE OKAY.
BILLY?!? OH GOSH. OH, THANK GODNESS.
I THINK I FRIED A FEW CIRCUITS.
I THOUGHT YOU... THE ELTARIANS ARE EVERYWHERE.
WE HAVE TO GET TO ZORDON BEFORE--
NO, NO... ALPHA, WE CAN'T GO THAT WAY.
I WAS JUST UP THERE. ZARTUS... HE DESTROYED THE CONTAINMENT CHAMBER.
HE...HE WHAT?
BUT IF ZORDON'S ENERGY HAS BEEN PURGED, THAT MEANS--
HOLD IT TOGETHER, ALPHA.
ZORDON'S NOT GONE QUITE YET...

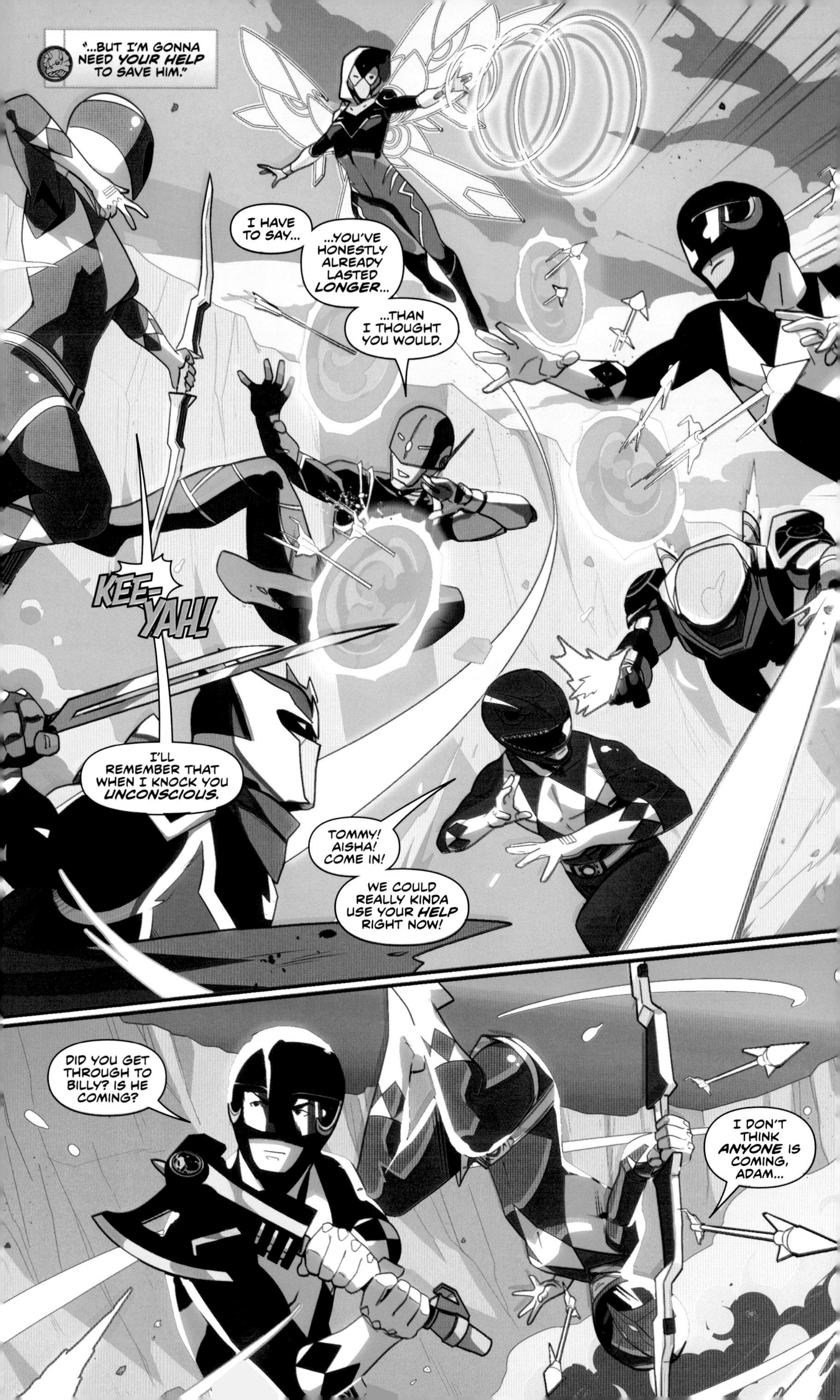
"...BUT I'M GONNA NEED YOUR HELP TO SAVE HIM."
I HAVE TO SAY...
...YOU'VE HONESTLY ALREADY LASTED LONGER...
...THAN I THOUGHT YOU WOULD.
KEE-YAH!
I'LL REMEMBER THAT WHEN I KNOCK YOU UNCONSCIOUS.
TOMMY! AISHA! COME IN!
WE COULD REALLY KINDA USE YOUR HELP RIGHT NOW!
DID YOU GET THROUGH TO BILLY? IS HE COMING?
I DON'T THINK ANYONE IS COMING, ADAM...

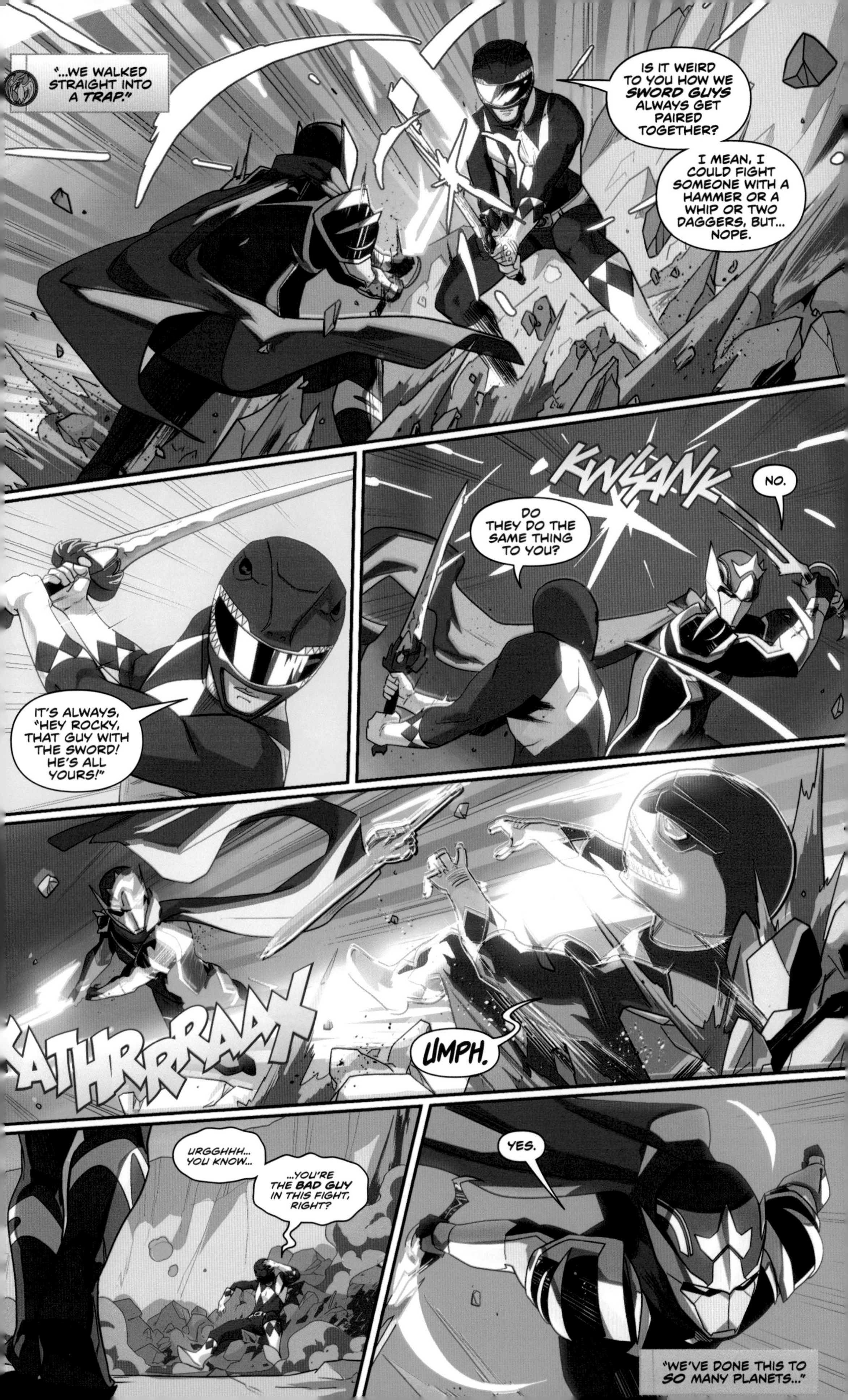
"...WE WALKED STRAIGHT INTO A *TRAP*."
IS IT WEIRD TO YOU HOW WE **SWORD GUYS** ALWAYS GET PAIRED TOGETHER?
I MEAN, I COULD FIGHT SOMEONE WITH A HAMMER OR A WHIP OR TWO DAGGERS, BUT... NOPE.
IT'S ALWAYS, "HEY ROCKY, THAT GUY WITH THE SWORD! HE'S ALL YOURS!"
KWLANK
DO THEY DO THE SAME THING TO YOU?
NO.
SATHRRRAAK
UMPH.
URGGHHH... YOU KNOW...
...YOU'RE THE **BAD GUY** IN THIS FIGHT, RIGHT?
YES.
"WE'VE DONE THIS TO SO MANY PLANETS..."

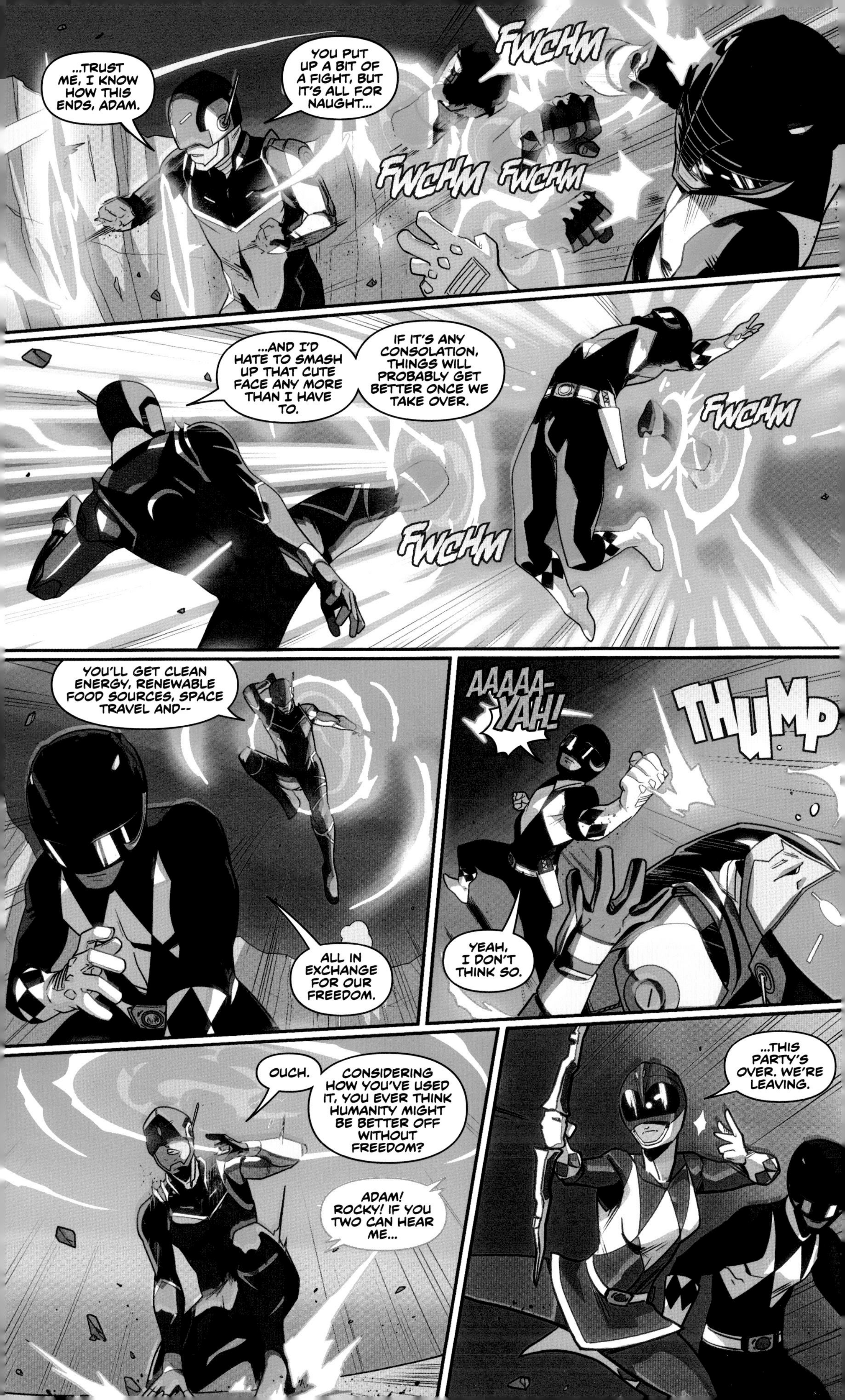

...TRUST ME, I KNOW HOW THIS ENDS, ADAM.
YOU PUT UP A BIT OF A FIGHT, BUT IT'S ALL FOR NAUGHT...
FWCHM
FWCHM FWCHM
...AND I'D HATE TO SMASH UP THAT CUTE FACE ANY MORE THAN I HAVE TO.
IF IT'S ANY CONSOLATION, THINGS WILL PROBABLY GET BETTER ONCE WE TAKE OVER.
FWCHM
FWCHM
YOU'LL GET CLEAN ENERGY, RENEWABLE FOOD SOURCES, SPACE TRAVEL AND--
ALL IN EXCHANGE FOR OUR FREEDOM.
AAAAA-YAH!
THUMP
YEAH, I DON'T THINK SO.
OUCH.
CONSIDERING HOW YOU'VE USED IT, YOU EVER THINK HUMANITY MIGHT BE BETTER OFF WITHOUT FREEDOM?
ADAM! ROCKY! IF YOU TWO CAN HEAR ME...
...THIS PARTY'S OVER. WE'RE LEAVING.

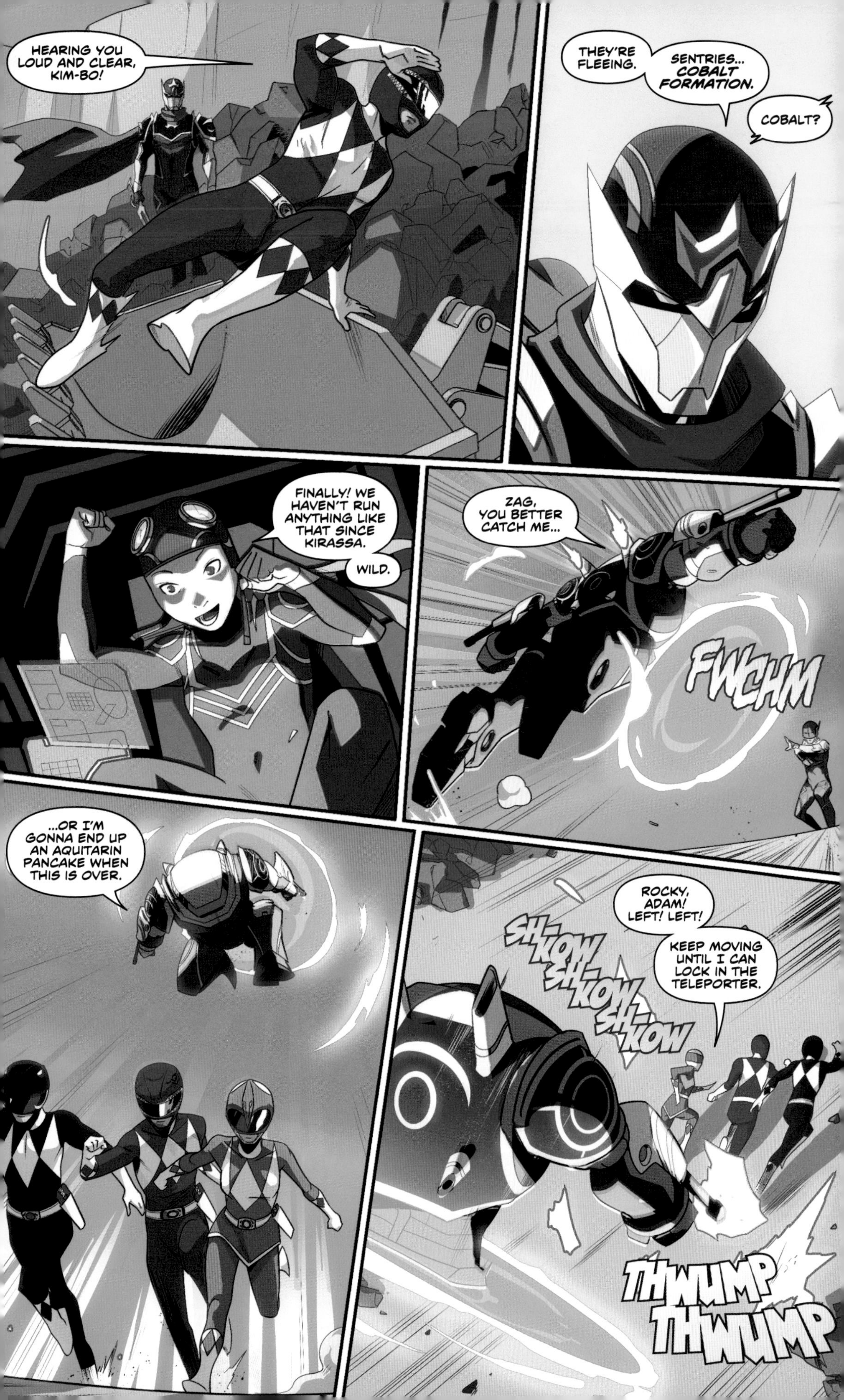

HEARING YOU LOUD AND CLEAR, KIM-BO!
THEY'RE FLEEING.
SENTRIES... COBALT FORMATION.
COBALT?
FINALLY! WE HAVEN'T RUN ANYTHING LIKE THAT SINCE KIRASSA.
WILD.
ZAG, YOU BETTER CATCH ME...
FWCHM
...OR I'M GONNA END UP AN AQUITARIN PANCAKE WHEN THIS IS OVER.
ROCKY, ADAM! LEFT! LEFT!
KEEP MOVING UNTIL I CAN LOCK IN THE TELEPORTER.
SH-KOW SH-KOW SH-KOW
THWUMP THWUMP

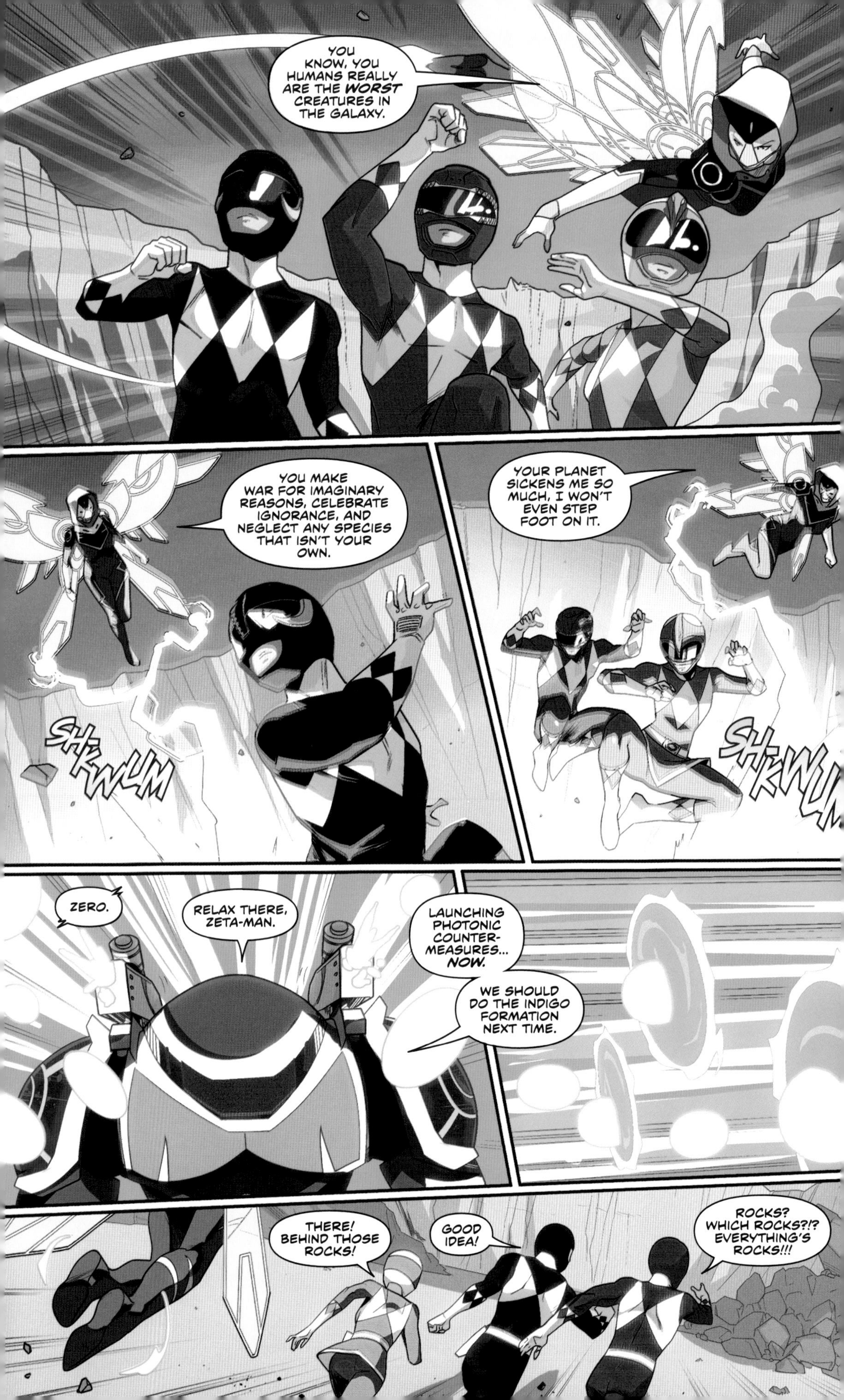

YOU KNOW, YOU HUMANS REALLY ARE THE **WORST** CREATURES IN THE GALAXY.
YOU MAKE WAR FOR IMAGINARY REASONS, CELEBRATE IGNORANCE, AND NEGLECT ANY SPECIES THAT ISN'T YOUR OWN.
SHKWUM
YOUR PLANET SICKENS ME SO MUCH, I WON'T EVEN STEP FOOT ON IT.
SHKWUM
ZERO.
RELAX THERE, ZETA-MAN.
LAUNCHING PHOTONIC COUNTER-MEASURES... **NOW.**
WE SHOULD DO THE INDIGO FORMATION NEXT TIME.
THERE! BEHIND THOSE ROCKS!
GOOD IDEA!
ROCKS? WHICH ROCKS?!? EVERYTHING'S ROCKS!!!

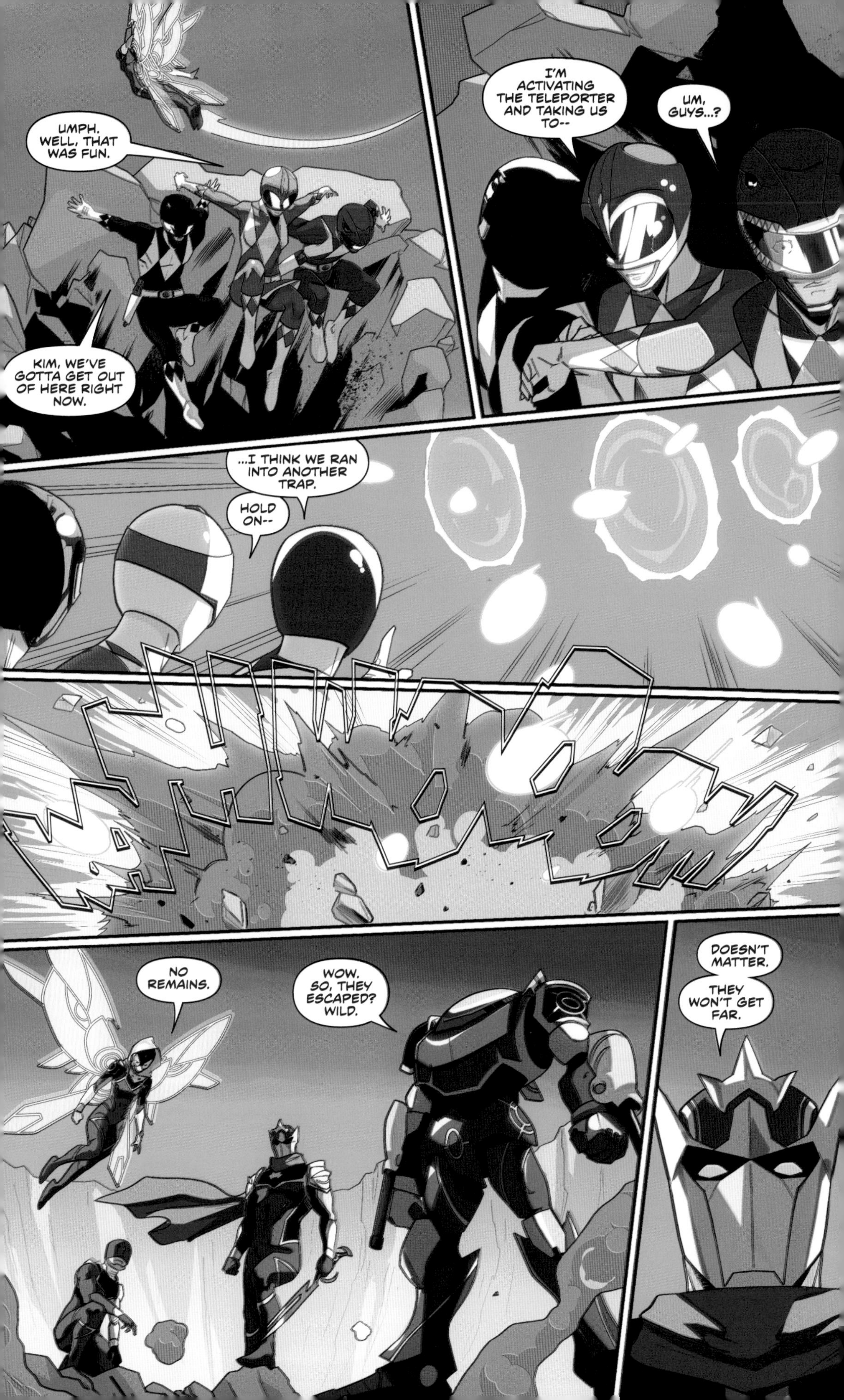
UMPH. WELL, THAT WAS FUN.
KIM, WE'VE GOTTA GET OUT OF HERE RIGHT NOW.
I'M ACTIVATING THE TELEPORTER AND TAKING US TO--
UM, GUYS...?
...I THINK WE RAN INTO ANOTHER TRAP.
HOLD ON--
NO REMAINS.
WOW. SO, THEY ESCAPED? WILD.
DOESN'T MATTER.
THEY WON'T GET FAR.

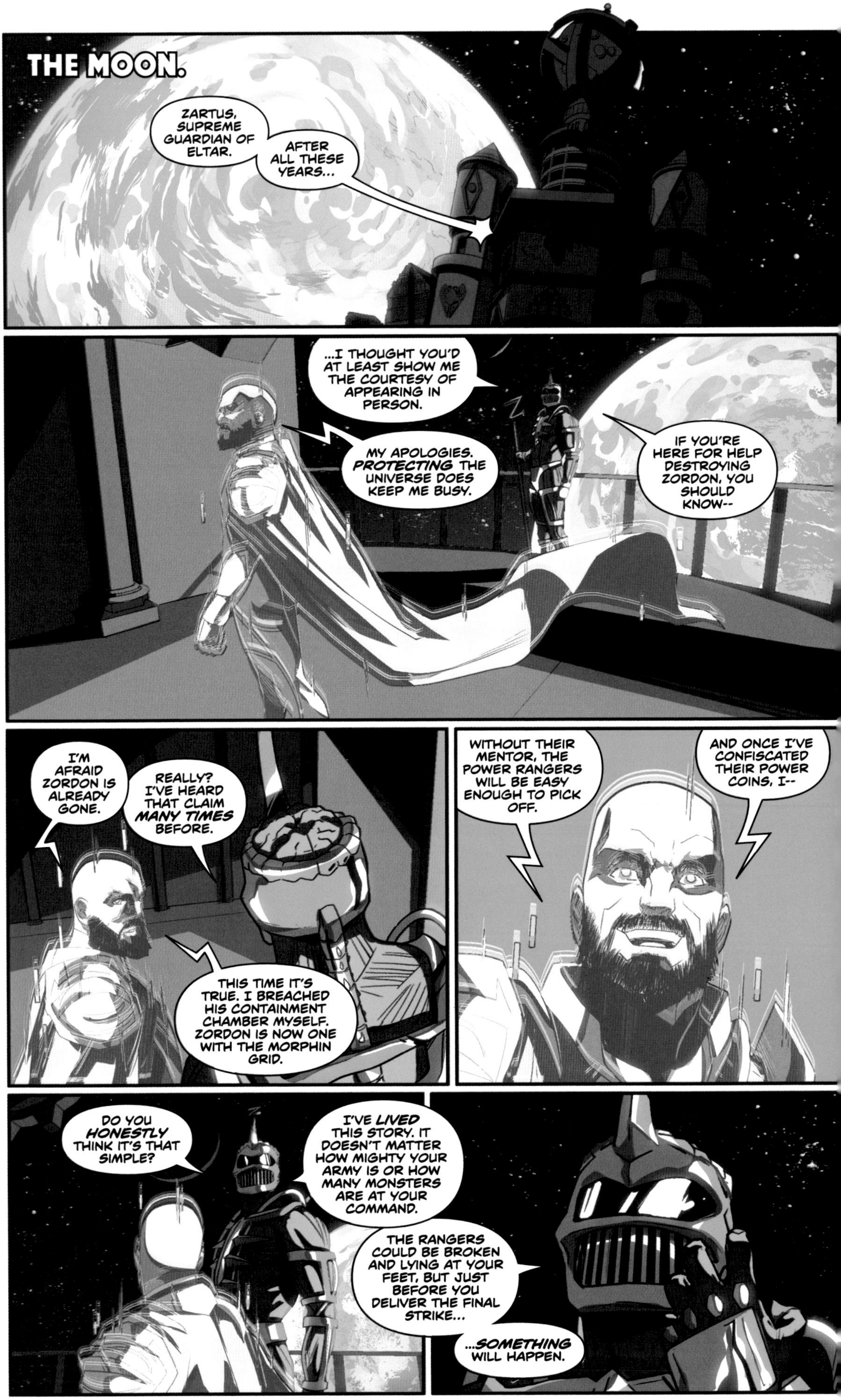
THE MOON.
ZARTUS, SUPREME GUARDIAN OF ELTAR.
AFTER ALL THESE YEARS...
...I THOUGHT YOU'D AT LEAST SHOW ME THE COURTESY OF APPEARING IN PERSON.
MY APOLOGIES. PROTECTING THE UNIVERSE DOES KEEP ME BUSY.
IF YOU'RE HERE FOR HELP DESTROYING ZORDON, YOU SHOULD KNOW--
I'M AFRAID ZORDON IS ALREADY GONE.
REALLY? I'VE HEARD THAT CLAIM MANY TIMES BEFORE.
THIS TIME IT'S TRUE. I BREACHED HIS CONTAINMENT CHAMBER MYSELF. ZORDON IS NOW ONE WITH THE MORPHIN GRID.
WITHOUT THEIR MENTOR, THE POWER RANGERS WILL BE EASY ENOUGH TO PICK OFF.
AND ONCE I'VE CONFISCATED THEIR POWER COINS, I--
DO YOU HONESTLY THINK IT'S THAT SIMPLE?
I'VE LIVED THIS STORY. IT DOESN'T MATTER HOW MIGHTY YOUR ARMY IS OR HOW MANY MONSTERS ARE AT YOUR COMMAND.
THE RANGERS COULD BE BROKEN AND LYING AT YOUR FEET, BUT JUST BEFORE YOU DELIVER THE FINAL STRIKE...
...SOMETHING WILL HAPPEN.

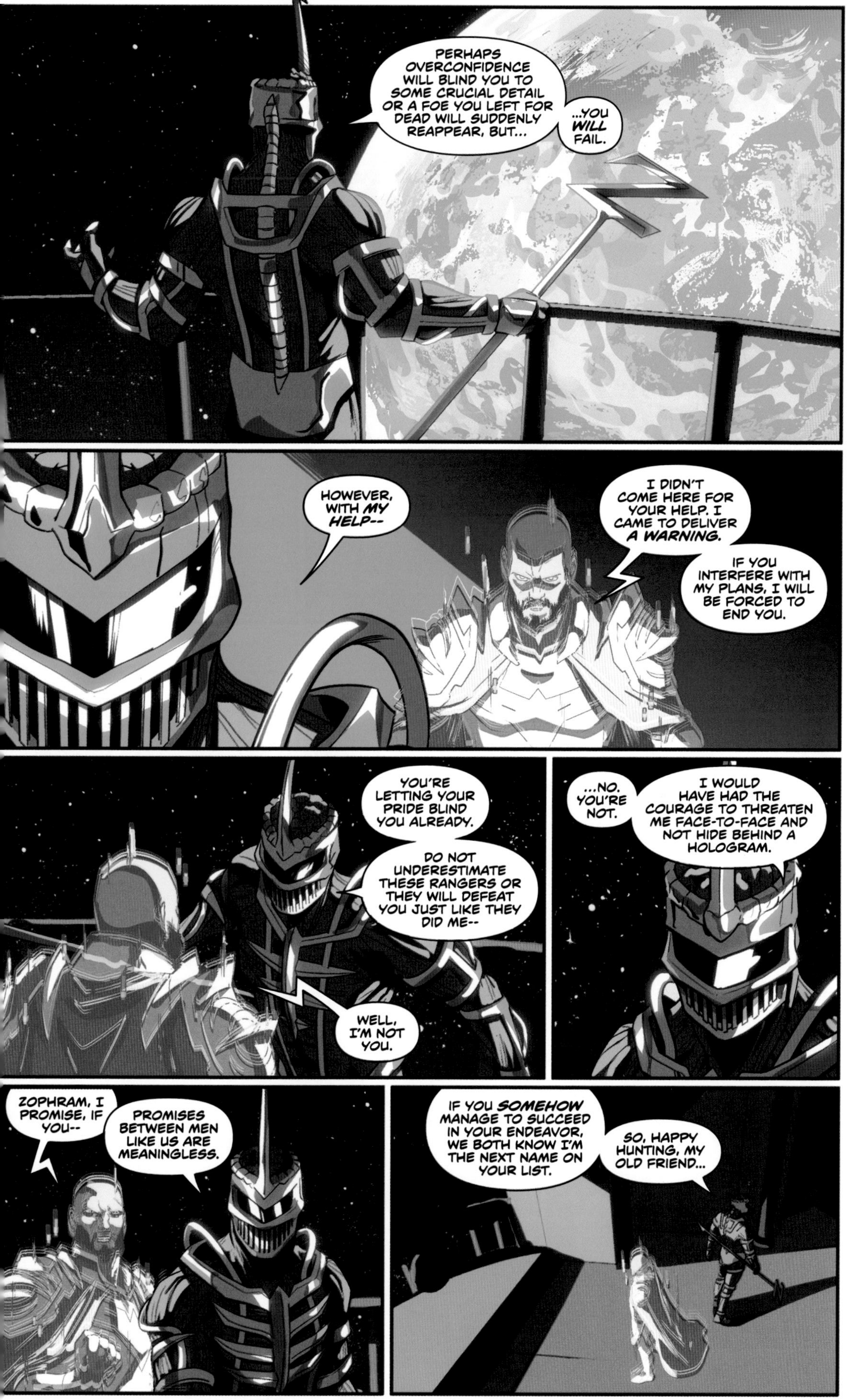
PERHAPS OVERCONFIDENCE WILL BLIND YOU TO SOME CRUCIAL DETAIL OR A FOE YOU LEFT FOR DEAD WILL SUDDENLY REAPPEAR, BUT...
...YOU *WILL* FAIL.
HOWEVER, WITH *MY HELP*--
I DIDN'T COME HERE FOR YOUR HELP. I CAME TO DELIVER *A WARNING.*
IF YOU INTERFERE WITH MY PLANS, I WILL BE FORCED TO END YOU.
YOU'RE LETTING YOUR PRIDE BLIND YOU ALREADY.
DO NOT UNDERESTIMATE THESE RANGERS OR THEY WILL DEFEAT YOU JUST LIKE THEY DID ME--
WELL, I'M NOT YOU.
...NO. YOU'RE NOT.
I WOULD HAVE HAD THE COURAGE TO THREATEN ME FACE-TO-FACE AND NOT HIDE BEHIND A HOLOGRAM.
ZOPHRAM, I PROMISE, IF YOU--
PROMISES BETWEEN MEN LIKE US ARE MEANINGLESS.
IF YOU *SOMEHOW* MANAGE TO SUCCEED IN YOUR ENDEAVOR, WE BOTH KNOW I'M THE NEXT NAME ON YOUR LIST.
SO, HAPPY HUNTING, MY OLD FRIEND...

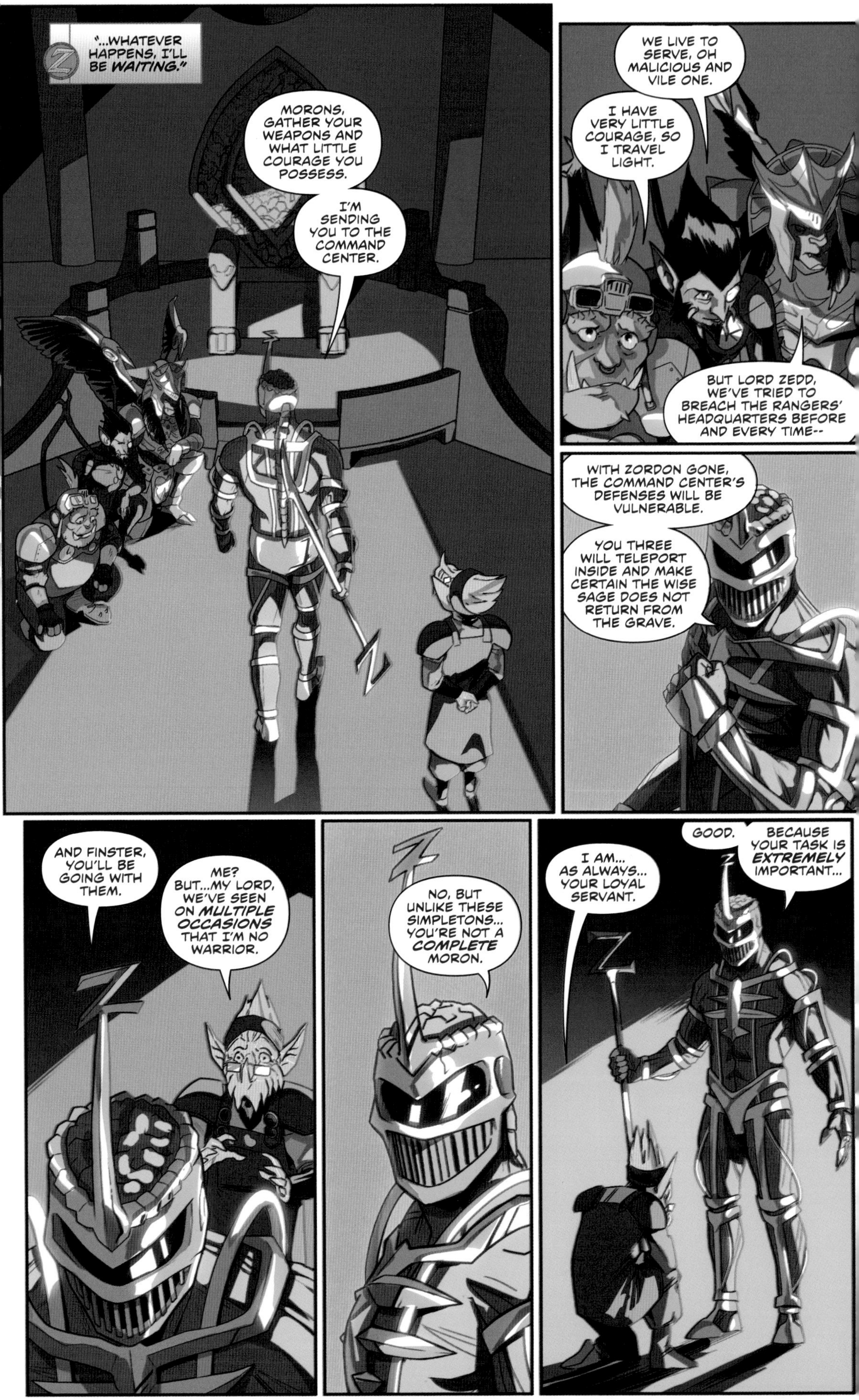
"...WHATEVER HAPPENS, I'LL BE WAITING."
MORONS, GATHER YOUR WEAPONS AND WHAT LITTLE COURAGE YOU POSSESS.
I'M SENDING YOU TO THE COMMAND CENTER.
WE LIVE TO SERVE, OH MALICIOUS AND VILE ONE.
I HAVE VERY LITTLE COURAGE, SO I TRAVEL LIGHT.
BUT LORD ZEDD, WE'VE TRIED TO BREACH THE RANGERS' HEADQUARTERS BEFORE AND EVERY TIME--
WITH ZORDON GONE, THE COMMAND CENTER'S DEFENSES WILL BE VULNERABLE.
YOU THREE WILL TELEPORT INSIDE AND MAKE CERTAIN THE WISE SAGE DOES NOT RETURN FROM THE GRAVE.
AND FINSTER, YOU'LL BE GOING WITH THEM.
ME? BUT...MY LORD, WE'VE SEEN ON MULTIPLE OCCASIONS THAT I'M NO WARRIOR.
NO, BUT UNLIKE THESE SIMPLETONS... YOU'RE NOT A COMPLETE MORON.
I AM... AS ALWAYS... YOUR LOYAL SERVANT.
GOOD.
BECAUSE YOUR TASK IS EXTREMELY IMPORTANT...

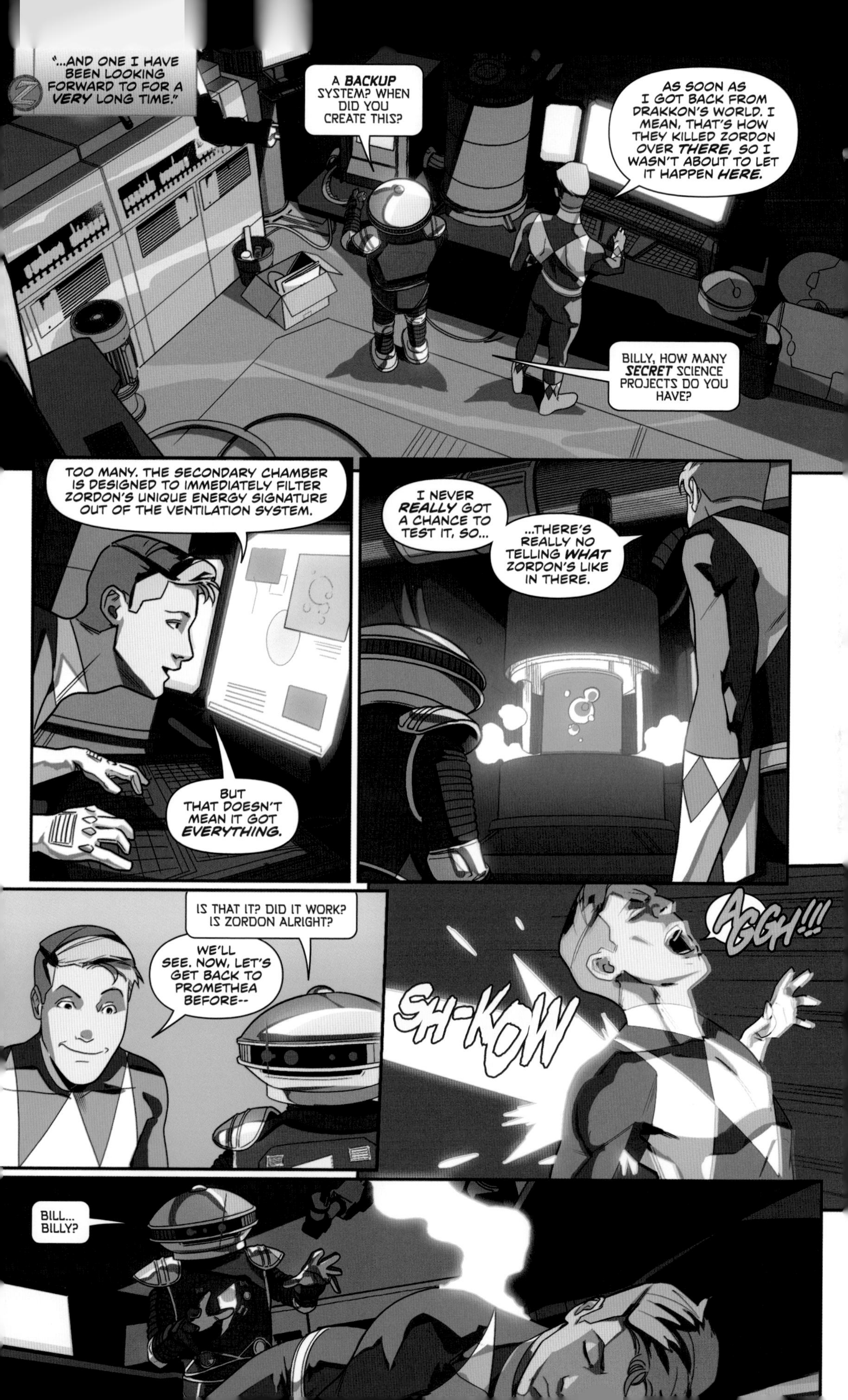
"...AND ONE I HAVE BEEN LOOKING FORWARD TO FOR A VERY LONG TIME."
A BACKUP SYSTEM? WHEN DID YOU CREATE THIS?
AS SOON AS I GOT BACK FROM DRAKKON'S WORLD. I MEAN, THAT'S HOW THEY KILLED ZORDON OVER THERE, SO I WASN'T ABOUT TO LET IT HAPPEN HERE.
BILLY, HOW MANY SECRET SCIENCE PROJECTS DO YOU HAVE?
TOO MANY. THE SECONDARY CHAMBER IS DESIGNED TO IMMEDIATELY FILTER ZORDON'S UNIQUE ENERGY SIGNATURE OUT OF THE VENTILATION SYSTEM.
BUT THAT DOESN'T MEAN IT GOT EVERYTHING.
I NEVER REALLY GOT A CHANCE TO TEST IT, SO...
...THERE'S REALLY NO TELLING WHAT ZORDON'S LIKE IN THERE.
IS THAT IT? DID IT WORK? IS ZORDON ALRIGHT?
WE'LL SEE. NOW, LET'S GET BACK TO PROMETHEA BEFORE--
SH-KOW
AGGH!!!
BILL... BILLY?

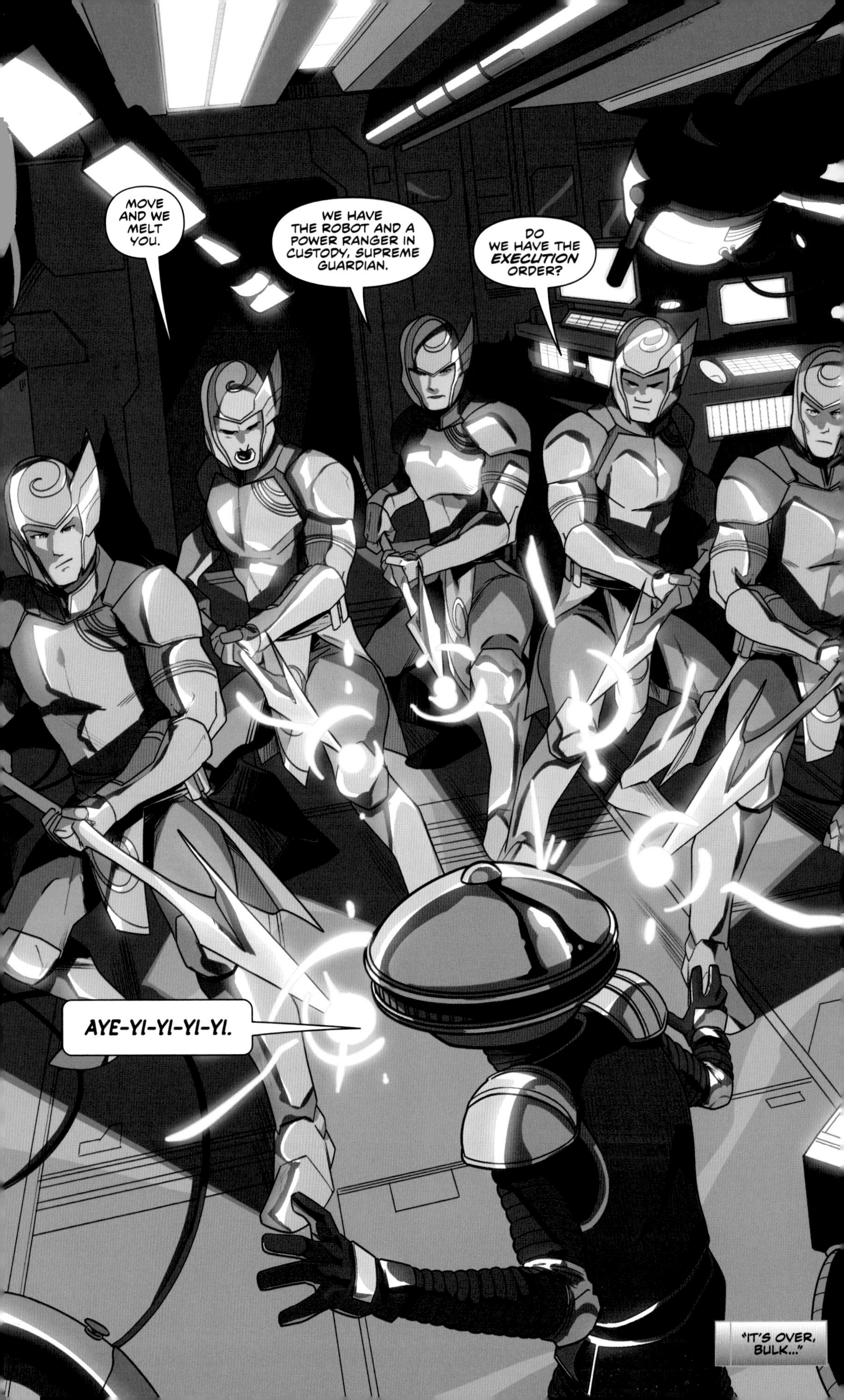
MOVE AND WE MELT YOU.
WE HAVE THE ROBOT AND A POWER RANGER IN CUSTODY, SUPREME GUARDIAN.
DO WE HAVE THE EXECUTION ORDER?
AYE-YI-YI-YI-YI.
"IT'S OVER, BULK..."

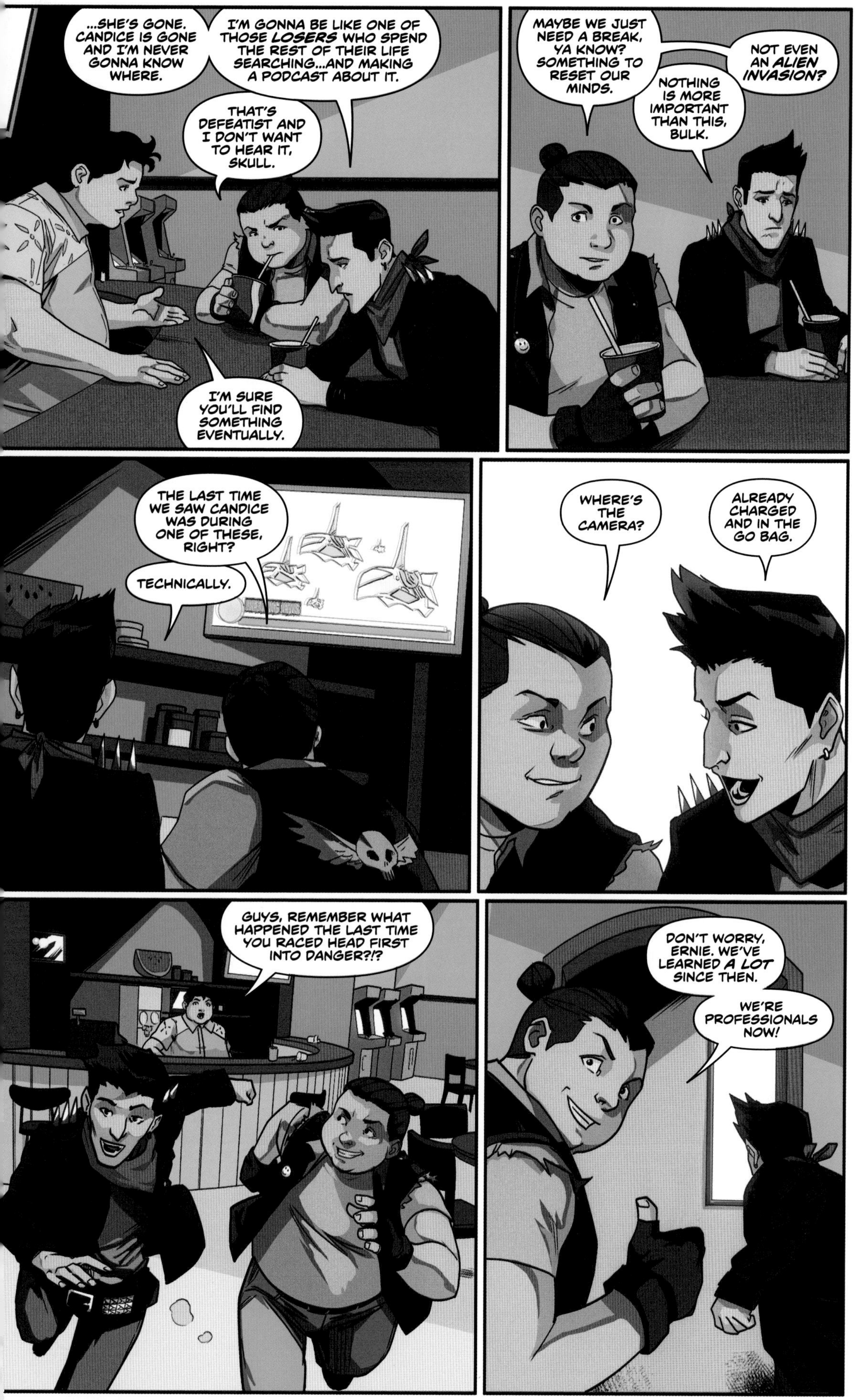
...SHE'S GONE. CANDICE IS GONE AND I'M NEVER GONNA KNOW WHERE.
I'M GONNA BE LIKE ONE OF THOSE LOSERS WHO SPEND THE REST OF THEIR LIFE SEARCHING...AND MAKING A PODCAST ABOUT IT.
THAT'S DEFEATIST AND I DON'T WANT TO HEAR IT, SKULL.
I'M SURE YOU'LL FIND SOMETHING EVENTUALLY.
MAYBE WE JUST NEED A BREAK, YA KNOW? SOMETHING TO RESET OUR MINDS.
NOTHING IS MORE IMPORTANT THAN THIS, BULK.
NOT EVEN AN ALIEN INVASION?
THE LAST TIME WE SAW CANDICE WAS DURING ONE OF THESE, RIGHT?
TECHNICALLY.
WHERE'S THE CAMERA?
ALREADY CHARGED AND IN THE GO BAG.
GUYS, REMEMBER WHAT HAPPENED THE LAST TIME YOU RACED HEAD FIRST INTO DANGER?!?
DON'T WORRY, ERNIE. WE'VE LEARNED A LOT SINCE THEN.
WE'RE PROFESSIONALS NOW!

PROMETHEA.

WHERE **WERE** YOU GUYS!?!

DIDN'T YOU GET ZORDON'S DISTRESS CALL?

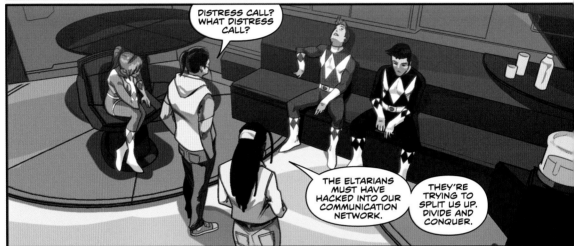

DISTRESS CALL? WHAT DISTRESS CALL?

THE ELTARIANS MUST HAVE HACKED INTO OUR COMMUNICATION NETWORK.

THEY'RE TRYING TO SPLIT US UP. DIVIDE AND CONQUER.

WELL, THANK GOD YOU GUYS GOT OUT BEFORE THEY DID ANY **REAL** DAMAGE.

YOU SURE YOU'RE OKAY?

I'M FINE, BUT SENTRY FORCE FOUR WASN'T MESSING AROUND.

WHAT ABOUT BILLY? AND ALPHA? AND ZORDON?

YEAH. WE CAN'T JUST ABANDON THEM OR WHATEVER.

NO ONE'S ABANDONING ANYONE, ROCKY.

WE CAME HERE TO FIND THE OMEGA RANGERS. ONCE WE CONTACT THEM, WE'LL COME UP WITH A RESCUE PLAN AND--

YOU'RE **ALREADY** OUT OF TIME, RANGERS.

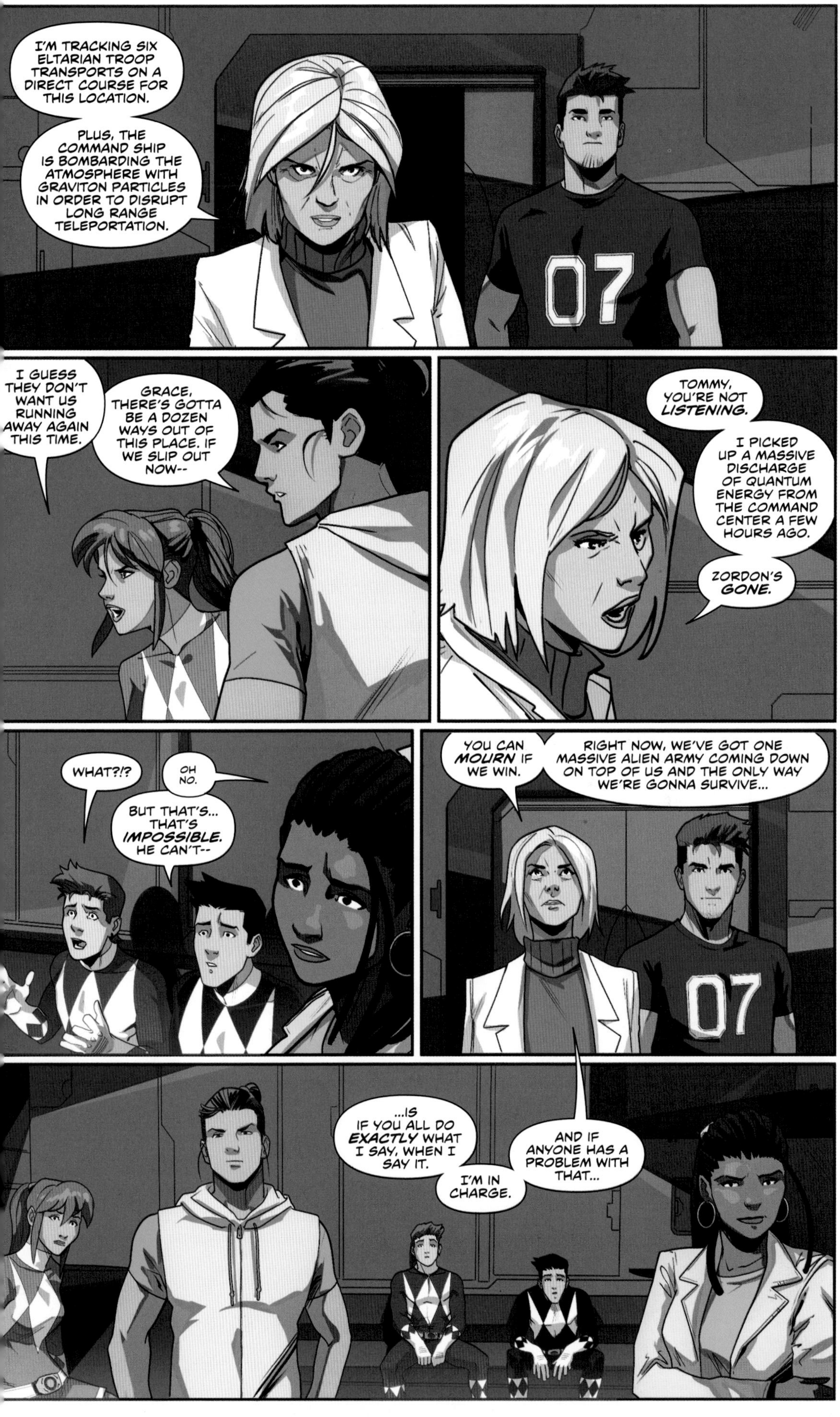

I'M TRACKING SIX ELTARIAN TROOP TRANSPORTS ON A DIRECT COURSE FOR THIS LOCATION.
PLUS, THE COMMAND SHIP IS BOMBARDING THE ATMOSPHERE WITH GRAVITON PARTICLES IN ORDER TO DISRUPT LONG RANGE TELEPORTATION.
I GUESS THEY DON'T WANT US RUNNING AWAY AGAIN THIS TIME.
GRACE, THERE'S GOTTA BE A DOZEN WAYS OUT OF THIS PLACE. IF WE SLIP OUT NOW--
TOMMY, YOU'RE NOT *LISTENING.*
I PICKED UP A MASSIVE DISCHARGE OF QUANTUM ENERGY FROM THE COMMAND CENTER A FEW HOURS AGO.
ZORDON'S *GONE.*
WHAT?!?
OH NO.
BUT THAT'S... THAT'S *IMPOSSIBLE.* HE CAN'T--
YOU CAN *MOURN* IF WE WIN.
RIGHT NOW, WE'VE GOT ONE MASSIVE ALIEN ARMY COMING DOWN ON TOP OF US AND THE ONLY WAY WE'RE GONNA SURVIVE...
...IS IF YOU ALL DO *EXACTLY* WHAT I SAY, WHEN I SAY IT.
AND IF ANYONE HAS A PROBLEM WITH THAT...
I'M IN CHARGE.
07

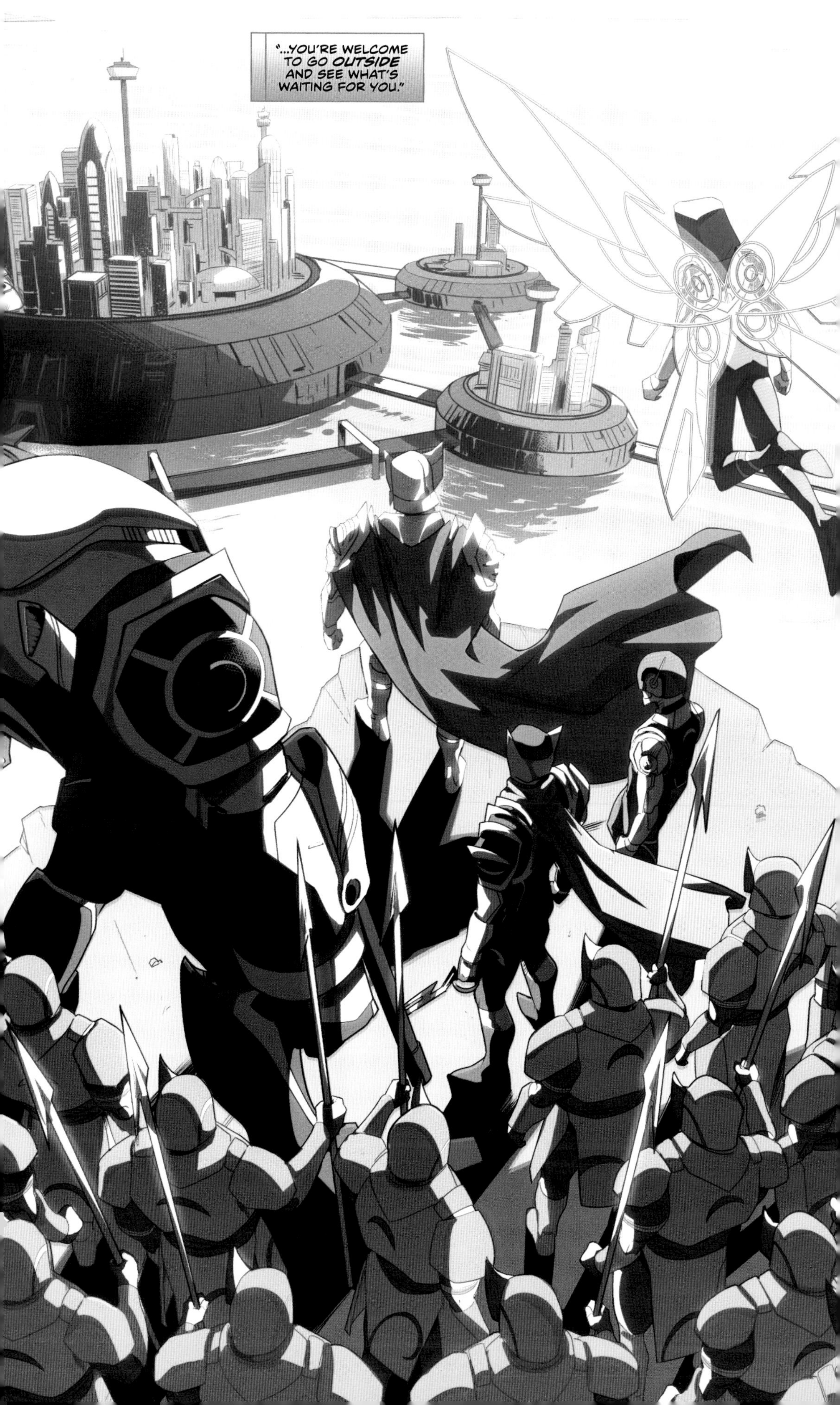
"...YOU'RE WELCOME TO GO OUTSIDE AND SEE WHAT'S WAITING FOR YOU."

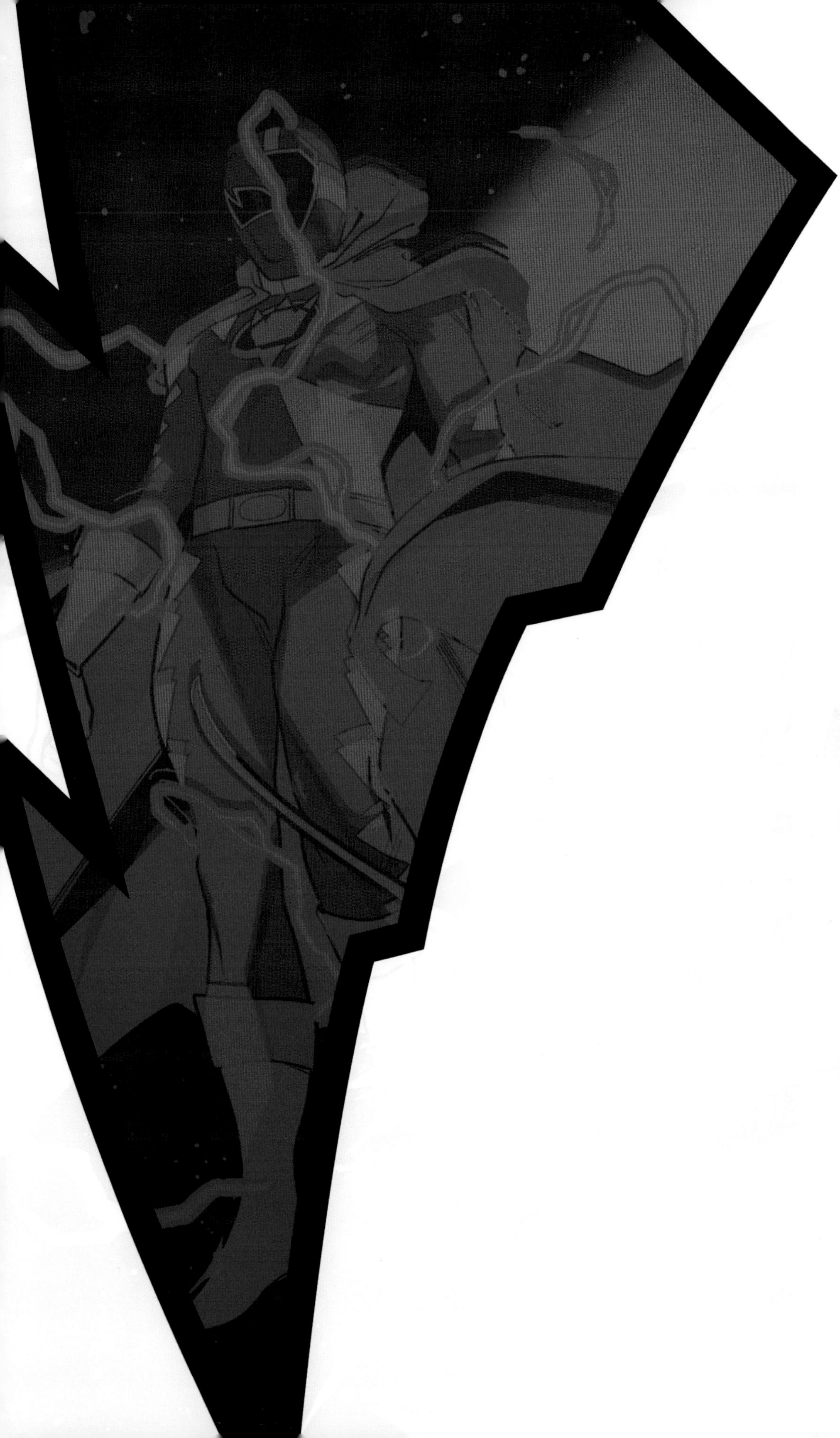

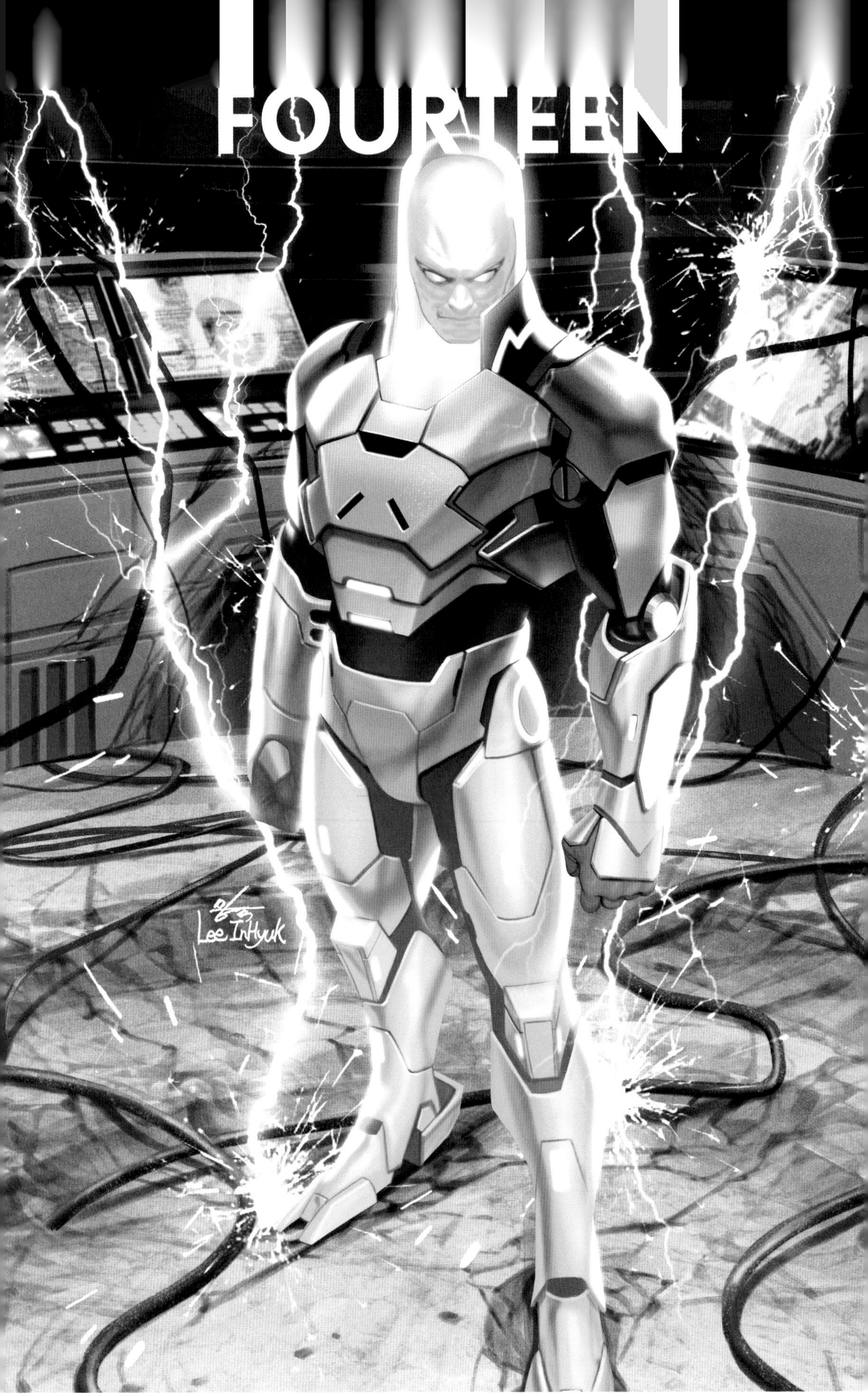
FOURTEEN
Lee InHyuk

INHYUK LEE | ISSUE FOURTEEN COVER

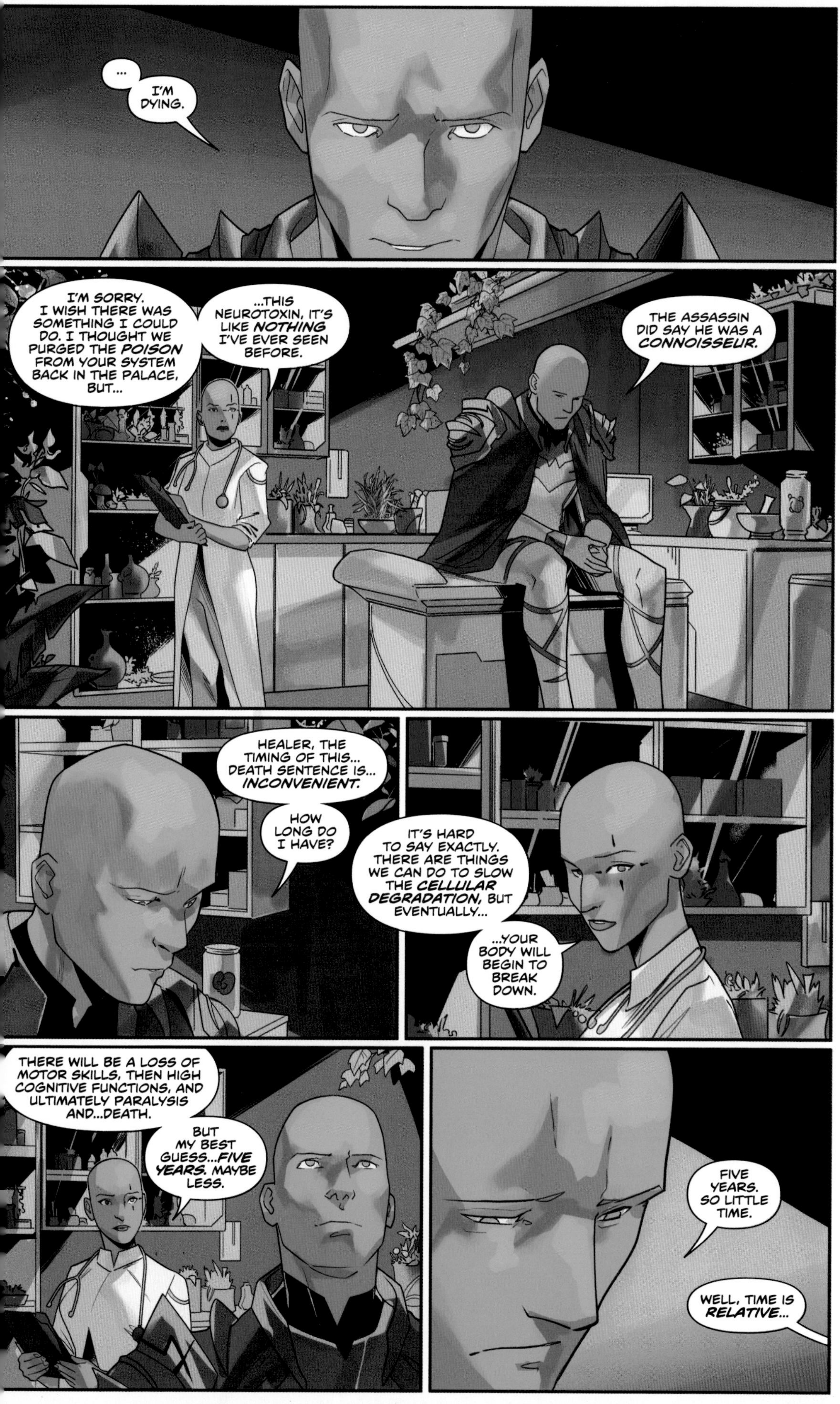
...
I'M DYING.
I'M SORRY. I WISH THERE WAS SOMETHING I COULD DO. I THOUGHT WE PURGED THE POISON FROM YOUR SYSTEM BACK IN THE PALACE, BUT...
...THIS NEUROTOXIN, IT'S LIKE NOTHING I'VE EVER SEEN BEFORE.
THE ASSASSIN DID SAY HE WAS A CONNOISSEUR.
HEALER, THE TIMING OF THIS... DEATH SENTENCE IS... INCONVENIENT.
HOW LONG DO I HAVE?
IT'S HARD TO SAY EXACTLY. THERE ARE THINGS WE CAN DO TO SLOW THE CELLULAR DEGRADATION, BUT EVENTUALLY...
...YOUR BODY WILL BEGIN TO BREAK DOWN.
THERE WILL BE A LOSS OF MOTOR SKILLS, THEN HIGH COGNITIVE FUNCTIONS, AND ULTIMATELY PARALYSIS AND...DEATH.
BUT MY BEST GUESS...FIVE YEARS. MAYBE LESS.
FIVE YEARS. SO LITTLE TIME.
WELL, TIME IS RELATIVE...

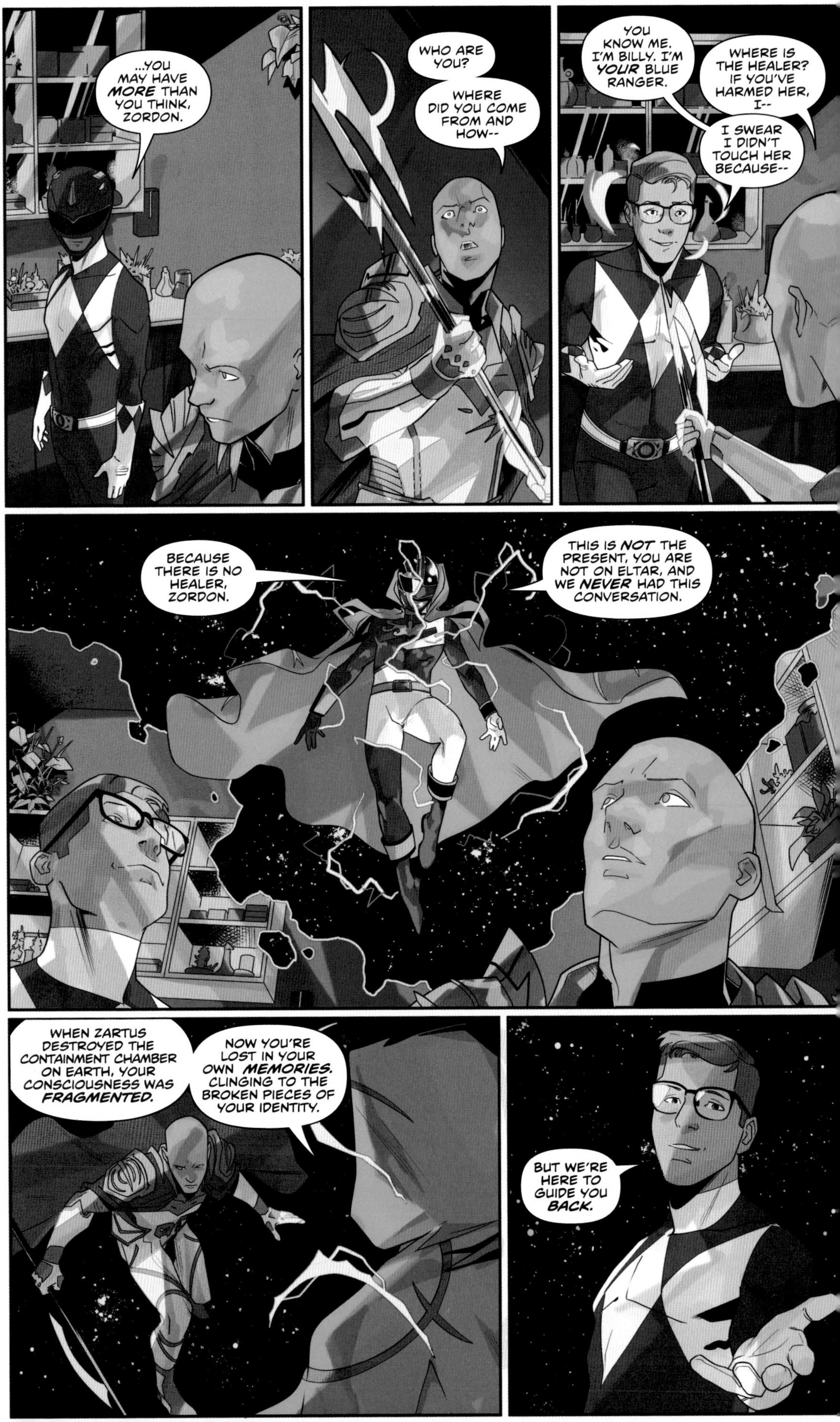
...YOU MAY HAVE MORE THAN YOU THINK, ZORDON.
WHO ARE YOU?
WHERE DID YOU COME FROM AND HOW--
YOU KNOW ME. I'M BILLY. I'M YOUR BLUE RANGER.
WHERE IS THE HEALER? IF YOU'VE HARMED HER, I--
I SWEAR I DIDN'T TOUCH HER BECAUSE--
BECAUSE THERE IS NO HEALER, ZORDON.
THIS IS NOT THE PRESENT, YOU ARE NOT ON ELTAR, AND WE NEVER HAD THIS CONVERSATION.
WHEN ZARTUS DESTROYED THE CONTAINMENT CHAMBER ON EARTH, YOUR CONSCIOUSNESS WAS FRAGMENTED.
NOW YOU'RE LOST IN YOUR OWN MEMORIES. CLINGING TO THE BROKEN PIECES OF YOUR IDENTITY.
BUT WE'RE HERE TO GUIDE YOU BACK.

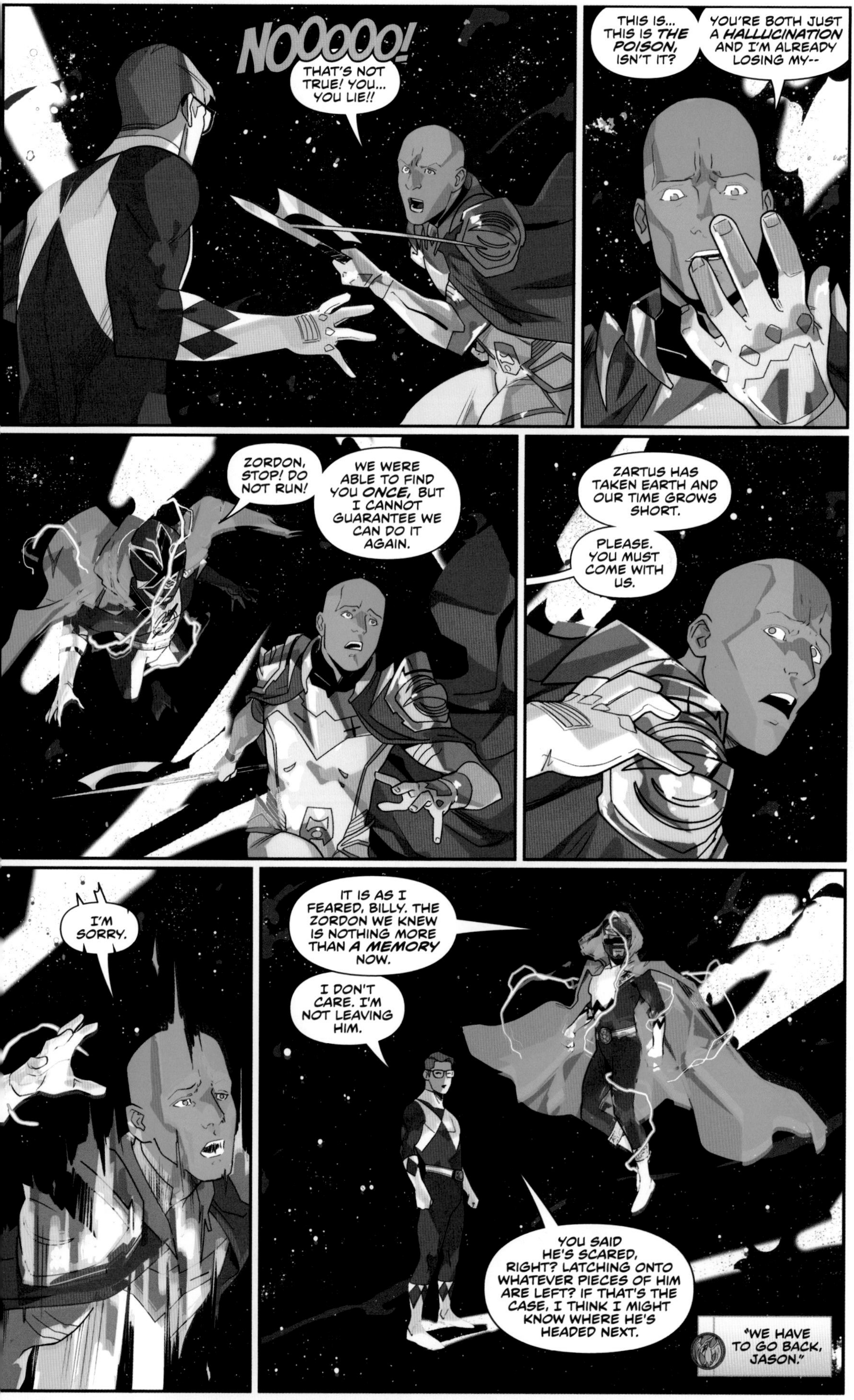
NOOOOO!
THAT'S NOT TRUE! YOU... YOU LIE!!
THIS IS... THIS IS THE POISON, ISN'T IT?
YOU'RE BOTH JUST A HALLUCINATION AND I'M ALREADY LOSING MY--
ZORDON, STOP! DO NOT RUN!
WE WERE ABLE TO FIND YOU ONCE, BUT I CANNOT GUARANTEE WE CAN DO IT AGAIN.
ZARTUS HAS TAKEN EARTH AND OUR TIME GROWS SHORT.
PLEASE. YOU MUST COME WITH US.
I'M SORRY.
IT IS AS I FEARED, BILLY. THE ZORDON WE KNEW IS NOTHING MORE THAN A MEMORY NOW.
I DON'T CARE. I'M NOT LEAVING HIM.
YOU SAID HE'S SCARED, RIGHT? LATCHING ONTO WHATEVER PIECES OF HIM ARE LEFT? IF THAT'S THE CASE, I THINK I MIGHT KNOW WHERE HE'S HEADED NEXT.
"WE HAVE TO GO BACK, JASON."

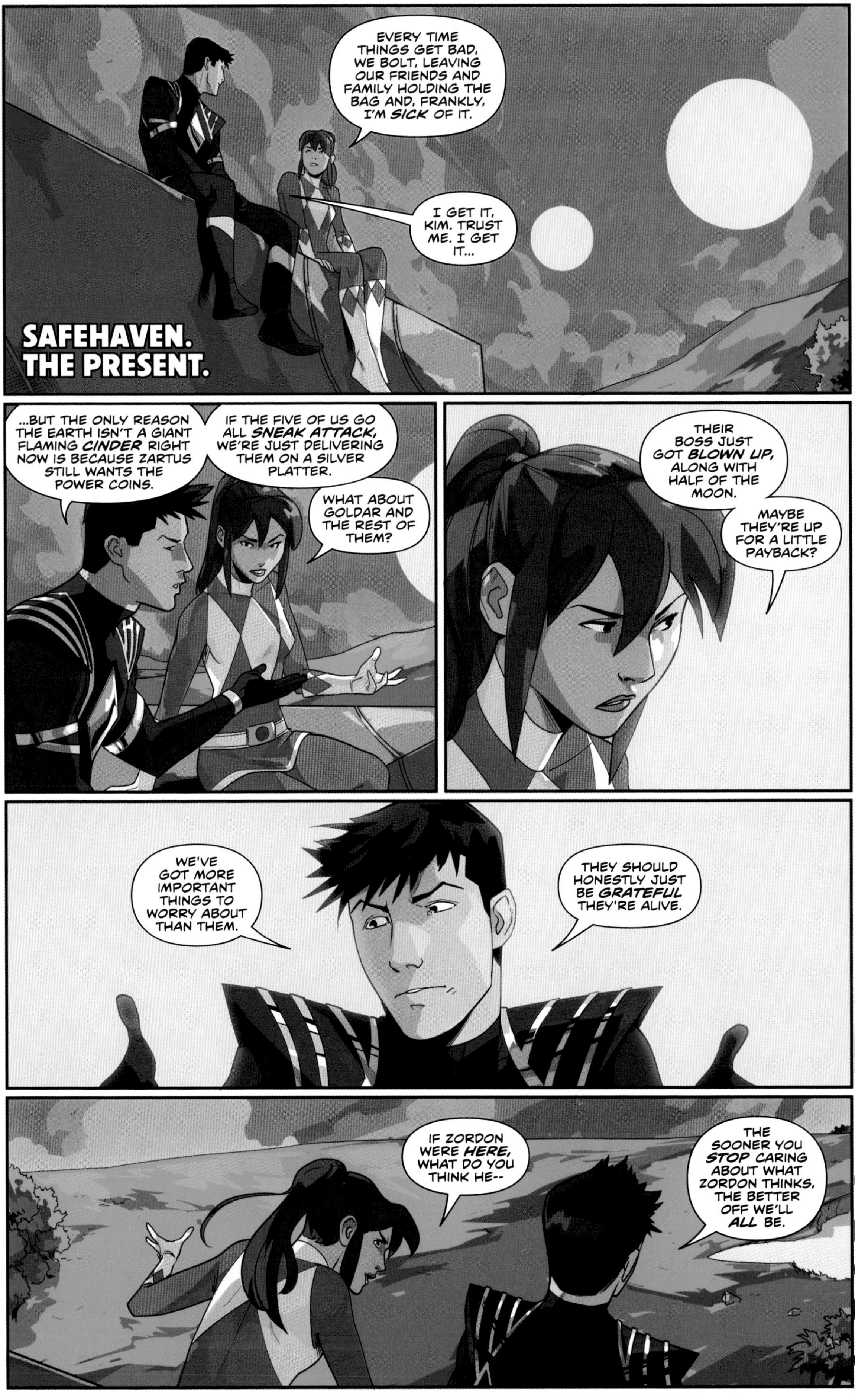
EVERY TIME THINGS GET BAD, WE BOLT, LEAVING OUR FRIENDS AND FAMILY HOLDING THE BAG AND, FRANKLY, I'M SICK OF IT.
I GET IT, KIM. TRUST ME. I GET IT...
SAFEHAVEN. THE PRESENT.
...BUT THE ONLY REASON THE EARTH ISN'T A GIANT FLAMING CINDER RIGHT NOW IS BECAUSE ZARTUS STILL WANTS THE POWER COINS.
IF THE FIVE OF US GO ALL SNEAK ATTACK, WE'RE JUST DELIVERING THEM ON A SILVER PLATTER.
WHAT ABOUT GOLDAR AND THE REST OF THEM?
THEIR BOSS JUST GOT BLOWN UP, ALONG WITH HALF OF THE MOON.
MAYBE THEY'RE UP FOR A LITTLE PAYBACK?
WE'VE GOT MORE IMPORTANT THINGS TO WORRY ABOUT THAN THEM.
THEY SHOULD HONESTLY JUST BE GRATEFUL THEY'RE ALIVE.
IF ZORDON WERE HERE, WHAT DO YOU THINK HE--
THE SOONER YOU STOP CARING ABOUT WHAT ZORDON THINKS, THE BETTER OFF WE'LL ALL BE.

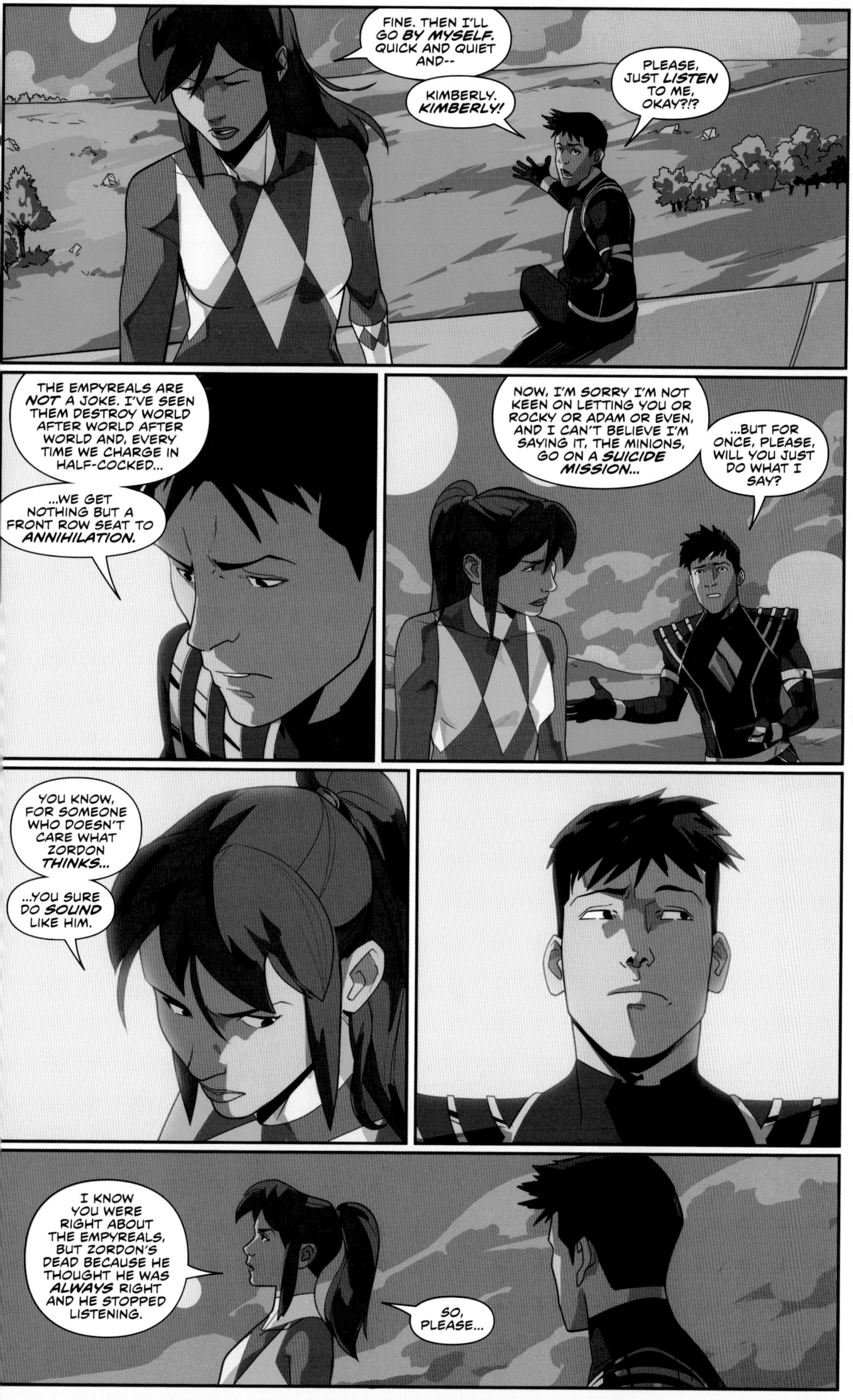
FINE. THEN I'LL GO BY MYSELF. QUICK AND QUIET AND--
KIMBERLY. KIMBERLY!
PLEASE, JUST LISTEN TO ME, OKAY?!?
THE EMPYREALS ARE NOT A JOKE. I'VE SEEN THEM DESTROY WORLD AFTER WORLD AFTER WORLD AND, EVERY TIME WE CHARGE IN HALF-COCKED...
...WE GET NOTHING BUT A FRONT ROW SEAT TO ANNIHILATION.
NOW, I'M SORRY I'M NOT KEEN ON LETTING YOU OR ROCKY OR ADAM OR EVEN, AND I CAN'T BELIEVE I'M SAYING IT, THE MINIONS, GO ON A SUICIDE MISSION...
...BUT FOR ONCE, PLEASE, WILL YOU JUST DO WHAT I SAY?
YOU KNOW, FOR SOMEONE WHO DOESN'T CARE WHAT ZORDON THINKS...
...YOU SURE DO SOUND LIKE HIM.
I KNOW YOU WERE RIGHT ABOUT THE EMPYREALS, BUT ZORDON'S DEAD BECAUSE HE THOUGHT HE WAS ALWAYS RIGHT AND HE STOPPED LISTENING.
SO, PLEASE...

"...DON'T MAKE THE **SAME** MISTAKE."

ACTIVATING POLARIZING COILS...**NOW!**

FWWZZZACK

ZZZZZZ ZZZZZZ ZZZZZZ ZZZZZZ

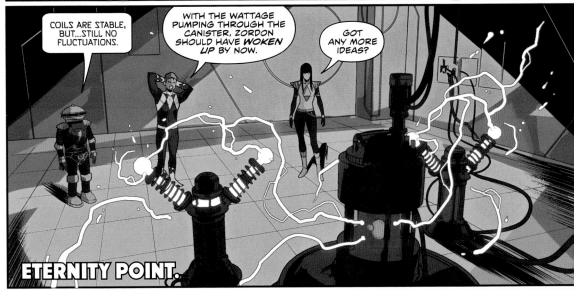

COILS ARE STABLE, BUT...STILL NO FLUCTUATIONS.

WITH THE WATTAGE PUMPING THROUGH THE CANISTER, ZORDON SHOULD HAVE **WOKEN UP** BY NOW.

GOT ANY MORE IDEAS?

ETERNITY POINT.

IT JUST DOESN'T MAKE SENSE.

WE SHOULD HAVE SEEN AT LEAST SOME SORT OF REACTION. I KNOW ZORDON IS IN THERE SOMEWHERE.

MAYBE IF WE FLIP THE POLARITY, THE SWITCH MIGHT--

GRRRRRWWWWWL

GAH!!

YALE, I TOLD YOU, I CAN'T PLAY RIGHT NOW, OKAY?

WE'RE TRYING TO RESURRECT A TEN-THOUSAND-YEAR-OLD ALIEN CONSCIOUSNESS, SO...CAN YOU MAYBE GO...FIND A STICK OR SOMETHING?

FRIEND YALE DOES NOT WANT TO PLAY.

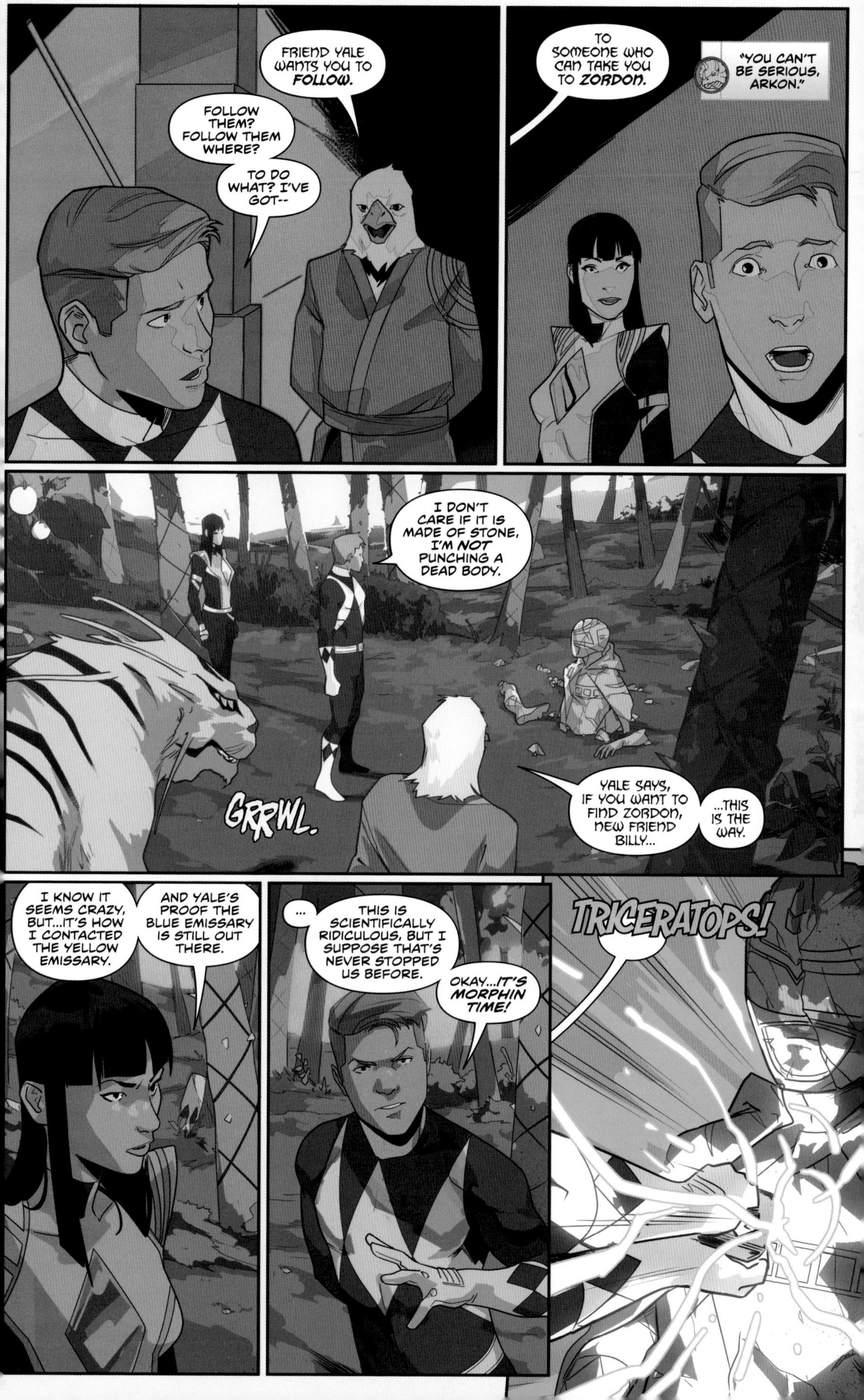
FRIEND YALE WANTS YOU TO FOLLOW.
FOLLOW THEM? FOLLOW THEM WHERE?
TO DO WHAT? I'VE GOT--
TO SOMEONE WHO CAN TAKE YOU TO ZORDON.
"YOU CAN'T BE SERIOUS, ARKON."
I DON'T CARE IF IT IS MADE OF STONE, I'M NOT PUNCHING A DEAD BODY.
GRRWL.
YALE SAYS, IF YOU WANT TO FIND ZORDON, NEW FRIEND BILLY...
...THIS IS THE WAY.
I KNOW IT SEEMS CRAZY, BUT...IT'S HOW I CONTACTED THE YELLOW EMISSARY.
AND YALE'S PROOF THE BLUE EMISSARY IS STILL OUT THERE.
...
THIS IS SCIENTIFICALLY RIDICULOUS, BUT I SUPPOSE THAT'S NEVER STOPPED US BEFORE.
OKAY...IT'S MORPHIN TIME!
TRICERATOPS!

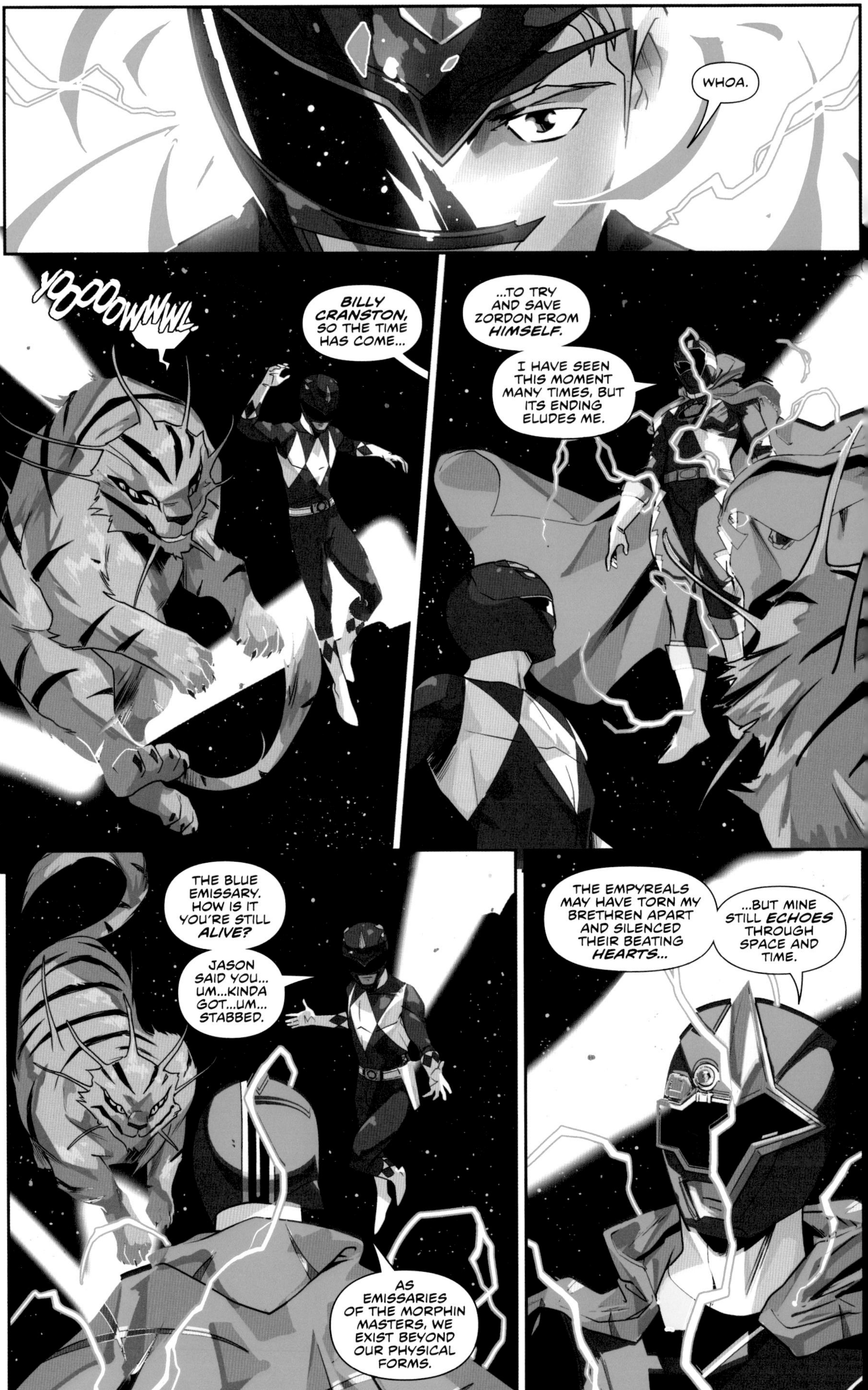
WHOA.
YOOOOOWWWL!
BILLY CRANSTON, SO THE TIME HAS COME...
...TO TRY AND SAVE ZORDON FROM HIMSELF.
I HAVE SEEN THIS MOMENT MANY TIMES, BUT ITS ENDING ELUDES ME.
THE BLUE EMISSARY. HOW IS IT YOU'RE STILL ALIVE?
JASON SAID YOU... UM...KINDA GOT...UM... STABBED.
AS EMISSARIES OF THE MORPHIN MASTERS, WE EXIST BEYOND OUR PHYSICAL FORMS.
THE EMPYREALS MAY HAVE TORN MY BRETHREN APART AND SILENCED THEIR BEATING HEARTS...
...BUT MINE STILL ECHOES THROUGH SPACE AND TIME.

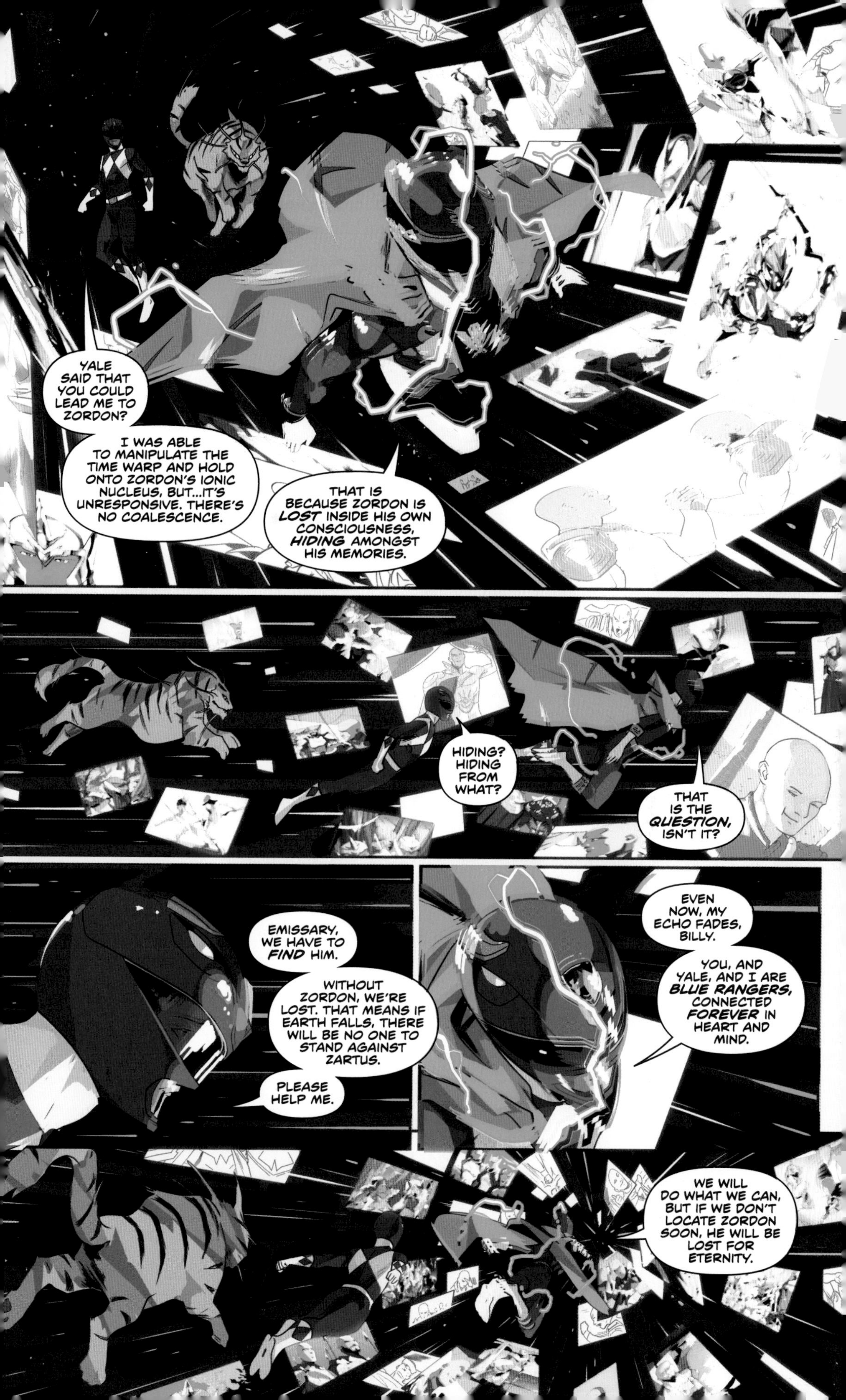
YALE SAID THAT YOU COULD LEAD ME TO ZORDON?
I WAS ABLE TO MANIPULATE THE TIME WARP AND HOLD ONTO ZORDON'S IONIC NUCLEUS, BUT...IT'S UNRESPONSIVE. THERE'S NO COALESCENCE.
THAT IS BECAUSE ZORDON IS LOST INSIDE HIS OWN CONSCIOUSNESS, HIDING AMONGST HIS MEMORIES.
HIDING? HIDING FROM WHAT?
THAT IS THE QUESTION, ISN'T IT?
EMISSARY, WE HAVE TO FIND HIM.
WITHOUT ZORDON, WE'RE LOST. THAT MEANS IF EARTH FALLS, THERE WILL BE NO ONE TO STAND AGAINST ZARTUS.
PLEASE HELP ME.
EVEN NOW, MY ECHO FADES, BILLY.
YOU, AND YALE, AND I ARE BLUE RANGERS, CONNECTED FOREVER IN HEART AND MIND.
WE WILL DO WHAT WE CAN, BUT IF WE DON'T LOCATE ZORDON SOON, HE WILL BE LOST FOR ETERNITY.

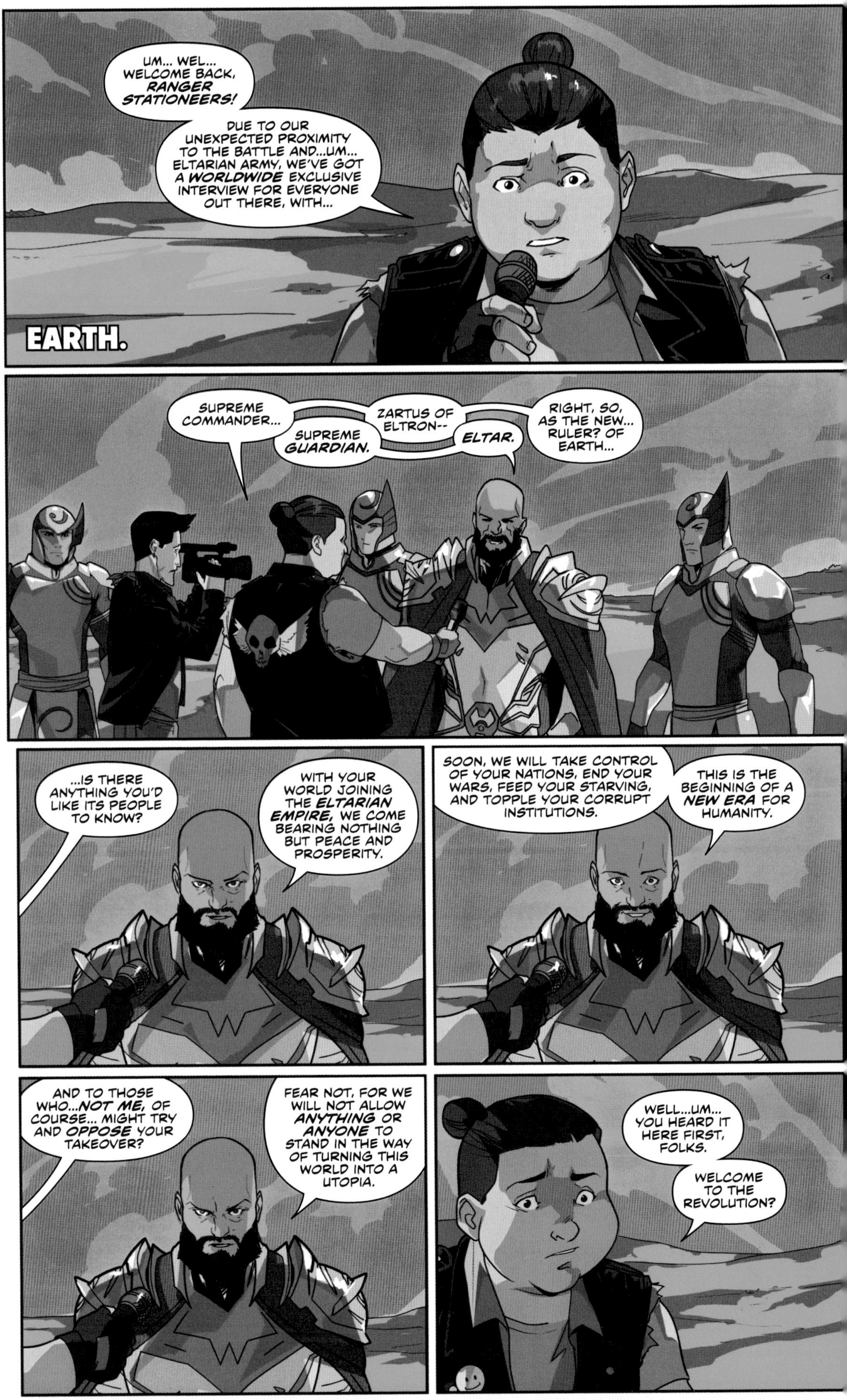
UM... WEL... WELCOME BACK, RANGER STATIONEERS!
DUE TO OUR UNEXPECTED PROXIMITY TO THE BATTLE AND...UM... ELTARIAN ARMY, WE'VE GOT A WORLDWIDE EXCLUSIVE INTERVIEW FOR EVERYONE OUT THERE, WITH...
EARTH.
SUPREME COMMANDER...
SUPREME GUARDIAN.
ZARTUS OF ELTRON--
ELTAR.
RIGHT, SO, AS THE NEW... RULER? OF EARTH...
...IS THERE ANYTHING YOU'D LIKE ITS PEOPLE TO KNOW?
WITH YOUR WORLD JOINING THE ELTARIAN EMPIRE, WE COME BEARING NOTHING BUT PEACE AND PROSPERITY.
SOON, WE WILL TAKE CONTROL OF YOUR NATIONS, END YOUR WARS, FEED YOUR STARVING, AND TOPPLE YOUR CORRUPT INSTITUTIONS.
THIS IS THE BEGINNING OF A NEW ERA FOR HUMANITY.
AND TO THOSE WHO...NOT ME, OF COURSE... MIGHT TRY AND OPPOSE YOUR TAKEOVER?
FEAR NOT, FOR WE WILL NOT ALLOW ANYTHING OR ANYONE TO STAND IN THE WAY OF TURNING THIS WORLD INTO A UTOPIA.
WELL...UM... YOU HEARD IT HERE FIRST, FOLKS.
WELCOME TO THE REVOLUTION?

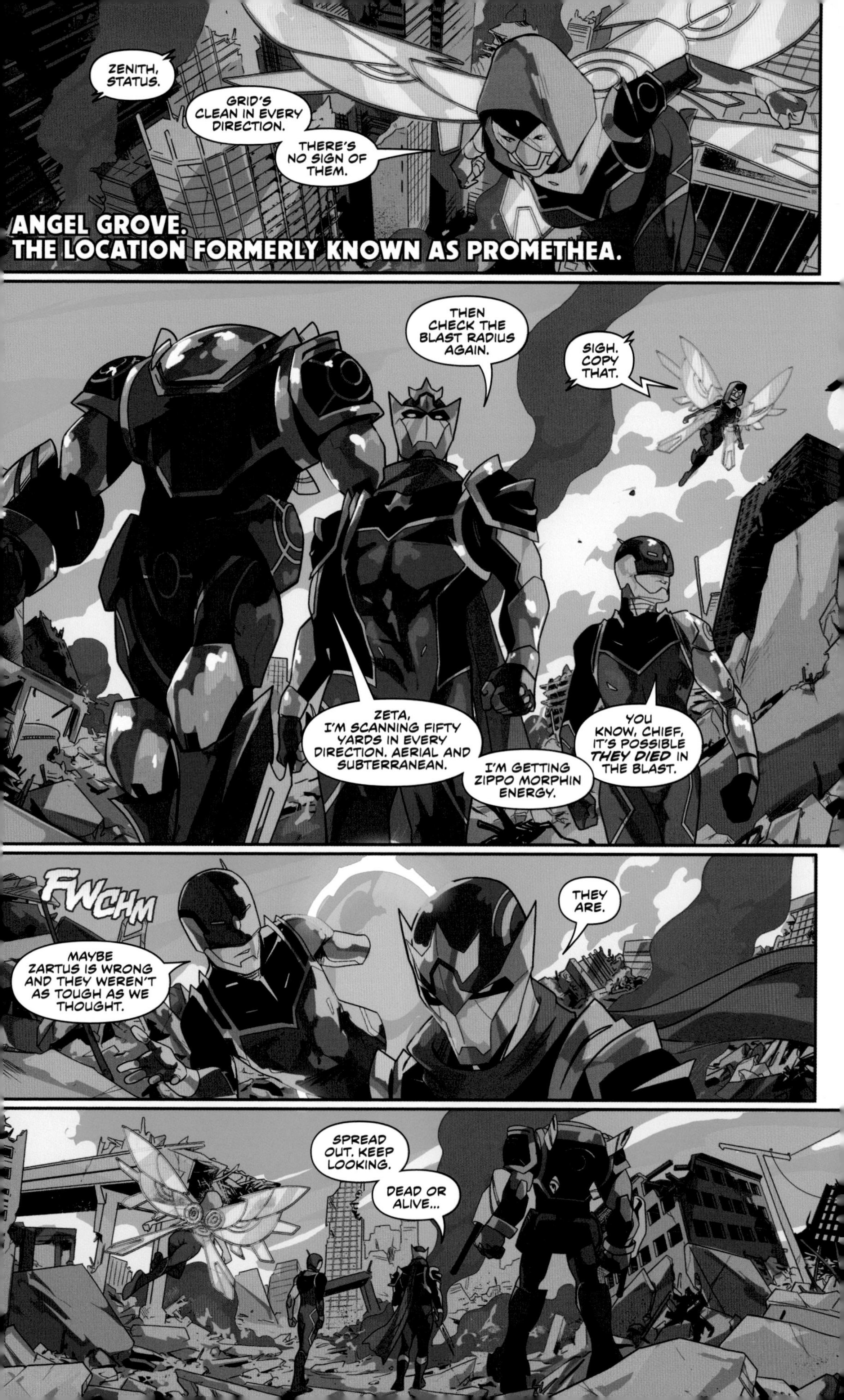
ZENITH, STATUS.
GRID'S CLEAN IN EVERY DIRECTION.
THERE'S NO SIGN OF THEM.
ANGEL GROVE. THE LOCATION FORMERLY KNOWN AS PROMETHEA.
THEN CHECK THE BLAST RADIUS AGAIN.
SIGH. COPY THAT.
ZETA, I'M SCANNING FIFTY YARDS IN EVERY DIRECTION. AERIAL AND SUBTERRANEAN.
I'M GETTING ZIPPO MORPHIN ENERGY.
YOU KNOW, CHIEF, IT'S POSSIBLE THEY DIED IN THE BLAST.
FWCHM
MAYBE ZARTUS IS WRONG AND THEY WEREN'T AS TOUGH AS WE THOUGHT.
THEY ARE.
SPREAD OUT. KEEP LOOKING.
DEAD OR ALIVE...

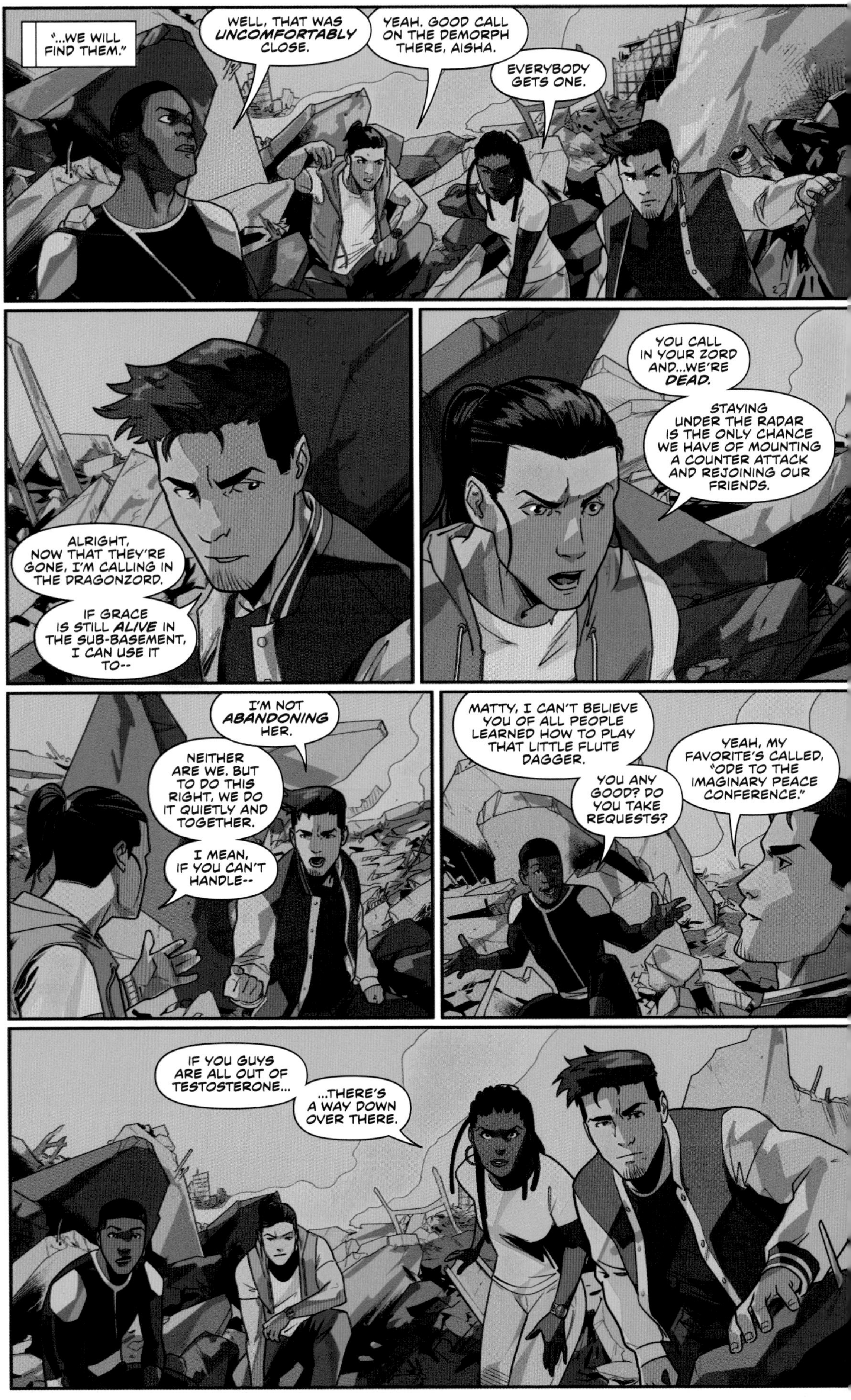
"...WE WILL FIND THEM."
WELL, THAT WAS *UNCOMFORTABLY* CLOSE.
YEAH. GOOD CALL ON THE DEMORPH THERE, AISHA.
EVERYBODY GETS ONE.
ALRIGHT, NOW THAT THEY'RE GONE, I'M CALLING IN THE DRAGONZORD.
IF GRACE IS STILL *ALIVE* IN THE SUB-BASEMENT, I CAN USE IT TO--
YOU CALL IN YOUR ZORD AND...WE'RE *DEAD.*
STAYING UNDER THE RADAR IS THE ONLY CHANCE WE HAVE OF MOUNTING A COUNTER ATTACK AND REJOINING OUR FRIENDS.
I'M NOT *ABANDONING* HER.
NEITHER ARE WE. BUT TO DO THIS RIGHT, WE DO IT QUIETLY AND TOGETHER.
I MEAN, IF YOU CAN'T HANDLE--
MATTY, I CAN'T BELIEVE YOU OF ALL PEOPLE LEARNED HOW TO PLAY THAT LITTLE FLUTE DAGGER.
YOU ANY GOOD? DO YOU TAKE REQUESTS?
YEAH, MY FAVORITE'S CALLED, "ODE TO THE IMAGINARY PEACE CONFERENCE."
IF YOU GUYS ARE ALL OUT OF TESTOSTERONE...
...THERE'S A WAY DOWN OVER THERE.

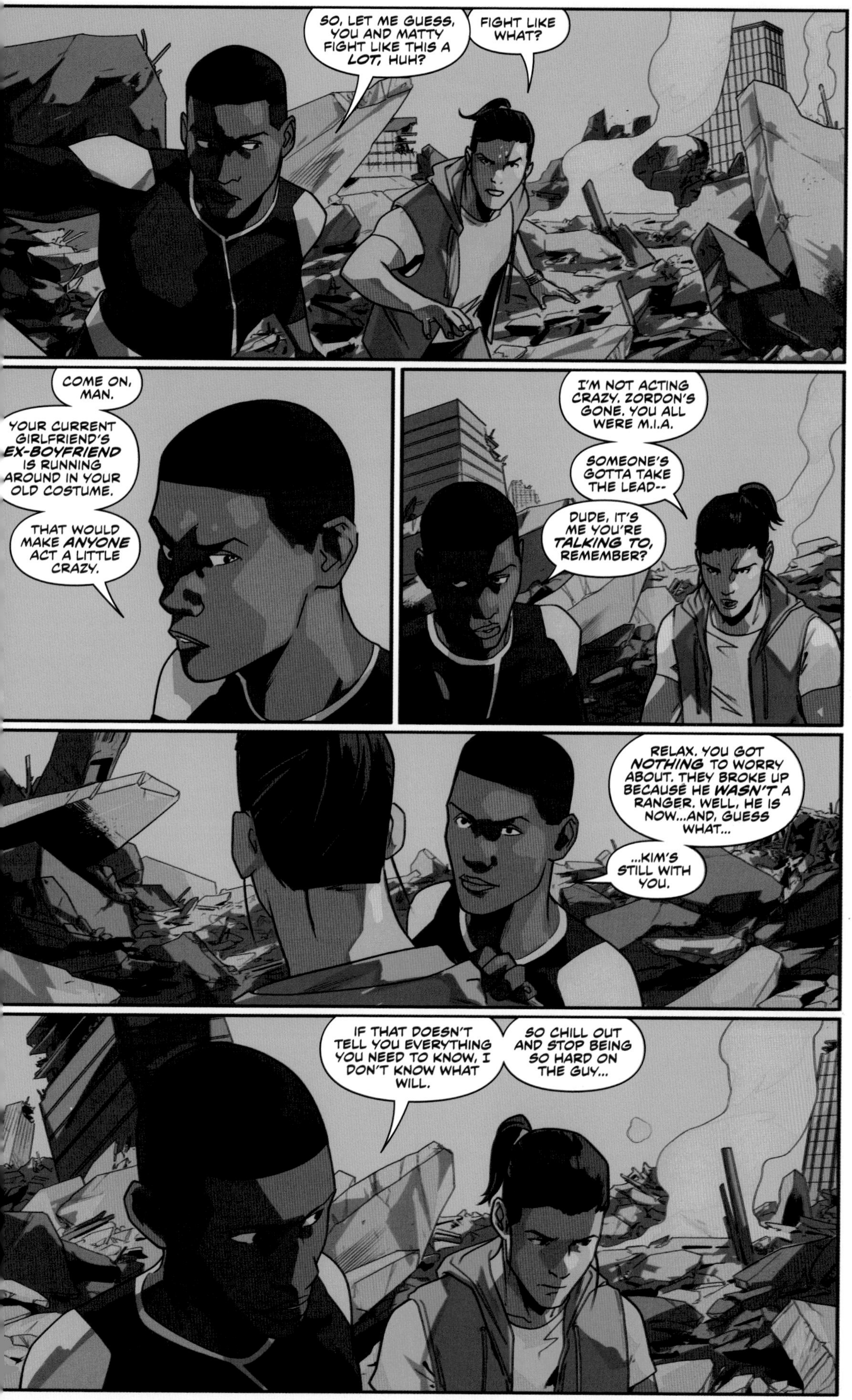
SO, LET ME GUESS, YOU AND MATTY FIGHT LIKE THIS A *LOT*, HUH?
FIGHT LIKE WHAT?
COME ON, MAN.
YOUR CURRENT GIRLFRIEND'S ***EX-BOYFRIEND*** IS RUNNING AROUND IN YOUR OLD COSTUME.
THAT WOULD MAKE ***ANYONE*** ACT A LITTLE CRAZY.
I'M NOT ACTING CRAZY. ZORDON'S GONE. YOU ALL WERE M.I.A.
SOMEONE'S GOTTA TAKE THE LEAD--
DUDE, IT'S ME YOU'RE ***TALKING TO***, REMEMBER?
RELAX. YOU GOT ***NOTHING*** TO WORRY ABOUT. THEY BROKE UP BECAUSE HE ***WASN'T*** A RANGER. WELL, HE IS NOW...AND, GUESS WHAT...
...KIM'S STILL WITH YOU.
IF THAT DOESN'T TELL YOU EVERYTHING YOU NEED TO KNOW, I DON'T KNOW WHAT WILL.
SO CHILL OUT AND STOP BEING SO HARD ON THE GUY...

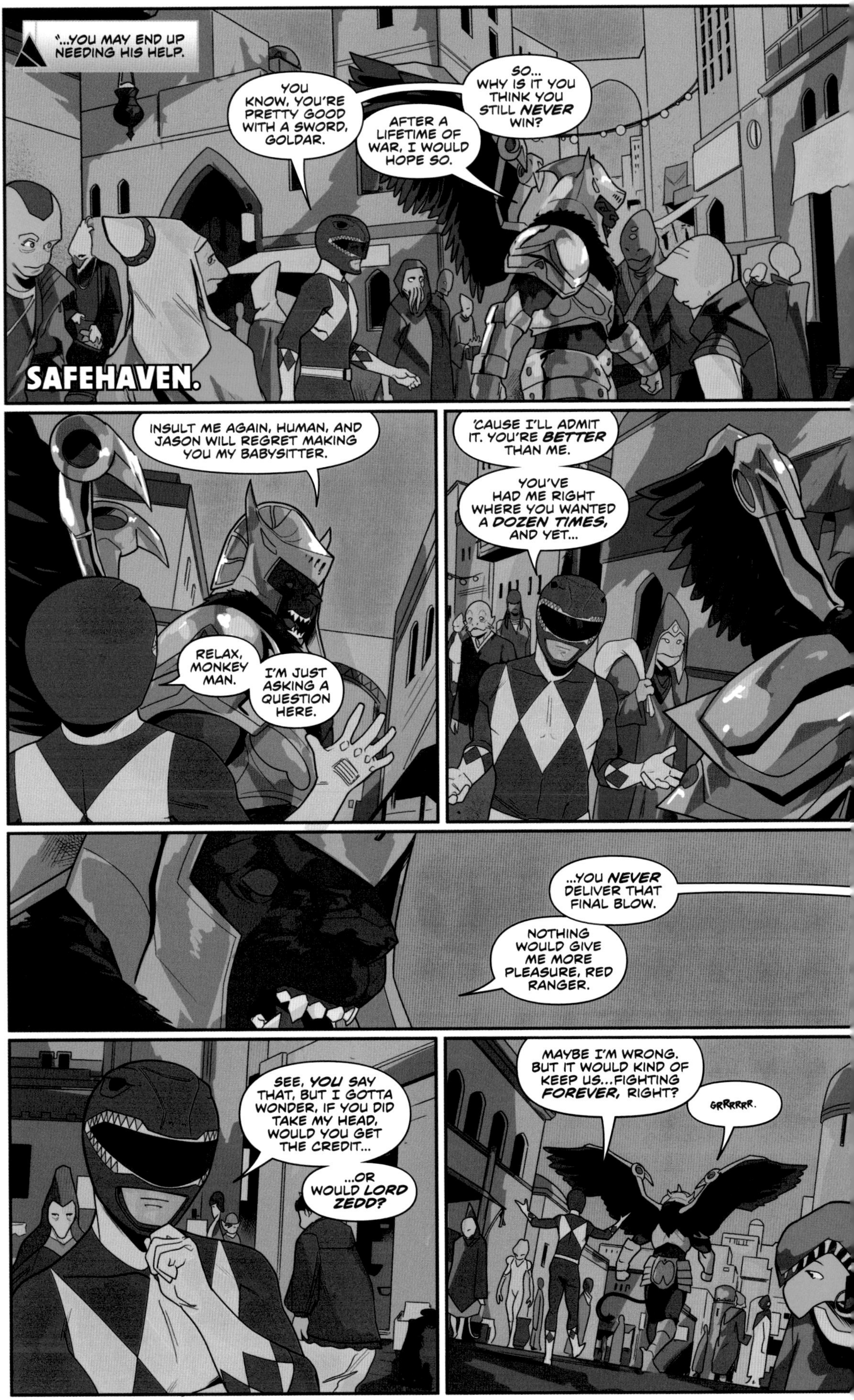
"...YOU MAY END UP NEEDING HIS HELP.
YOU KNOW, YOU'RE PRETTY GOOD WITH A SWORD, GOLDAR.
AFTER A LIFETIME OF WAR, I WOULD HOPE SO.
SO... WHY IS IT YOU THINK YOU STILL NEVER WIN?
SAFEHAVEN.
INSULT ME AGAIN, HUMAN, AND JASON WILL REGRET MAKING YOU MY BABYSITTER.
RELAX, MONKEY MAN.
I'M JUST ASKING A QUESTION HERE.
'CAUSE I'LL ADMIT IT. YOU'RE BETTER THAN ME.
YOU'VE HAD ME RIGHT WHERE YOU WANTED A DOZEN TIMES, AND YET...
...YOU NEVER DELIVER THAT FINAL BLOW.
NOTHING WOULD GIVE ME MORE PLEASURE, RED RANGER.
SEE, YOU SAY THAT, BUT I GOTTA WONDER, IF YOU DID TAKE MY HEAD, WOULD YOU GET THE CREDIT...
...OR WOULD LORD ZEDD?
MAYBE I'M WRONG. BUT IT WOULD KIND OF KEEP US...FIGHTING FOREVER, RIGHT?
GRRRRRR.

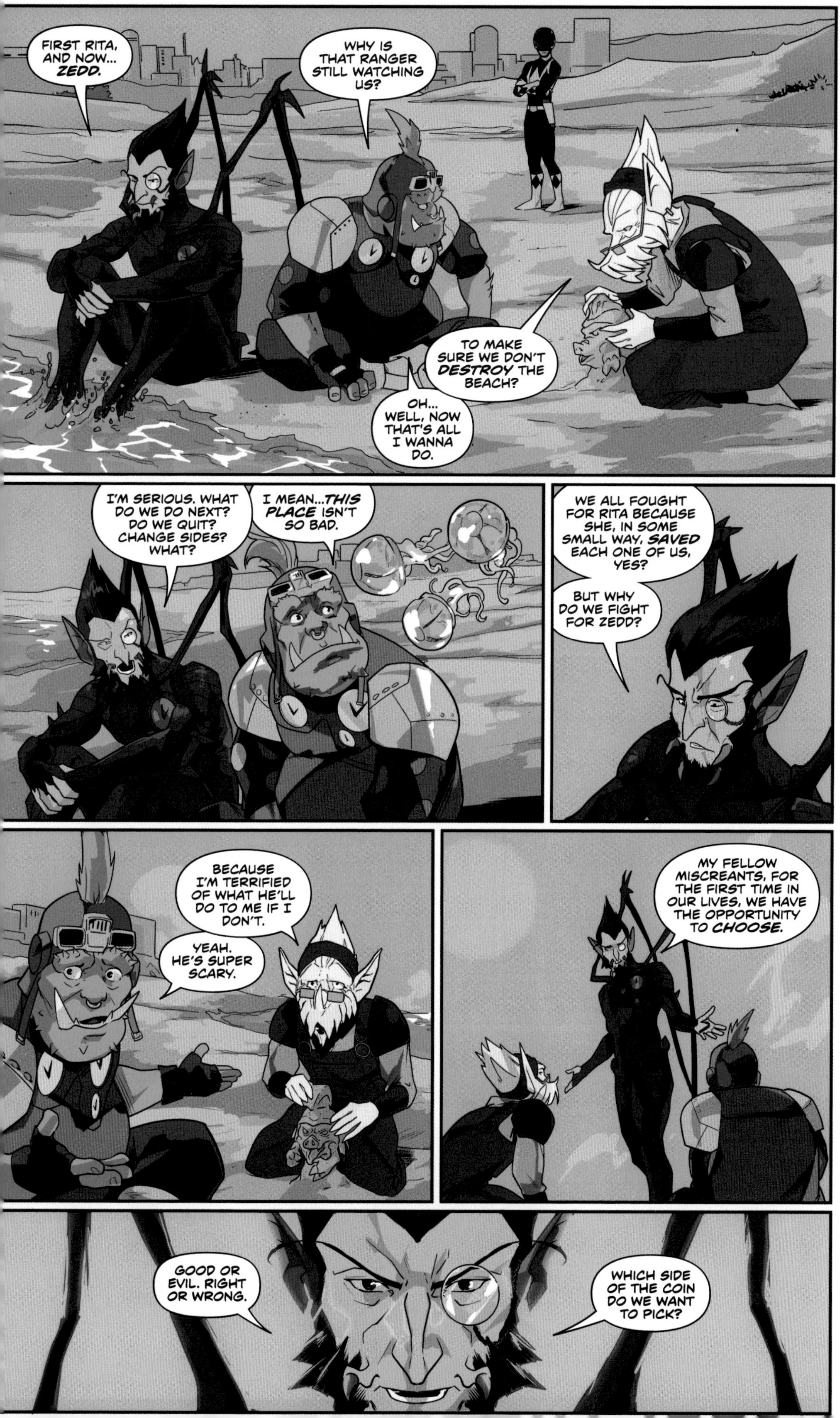
FIRST RITA, AND NOW... ZEDD.
WHY IS THAT RANGER STILL WATCHING US?
TO MAKE SURE WE DON'T DESTROY THE BEACH?
OH... WELL, NOW THAT'S ALL I WANNA DO.
I'M SERIOUS. WHAT DO WE DO NEXT? DO WE QUIT? CHANGE SIDES? WHAT?
I MEAN...THIS PLACE ISN'T SO BAD.
WE ALL FOUGHT FOR RITA BECAUSE SHE, IN SOME SMALL WAY, SAVED EACH ONE OF US, YES?
BUT WHY DO WE FIGHT FOR ZEDD?
BECAUSE I'M TERRIFIED OF WHAT HE'LL DO TO ME IF I DON'T.
YEAH. HE'S SUPER SCARY.
MY FELLOW MISCREANTS, FOR THE FIRST TIME IN OUR LIVES, WE HAVE THE OPPORTUNITY TO CHOOSE.
GOOD OR EVIL. RIGHT OR WRONG.
WHICH SIDE OF THE COIN DO WE WANT TO PICK?

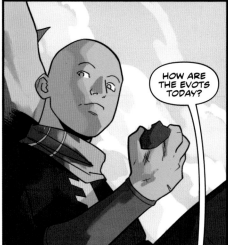

HOW ARE THE EVOTS TODAY?

I HEAR THE RIPEST ONES ARE AT THE VERY TOP, RIGHT?

BECAUSE THEY GET THE MOST SUNSHINE.

ABSOLUTELY. WOULD YOU CARE FOR SOME?

I'VE GOT PLENTY UP HERE.

IF IT'S NOT TOO MUCH TROUBLE. SURE.

NO TROUBLE AT ALL.

THIS WAY YOU DON'T HAVE TO SCRATCH YOURSELF UP GETTING UP THERE.

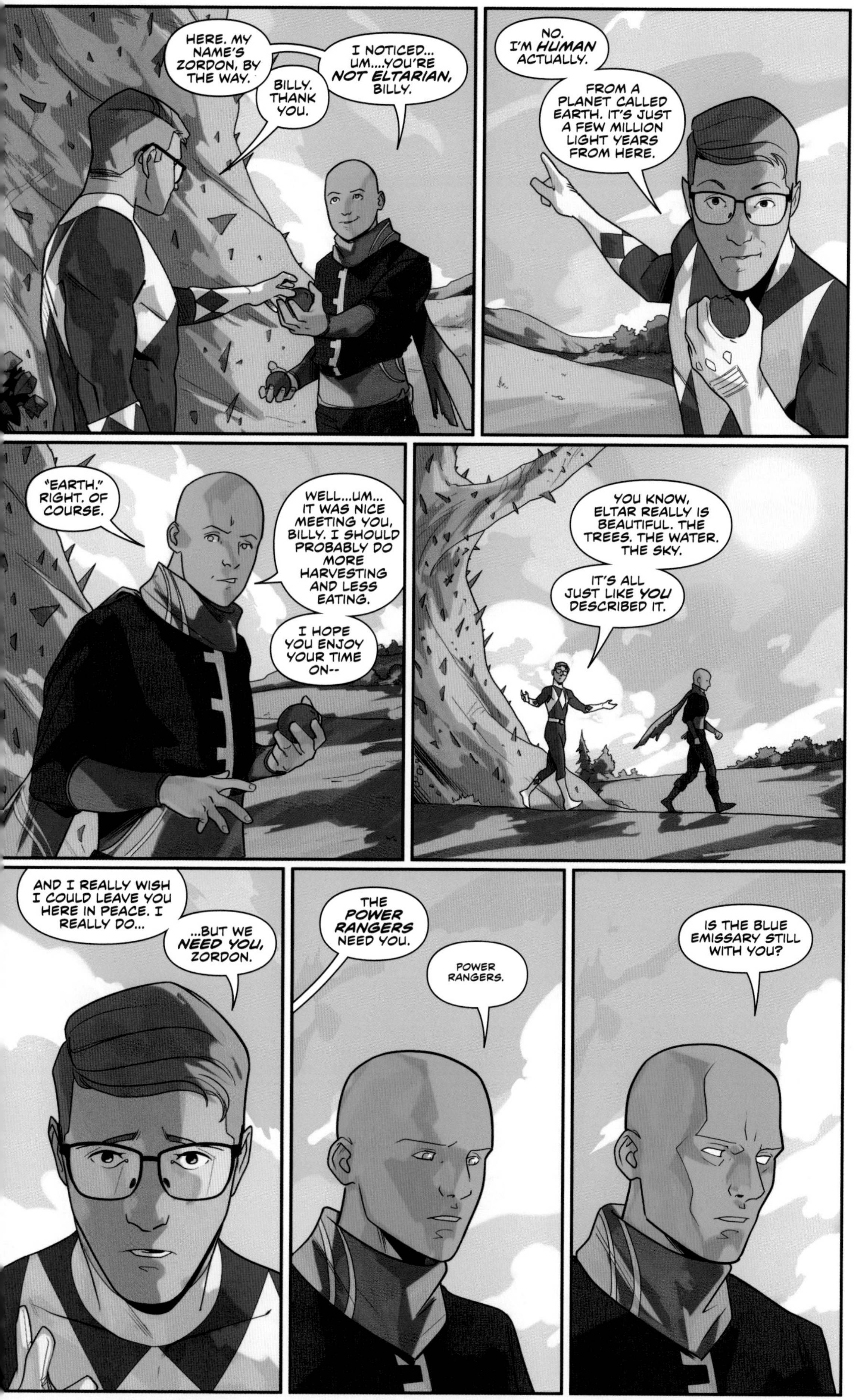
HERE. MY NAME'S ZORDON, BY THE WAY.
BILLY. THANK YOU.
I NOTICED... UM...YOU'RE NOT ELTARIAN, BILLY.
NO. I'M HUMAN ACTUALLY.
FROM A PLANET CALLED EARTH. IT'S JUST A FEW MILLION LIGHT YEARS FROM HERE.
"EARTH." RIGHT. OF COURSE.
WELL...UM... IT WAS NICE MEETING YOU, BILLY. I SHOULD PROBABLY DO MORE HARVESTING AND LESS EATING.
I HOPE YOU ENJOY YOUR TIME ON--
YOU KNOW, ELTAR REALLY IS BEAUTIFUL. THE TREES. THE WATER. THE SKY.
IT'S ALL JUST LIKE YOU DESCRIBED IT.
AND I REALLY WISH I COULD LEAVE YOU HERE IN PEACE. I REALLY DO...
...BUT WE NEED YOU, ZORDON.
THE POWER RANGERS NEED YOU.
POWER RANGERS.
IS THE BLUE EMISSARY STILL WITH YOU?

I HAVE SEEN YOUR STORY, SAGE OF ELTAR.

AND THIS IS *NOT* THE ENDING.

ZORDON, PLEASE. WE'RE IN TROUBLE. WE NEED YOUR GUIDANCE--

MY *GUIDANCE?* MY GUIDANCE HAS LED US TO THE BRINK OF *DESTRUCTION.*

BELIEVE ME, YOU'RE BETTER OFF WITHOUT ME.

THAT'S NOT TRUE. YOU'RE THE ONLY--

BILLY, WHEN I SACRIFICED MY BODY TO STOP RITA, I GAVE UP ANY CHANCE OF EVER HAVING LOVE OR CHILDREN OR EVEN A FAMILY.

I LOST EVERYTHING, BUT I THOUGHT IT WAS WORTH IT BECAUSE...

...I *BELIEVED* IN ELTAR.

MY WORLD WAS *EVERYTHING* RIGHT, NOBLE AND TRUE IN THE UNIVERSE.

BUT TO HOLD ONTO THAT BELIEF, I *IGNORED* EVERYTHING AND EVERYONE THAT CHALLENGED IT. INCLUDING THE PEOPLE I CARED ABOUT MOST.

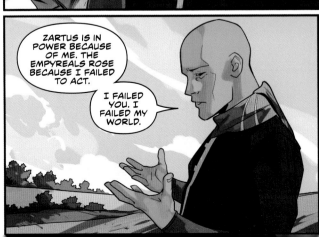

ZARTUS IS IN POWER BECAUSE OF ME. THE EMPYREALS ROSE BECAUSE I FAILED TO ACT.

I FAILED YOU. I FAILED MY WORLD.

I FAILED *EVERYONE.*

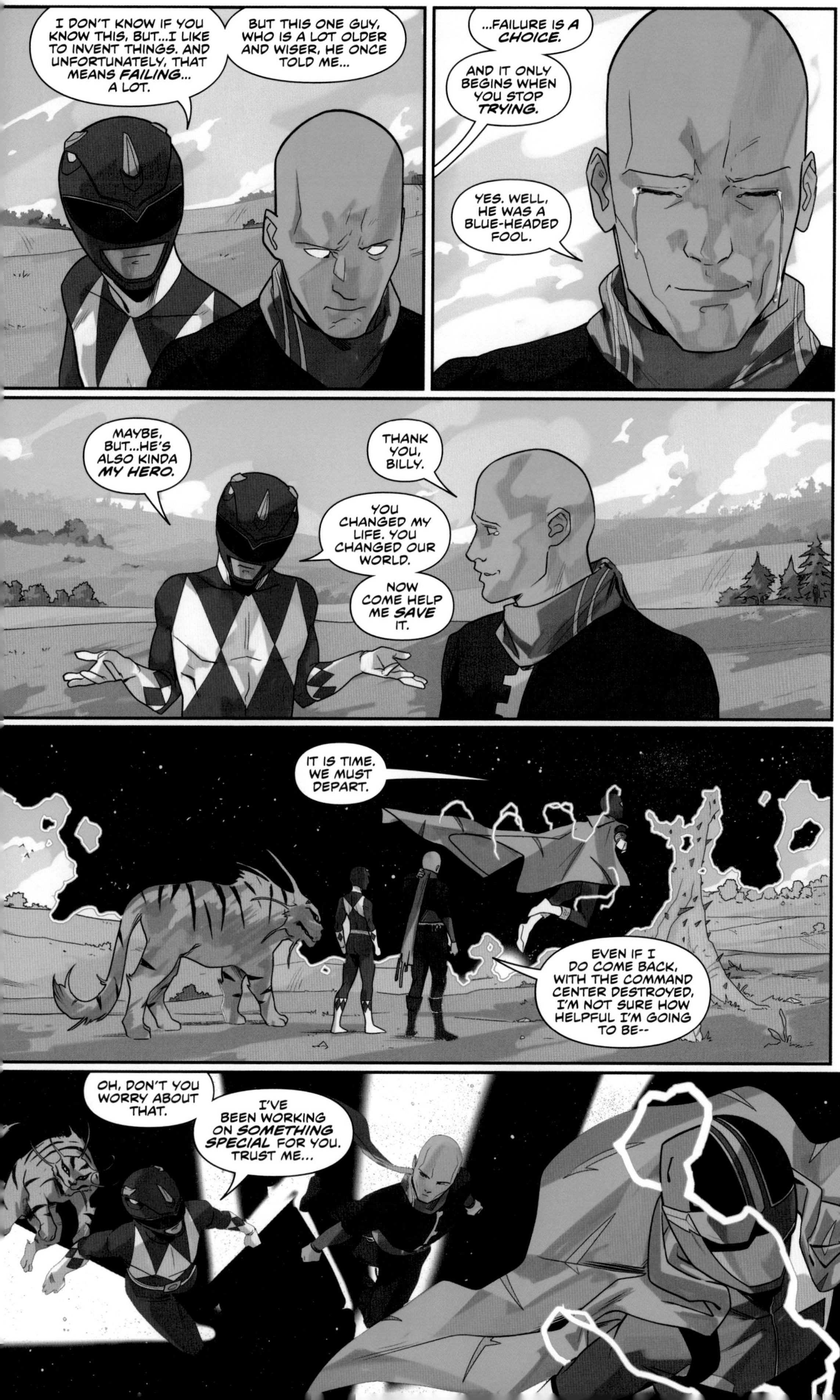
I DON'T KNOW IF YOU KNOW THIS, BUT...I LIKE TO INVENT THINGS. AND UNFORTUNATELY, THAT MEANS FAILING... A LOT.
BUT THIS ONE GUY, WHO IS A LOT OLDER AND WISER, HE ONCE TOLD ME...
...FAILURE IS A CHOICE.
AND IT ONLY BEGINS WHEN YOU STOP TRYING.
YES. WELL, HE WAS A BLUE-HEADED FOOL.
MAYBE, BUT...HE'S ALSO KINDA MY HERO.
THANK YOU, BILLY.
YOU CHANGED MY LIFE. YOU CHANGED OUR WORLD.
NOW COME HELP ME SAVE IT.
IT IS TIME. WE MUST DEPART.
EVEN IF I DO COME BACK, WITH THE COMMAND CENTER DESTROYED, I'M NOT SURE HOW HELPFUL I'M GOING TO BE--
OH, DON'T YOU WORRY ABOUT THAT.
I'VE BEEN WORKING ON SOMETHING SPECIAL FOR YOU. TRUST ME...

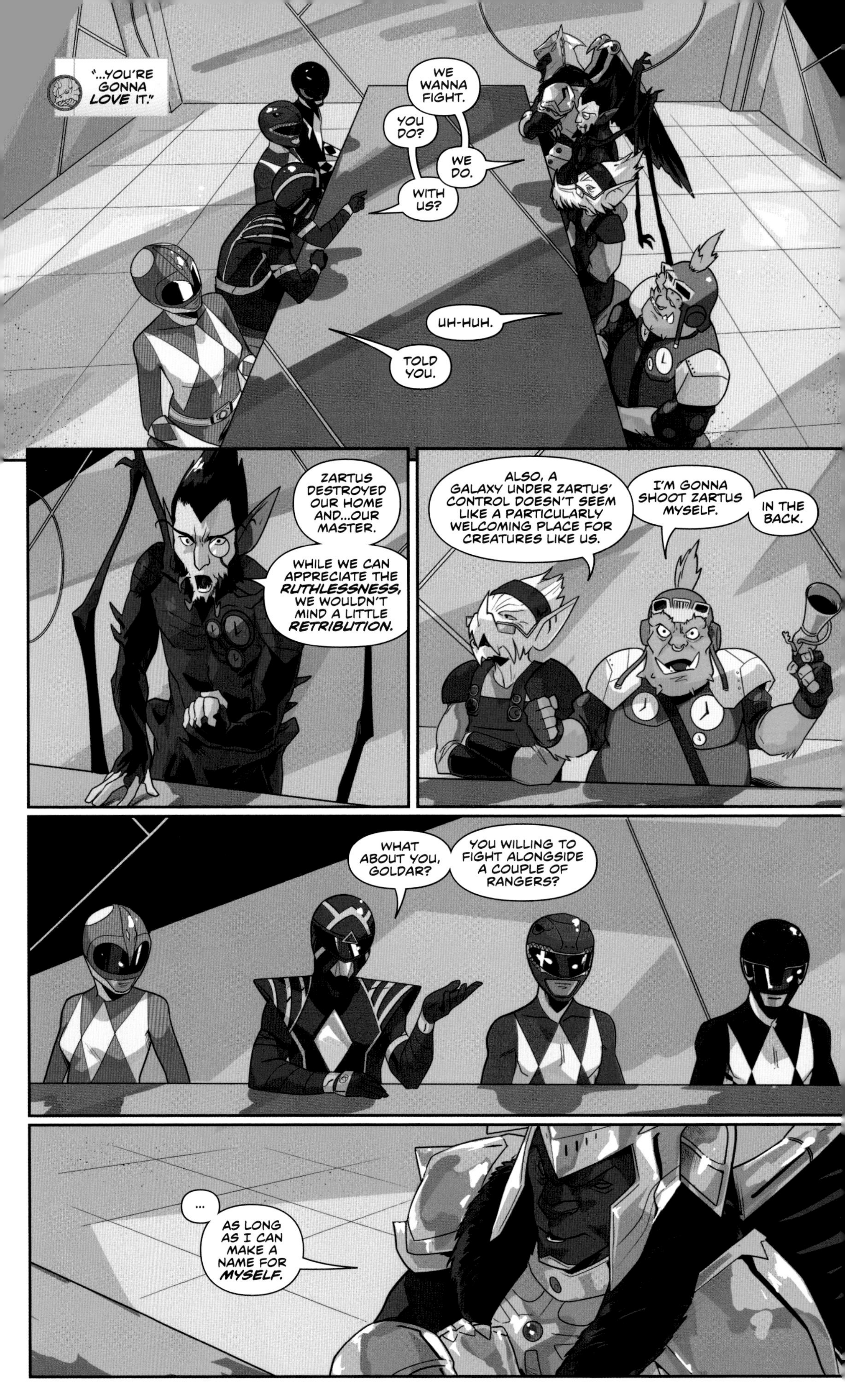
"...YOU'RE GONNA LOVE IT."
WE WANNA FIGHT.
YOU DO?
WE DO.
WITH US?
UH-HUH.
TOLD YOU.
ZARTUS DESTROYED OUR HOME AND...OUR MASTER.
WHILE WE CAN APPRECIATE THE RUTHLESSNESS, WE WOULDN'T MIND A LITTLE RETRIBUTION.
ALSO, A GALAXY UNDER ZARTUS' CONTROL DOESN'T SEEM LIKE A PARTICULARLY WELCOMING PLACE FOR CREATURES LIKE US.
I'M GONNA SHOOT ZARTUS MYSELF.
IN THE BACK.
WHAT ABOUT YOU, GOLDAR?
YOU WILLING TO FIGHT ALONGSIDE A COUPLE OF RANGERS?
...
AS LONG AS I CAN MAKE A NAME FOR MYSELF.

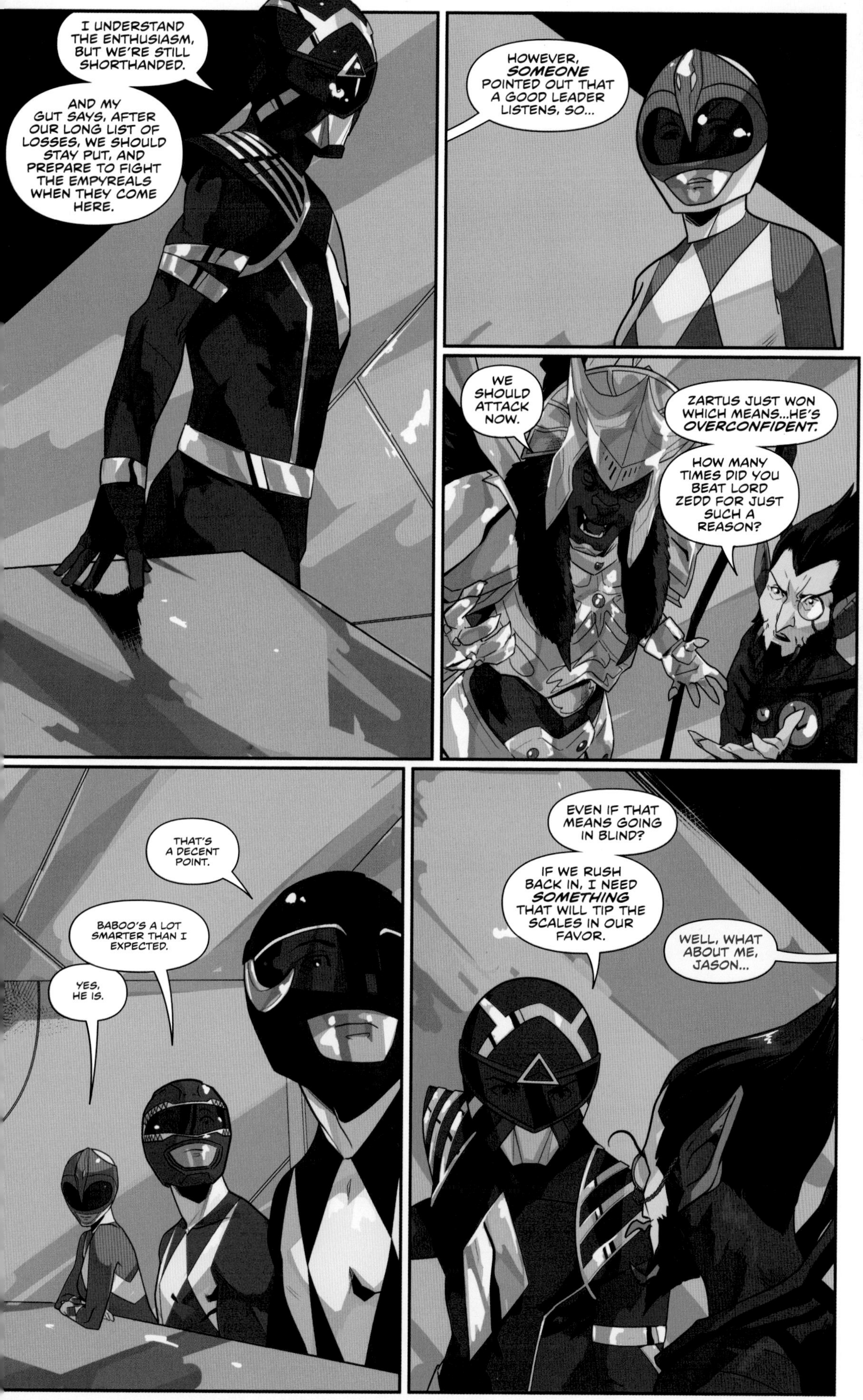
I UNDERSTAND THE ENTHUSIASM, BUT WE'RE STILL SHORTHANDED.
AND MY GUT SAYS, AFTER OUR LONG LIST OF LOSSES, WE SHOULD STAY PUT, AND PREPARE TO FIGHT THE EMPYREALS WHEN THEY COME HERE.
HOWEVER, *SOMEONE* POINTED OUT THAT A GOOD LEADER LISTENS, SO...
WE SHOULD ATTACK NOW.
ZARTUS JUST WON WHICH MEANS...HE'S *OVERCONFIDENT.*
HOW MANY TIMES DID YOU BEAT LORD ZEDD FOR JUST SUCH A REASON?
THAT'S A DECENT POINT.
BABOO'S A LOT SMARTER THAN I EXPECTED.
YES, HE IS.
EVEN IF THAT MEANS GOING IN BLIND?
IF WE RUSH BACK IN, I NEED *SOMETHING* THAT WILL TIP THE SCALES IN OUR FAVOR.
WELL, WHAT ABOUT ME, JASON...

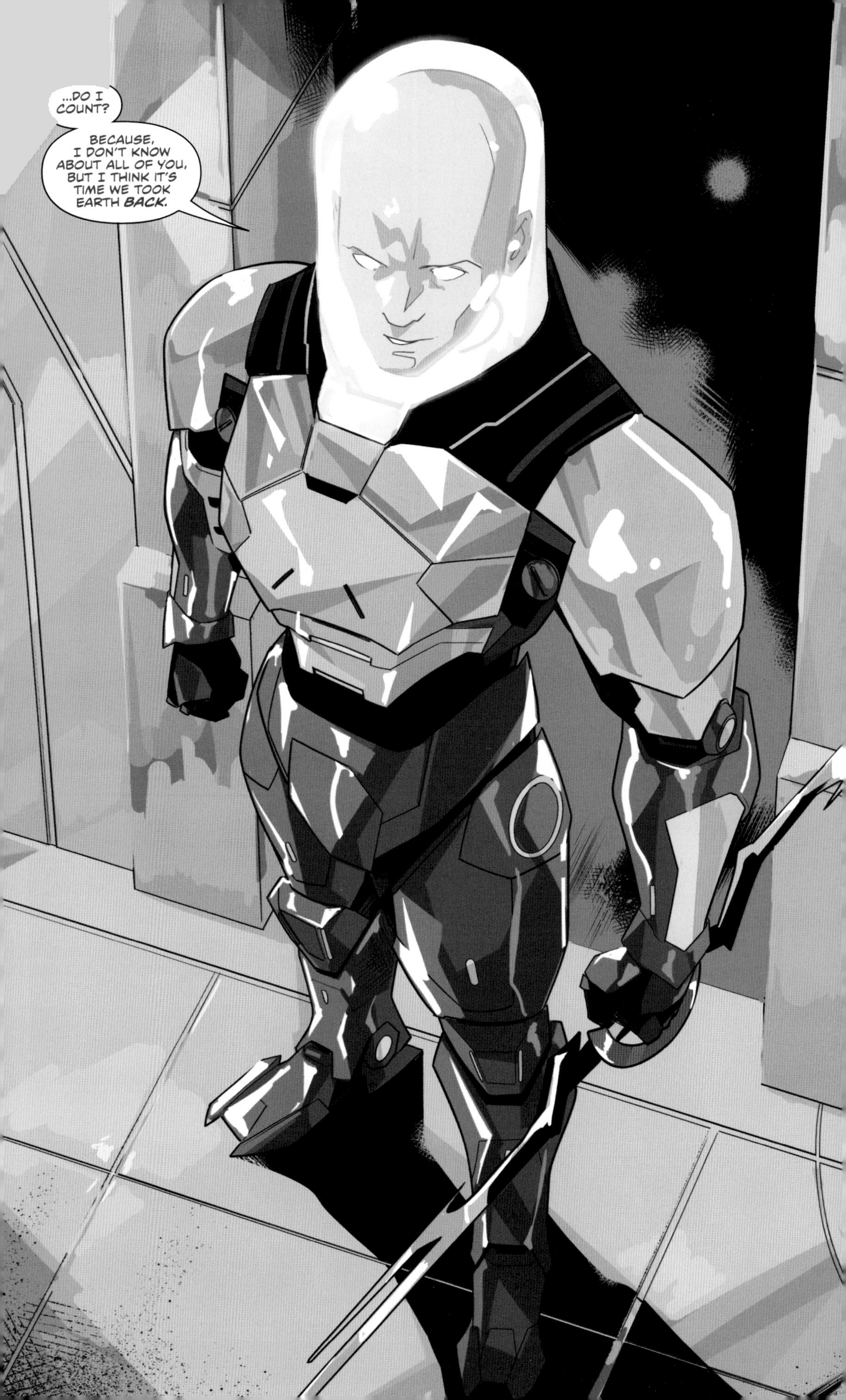
...DO I COUNT?
BECAUSE, I DON'T KNOW ABOUT ALL OF YOU, BUT I THINK IT'S TIME WE TOOK EARTH BACK.

CHAPTER FIFTEEN

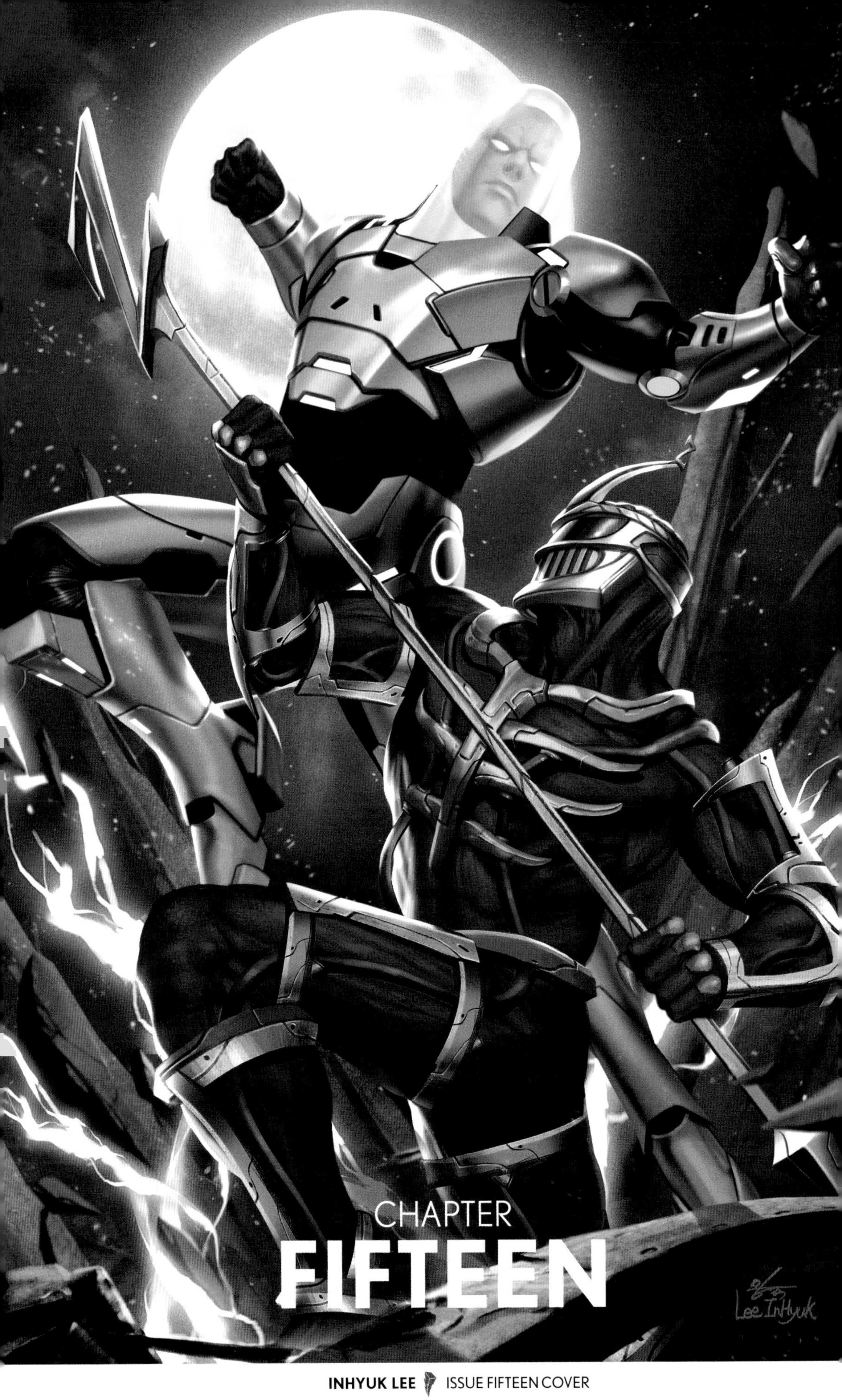
Lee InHyuk

INHYUK LEE ISSUE FIFTEEN COVER

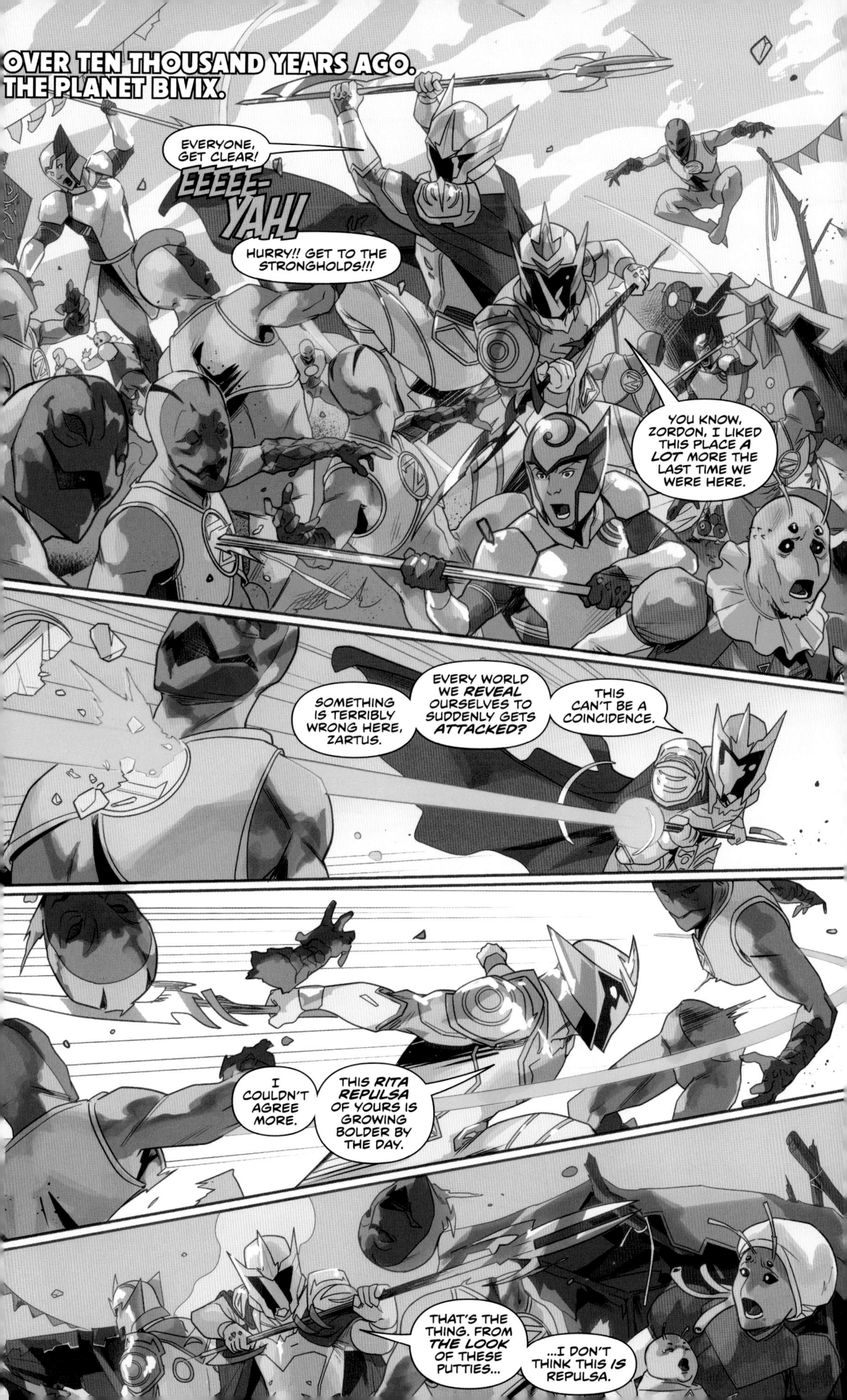
OVER TEN THOUSAND YEARS AGO. THE PLANET BIVIX.
EVERYONE, GET CLEAR!
EEEEE-YAH!
HURRY!! GET TO THE STRONGHOLDS!!!
YOU KNOW, ZORDON, I LIKED THIS PLACE A LOT MORE THE LAST TIME WE WERE HERE.
SOMETHING IS TERRIBLY WRONG HERE, ZARTUS.
EVERY WORLD WE REVEAL OURSELVES TO SUDDENLY GETS ATTACKED?
THIS CAN'T BE A COINCIDENCE.
I COULDN'T AGREE MORE.
THIS RITA REPULSA OF YOURS IS GROWING BOLDER BY THE DAY.
THAT'S THE THING. FROM THE LOOK OF THESE PUTTIES...
...I DON'T THINK THIS IS REPULSA.

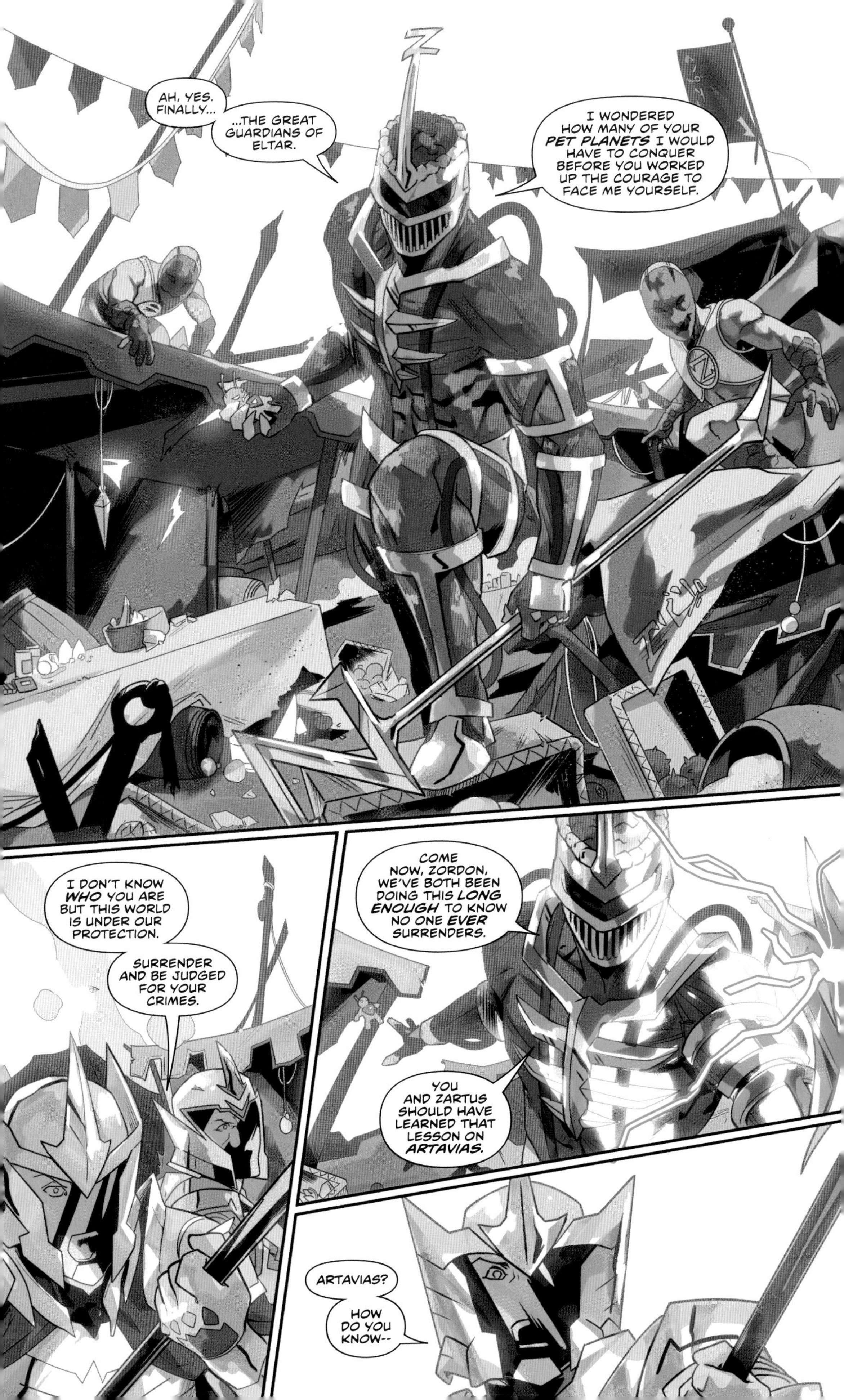

AH, YES. FINALLY...
...THE GREAT GUARDIANS OF ELTAR.
I WONDERED HOW MANY OF YOUR *PET PLANETS* I WOULD HAVE TO CONQUER BEFORE YOU WORKED UP THE COURAGE TO FACE ME YOURSELF.
I DON'T KNOW *WHO* YOU ARE BUT THIS WORLD IS UNDER OUR PROTECTION.
SURRENDER AND BE JUDGED FOR YOUR CRIMES.
COME NOW, ZORDON, WE'VE BOTH BEEN DOING THIS *LONG ENOUGH* TO KNOW NO ONE *EVER* SURRENDERS.
YOU AND ZARTUS SHOULD HAVE LEARNED THAT LESSON ON *ARTAVIAS.*
ARTAVIAS?
HOW DO YOU KNOW--

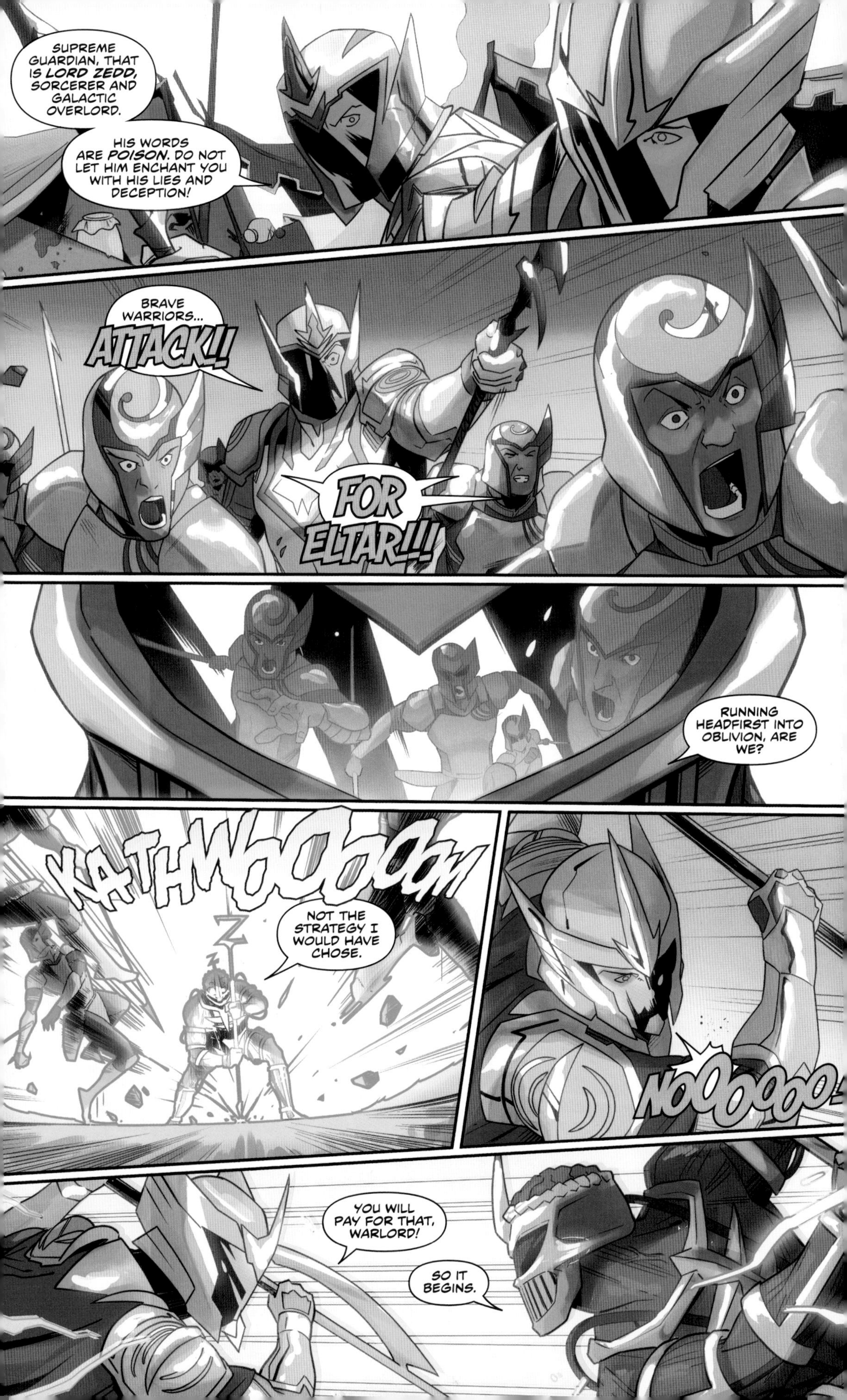
SUPREME GUARDIAN, THAT IS LORD ZEDD, SORCERER AND GALACTIC OVERLORD.
HIS WORDS ARE POISON. DO NOT LET HIM ENCHANT YOU WITH HIS LIES AND DECEPTION!
BRAVE WARRIORS... ATTACK!!
FOR ELTAR!!!
RUNNING HEADFIRST INTO OBLIVION, ARE WE?
KATHWOOOOOM
NOT THE STRATEGY I WOULD HAVE CHOSE.
NOOOOOOO
YOU WILL PAY FOR THAT, WARLORD!
SO IT BEGINS.

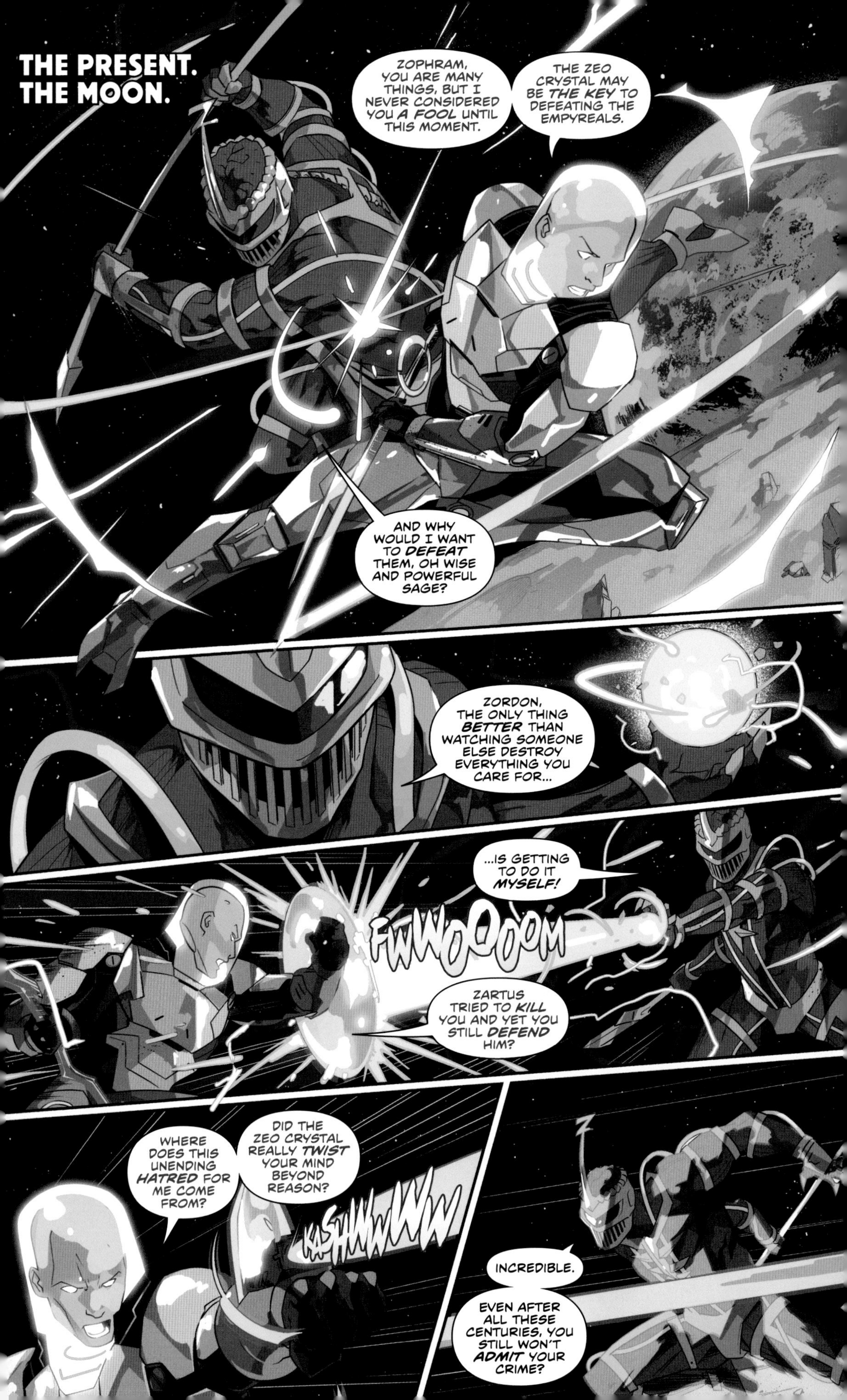
THE PRESENT. THE MOON.
ZOPHRAM, YOU ARE MANY THINGS, BUT I NEVER CONSIDERED YOU A FOOL UNTIL THIS MOMENT.
THE ZEO CRYSTAL MAY BE THE KEY TO DEFEATING THE EMPYREALS.
AND WHY WOULD I WANT TO DEFEAT THEM, OH WISE AND POWERFUL SAGE?
ZORDON, THE ONLY THING BETTER THAN WATCHING SOMEONE ELSE DESTROY EVERYTHING YOU CARE FOR...
...IS GETTING TO DO IT MYSELF!
FWWOOOOM
ZARTUS TRIED TO KILL YOU AND YET YOU STILL DEFEND HIM?
WHERE DOES THIS UNENDING HATRED FOR ME COME FROM?
DID THE ZEO CRYSTAL REALLY TWIST YOUR MIND BEYOND REASON?
KASHWWWW
INCREDIBLE.
EVEN AFTER ALL THESE CENTURIES, YOU STILL WON'T ADMIT YOUR CRIME?

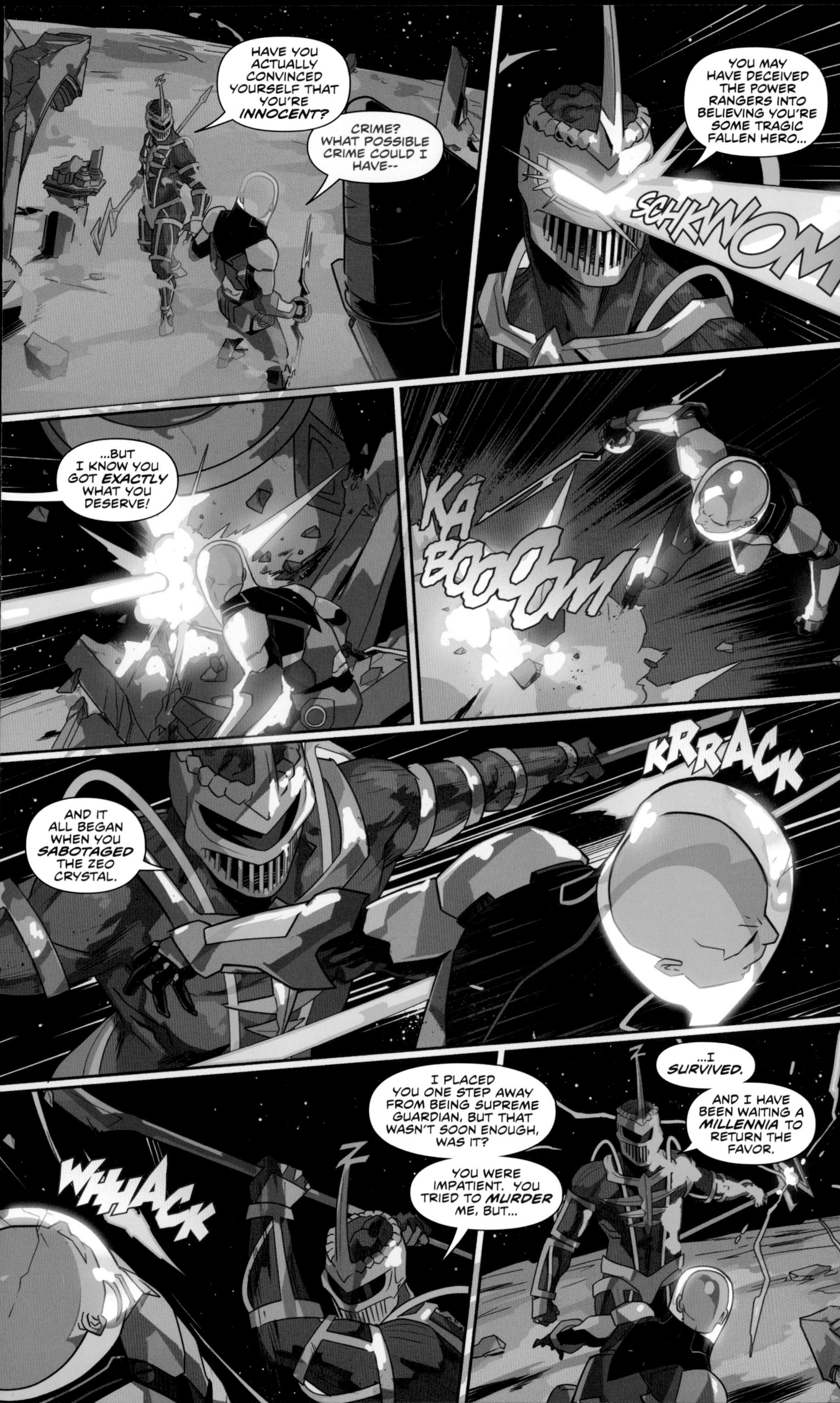
HAVE YOU ACTUALLY CONVINCED YOURSELF THAT YOU'RE *INNOCENT?*
CRIME? WHAT POSSIBLE CRIME COULD I HAVE--
YOU MAY HAVE DECEIVED THE POWER RANGERS INTO BELIEVING YOU'RE SOME TRAGIC FALLEN HERO...
SCHKWOM
...BUT I KNOW YOU GOT *EXACTLY* WHAT YOU DESERVE!
KA BOOOOM
KRRACK
AND IT ALL BEGAN WHEN YOU *SABOTAGED* THE ZEO CRYSTAL.
WHHACK
I PLACED YOU ONE STEP AWAY FROM BEING SUPREME GUARDIAN, BUT THAT WASN'T SOON ENOUGH, WAS IT?
YOU WERE IMPATIENT. YOU TRIED TO *MURDER* ME, BUT...
...I *SURVIVED.*
AND I HAVE BEEN WAITING A *MILLENNIA* TO RETURN THE FAVOR.

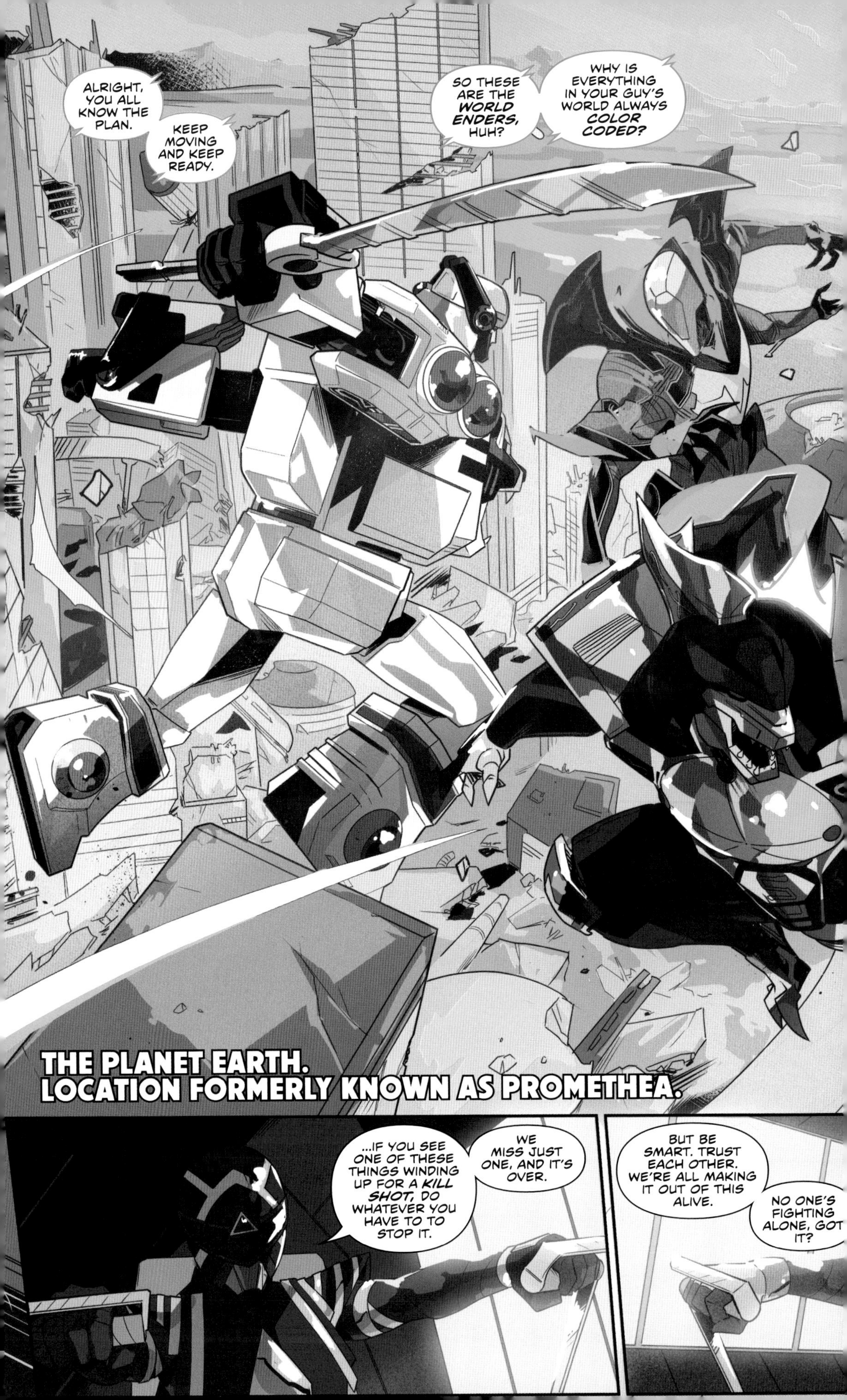
ALRIGHT, YOU ALL KNOW THE PLAN.
KEEP MOVING AND KEEP READY.
SO THESE ARE THE WORLD ENDERS, HUH?
WHY IS EVERYTHING IN YOUR GUY'S WORLD ALWAYS COLOR CODED?
THE PLANET EARTH.
LOCATION FORMERLY KNOWN AS PROMETHEA.
...IF YOU SEE ONE OF THESE THINGS WINDING UP FOR A KILL SHOT, DO WHATEVER YOU HAVE TO TO STOP IT.
WE MISS JUST ONE, AND IT'S OVER.
BUT BE SMART. TRUST EACH OTHER. WE'RE ALL MAKING IT OUT OF THIS ALIVE.
NO ONE'S FIGHTING ALONE, GOT IT?

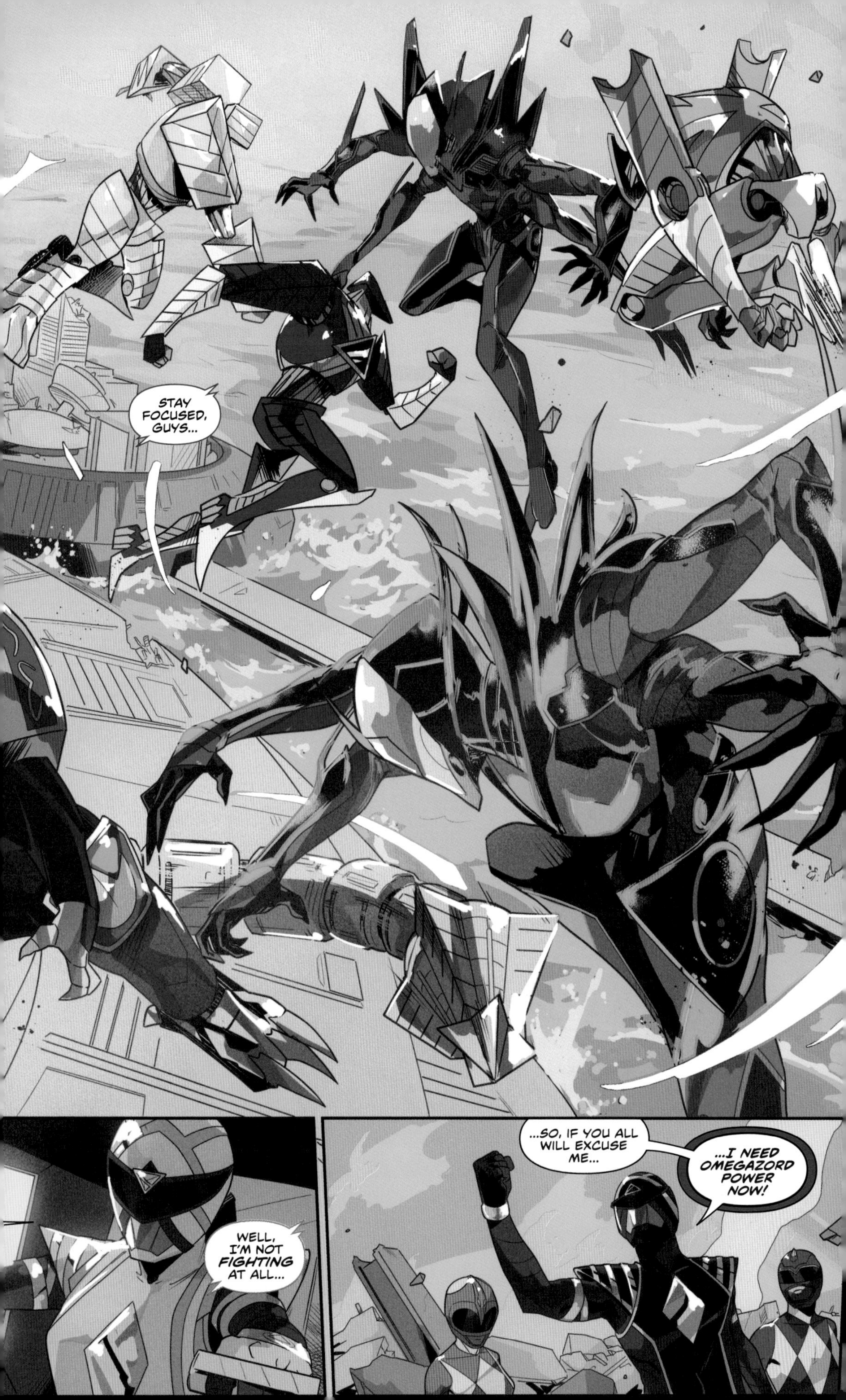
STAY FOCUSED, GUYS...
WELL, I'M NOT *FIGHTING* AT ALL...
...SO, IF YOU ALL WILL EXCUSE ME...
...I NEED OMEGAZORD POWER NOW!

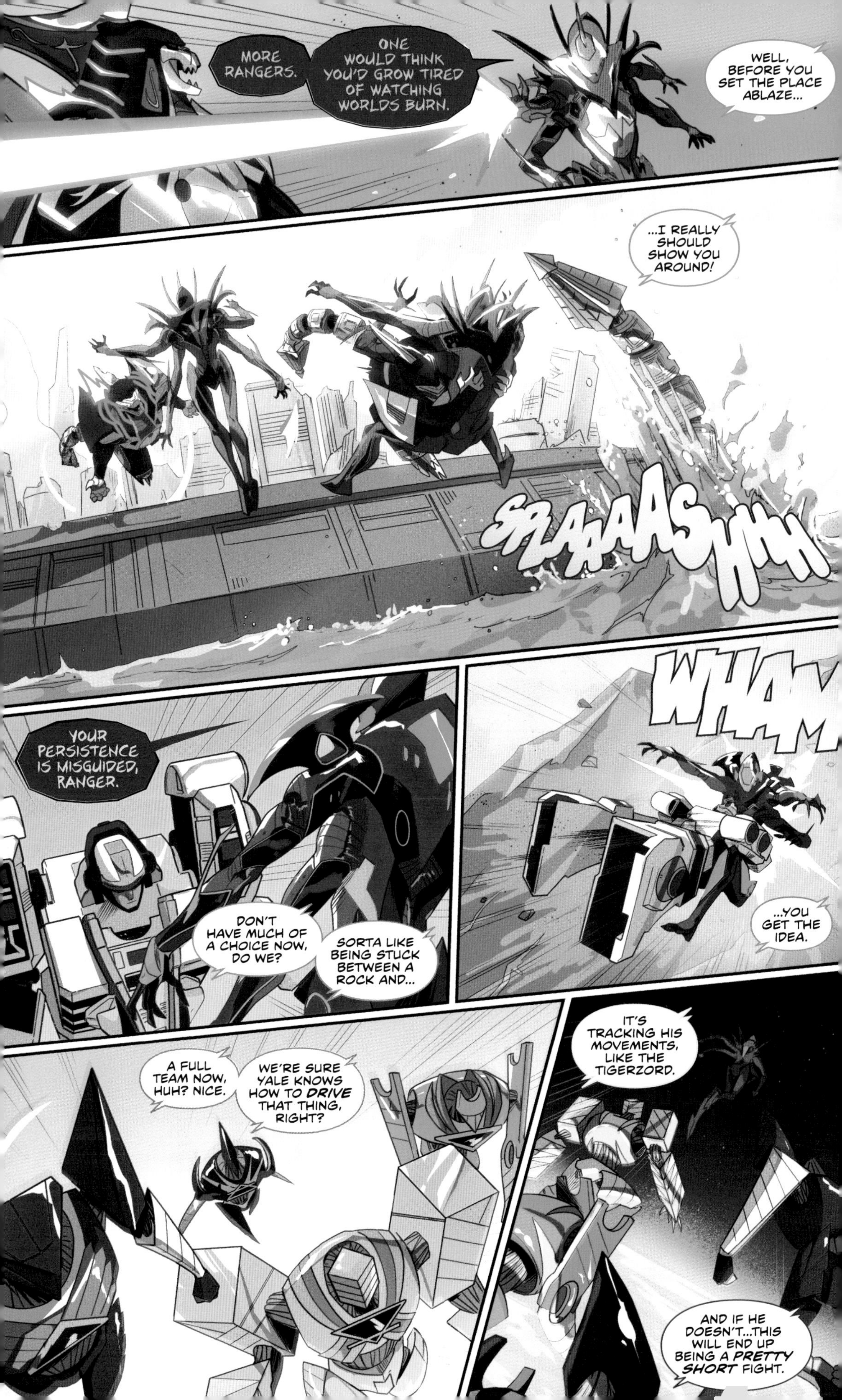
MORE RANGERS.
ONE WOULD THINK YOU'D GROW TIRED OF WATCHING WORLDS BURN.
WELL, BEFORE YOU SET THE PLACE ABLAZE...
...I REALLY SHOULD SHOW YOU AROUND!
SPLAAAASHHH
YOUR PERSISTENCE IS MISGUIDED, RANGER.
DON'T HAVE MUCH OF A CHOICE NOW, DO WE?
SORTA LIKE BEING STUCK BETWEEN A ROCK AND...
WHAM
...YOU GET THE IDEA.
A FULL TEAM NOW, HUH? NICE.
WE'RE SURE YALE KNOWS HOW TO *DRIVE* THAT THING, RIGHT?
IT'S TRACKING HIS MOVEMENTS, LIKE THE TIGERZORD.
AND IF HE DOESN'T...THIS WILL END UP BEING A *PRETTY SHORT* FIGHT.

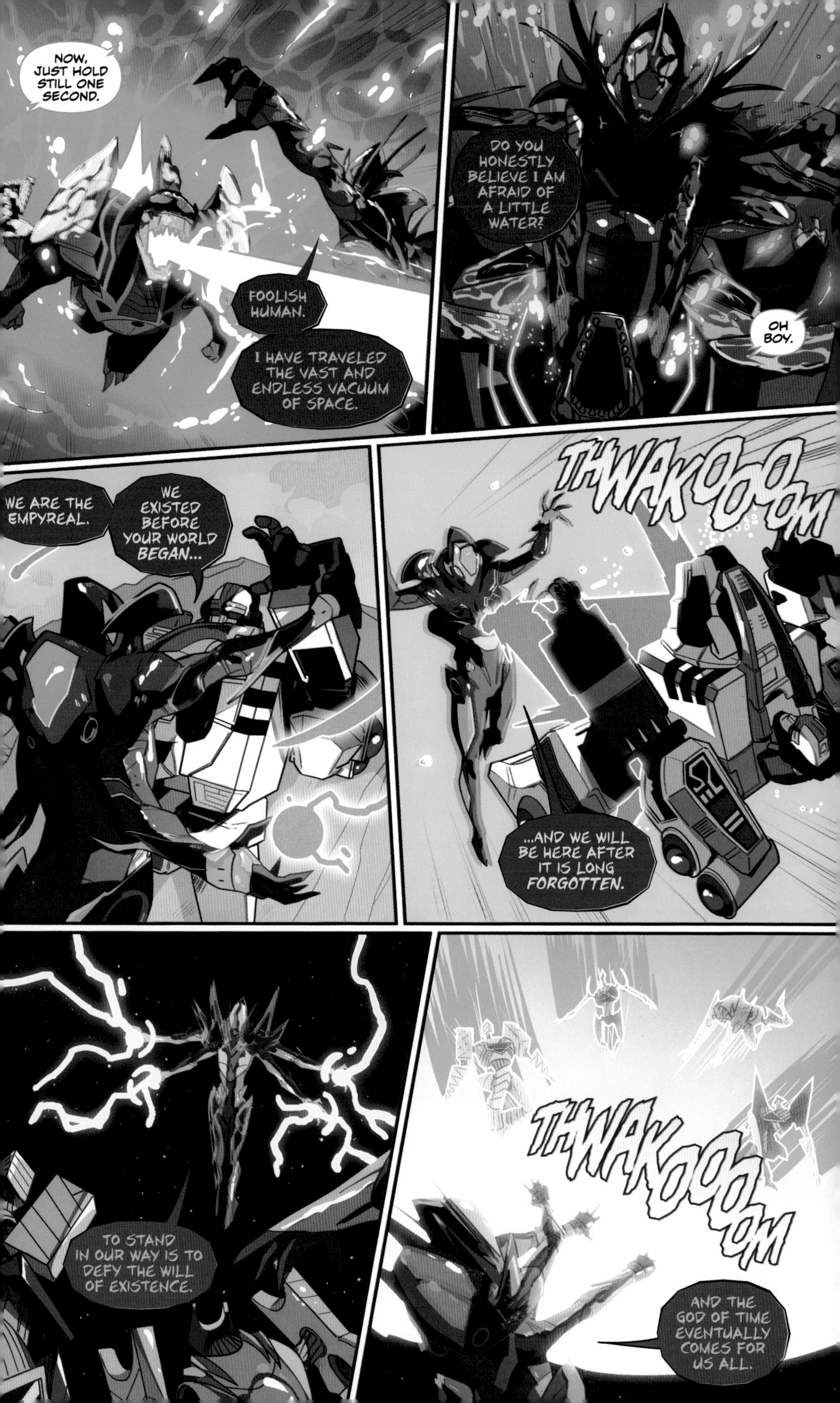
NOW, JUST HOLD STILL ONE SECOND.
FOOLISH HUMAN.
I HAVE TRAVELED THE VAST AND ENDLESS VACUUM OF SPACE.
DO YOU HONESTLY BELIEVE I AM AFRAID OF A LITTLE WATER?
OH BOY.
WE ARE THE EMPYREAL.
WE EXISTED BEFORE YOUR WORLD BEGAN...
THWAKOOOOM
...AND WE WILL BE HERE AFTER IT IS LONG FORGOTTEN.
TO STAND IN OUR WAY IS TO DEFY THE WILL OF EXISTENCE.
THWAKOOOOOM
AND THE GOD OF TIME EVENTUALLY COMES FOR US ALL.

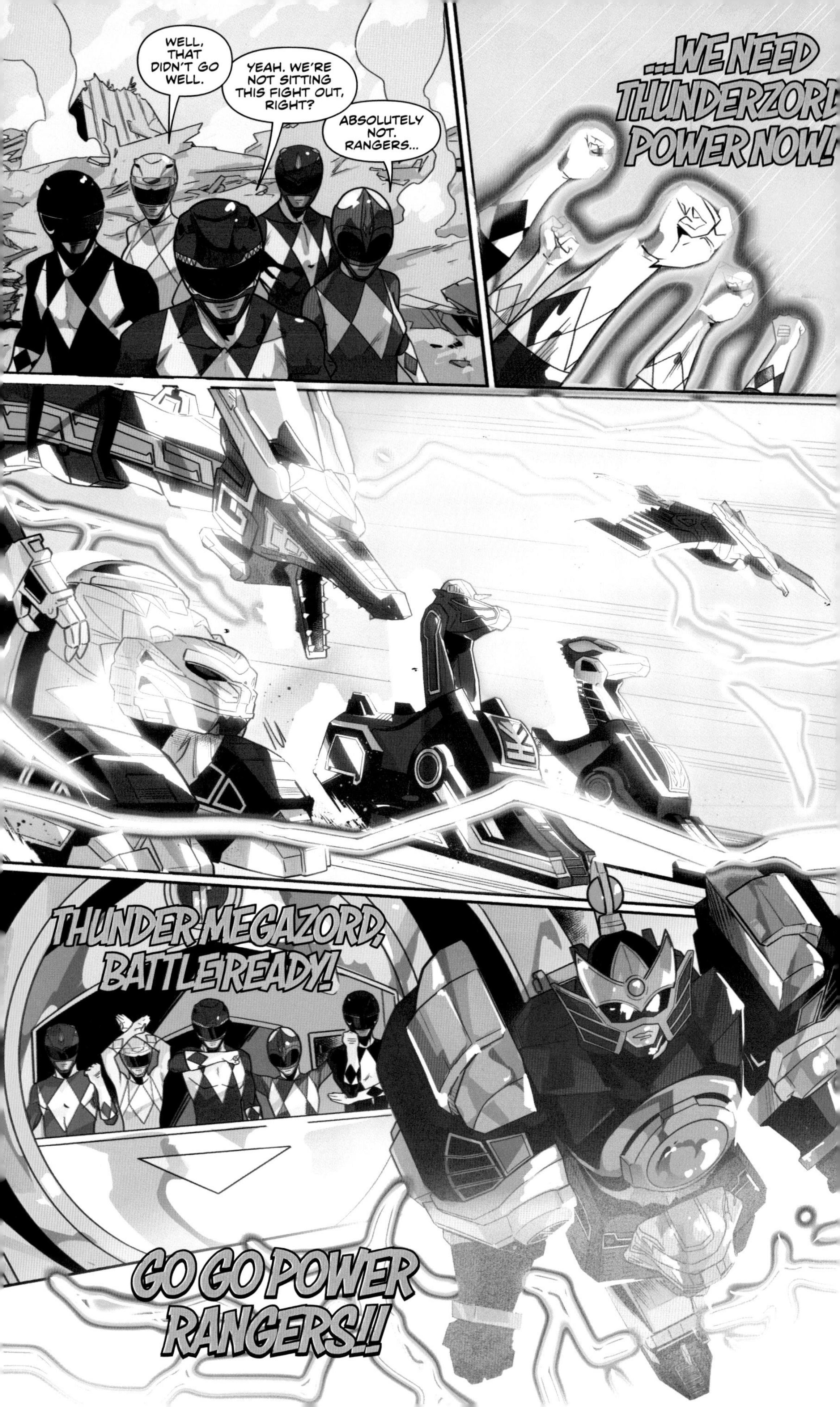
WELL, THAT DIDN'T GO WELL.
YEAH. WE'RE NOT SITTING THIS FIGHT OUT, RIGHT?
ABSOLUTELY NOT. RANGERS...
...WE NEED THUNDERZORD POWER NOW!
THUNDER MEGAZORD, BATTLE READY!
GO GO POWER RANGERS!!

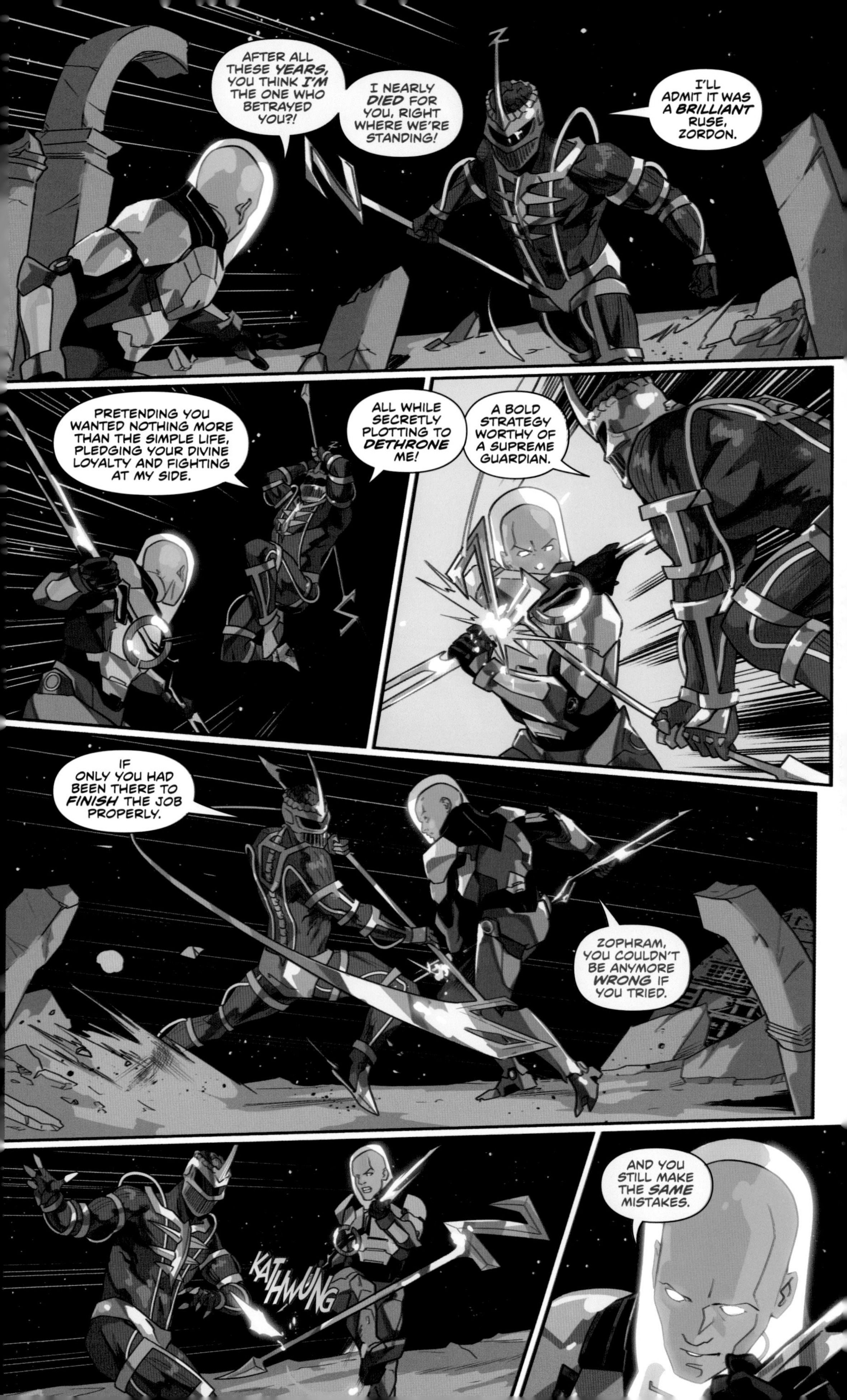
AFTER ALL THESE YEARS, YOU THINK I'M THE ONE WHO BETRAYED YOU?!
I NEARLY DIED FOR YOU, RIGHT WHERE WE'RE STANDING!
I'LL ADMIT IT WAS A BRILLIANT RUSE, ZORDON.
PRETENDING YOU WANTED NOTHING MORE THAN THE SIMPLE LIFE, PLEDGING YOUR DIVINE LOYALTY AND FIGHTING AT MY SIDE.
ALL WHILE SECRETLY PLOTTING TO DETHRONE ME!
A BOLD STRATEGY WORTHY OF A SUPREME GUARDIAN.
IF ONLY YOU HAD BEEN THERE TO FINISH THE JOB PROPERLY.
ZOPHRAM, YOU COULDN'T BE ANYMORE WRONG IF YOU TRIED.
KATHWUNG
AND YOU STILL MAKE THE SAME MISTAKES.

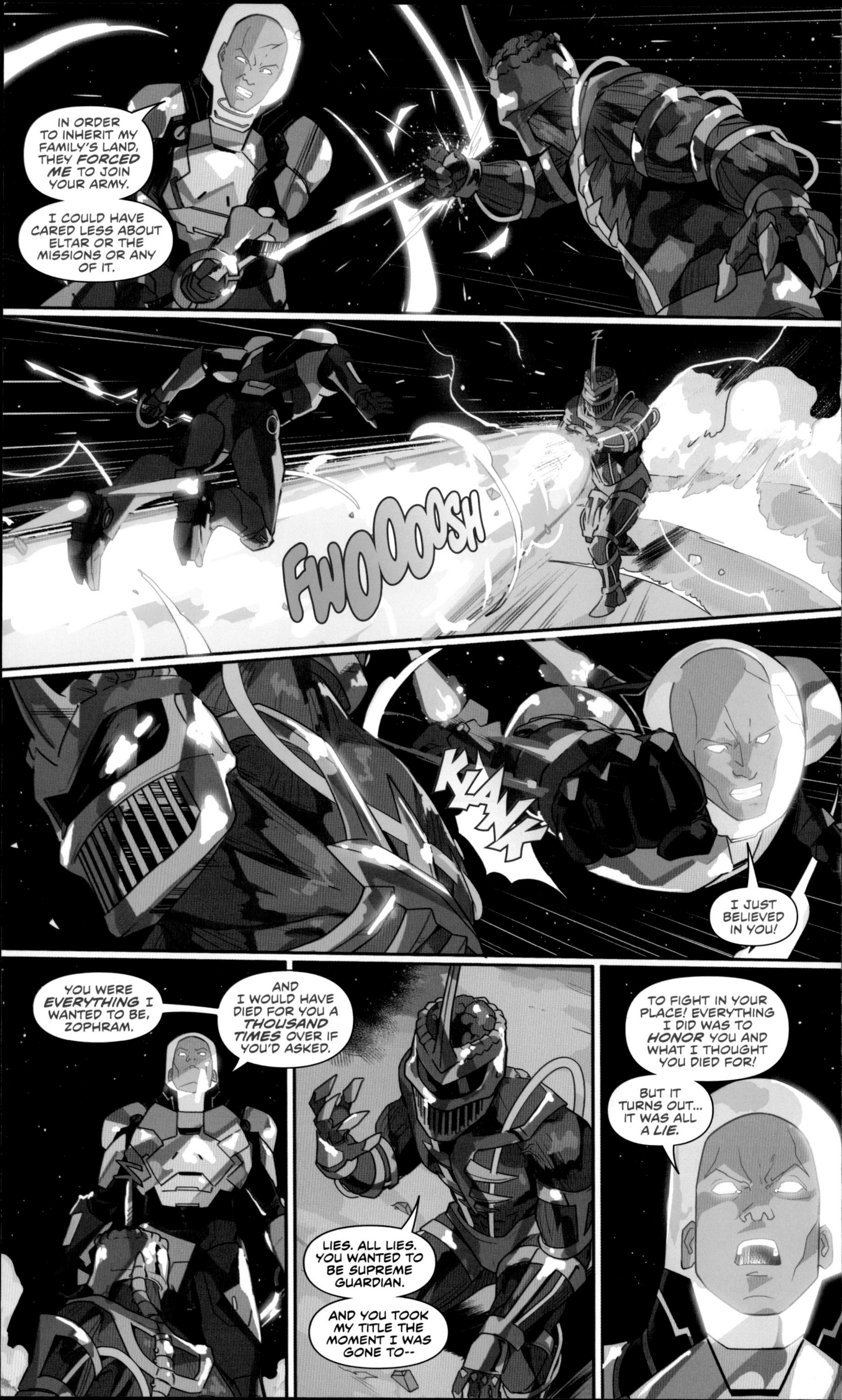
IN ORDER TO INHERIT MY FAMILY'S LAND, THEY *FORCED ME* TO JOIN YOUR ARMY.
I COULD HAVE CARED LESS ABOUT ELTAR OR THE MISSIONS OR ANY OF IT.
FWOOOOSH
KLANK
I JUST BELIEVED IN YOU!
YOU WERE *EVERYTHING* I WANTED TO BE, ZOPHRAM.
AND I WOULD HAVE DIED FOR YOU A *THOUSAND TIMES* OVER IF YOU'D ASKED.
LIES. ALL LIES. YOU WANTED TO BE SUPREME GUARDIAN.
AND YOU TOOK MY TITLE THE MOMENT I WAS GONE TO--
TO FIGHT IN YOUR PLACE! EVERYTHING I DID WAS TO *HONOR* YOU AND WHAT I THOUGHT YOU DIED FOR!
BUT IT TURNS OUT... IT WAS ALL A *LIE.*

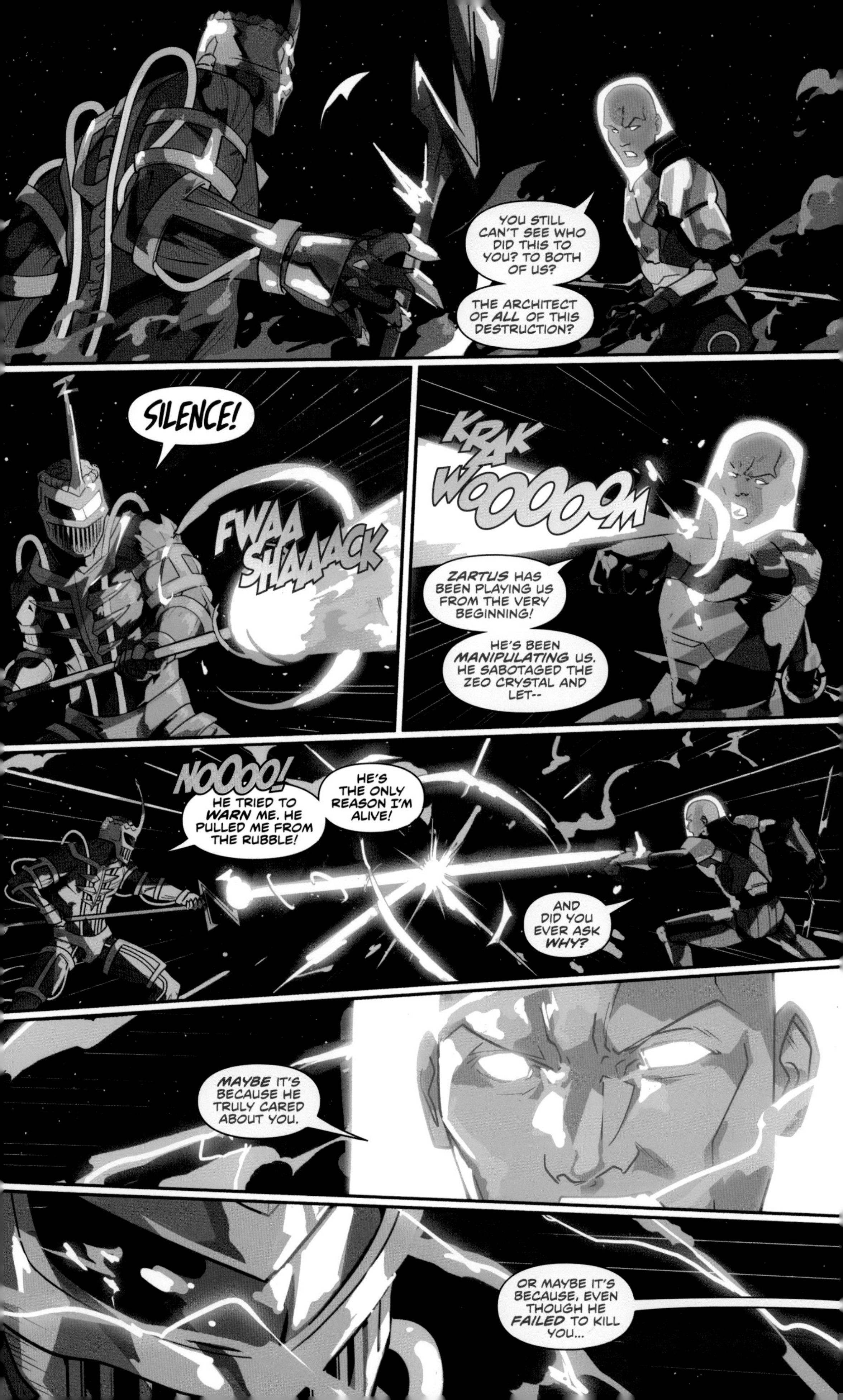

YOU STILL CAN'T SEE WHO DID THIS TO YOU? TO BOTH OF US?
THE ARCHITECT OF ALL OF THIS DESTRUCTION?
SILENCE!
FWAA SHAAACK
KRAK A WOOOOOOM
ZARTUS HAS BEEN PLAYING US FROM THE VERY BEGINNING!
HE'S BEEN MANIPULATING US. HE SABOTAGED THE ZEO CRYSTAL AND LET--
NOOOO!
HE TRIED TO WARN ME. HE PULLED ME FROM THE RUBBLE!
HE'S THE ONLY REASON I'M ALIVE!
AND DID YOU EVER ASK WHY?
MAYBE IT'S BECAUSE HE TRULY CARED ABOUT YOU.
OR MAYBE IT'S BECAUSE, EVEN THOUGH HE FAILED TO KILL YOU...

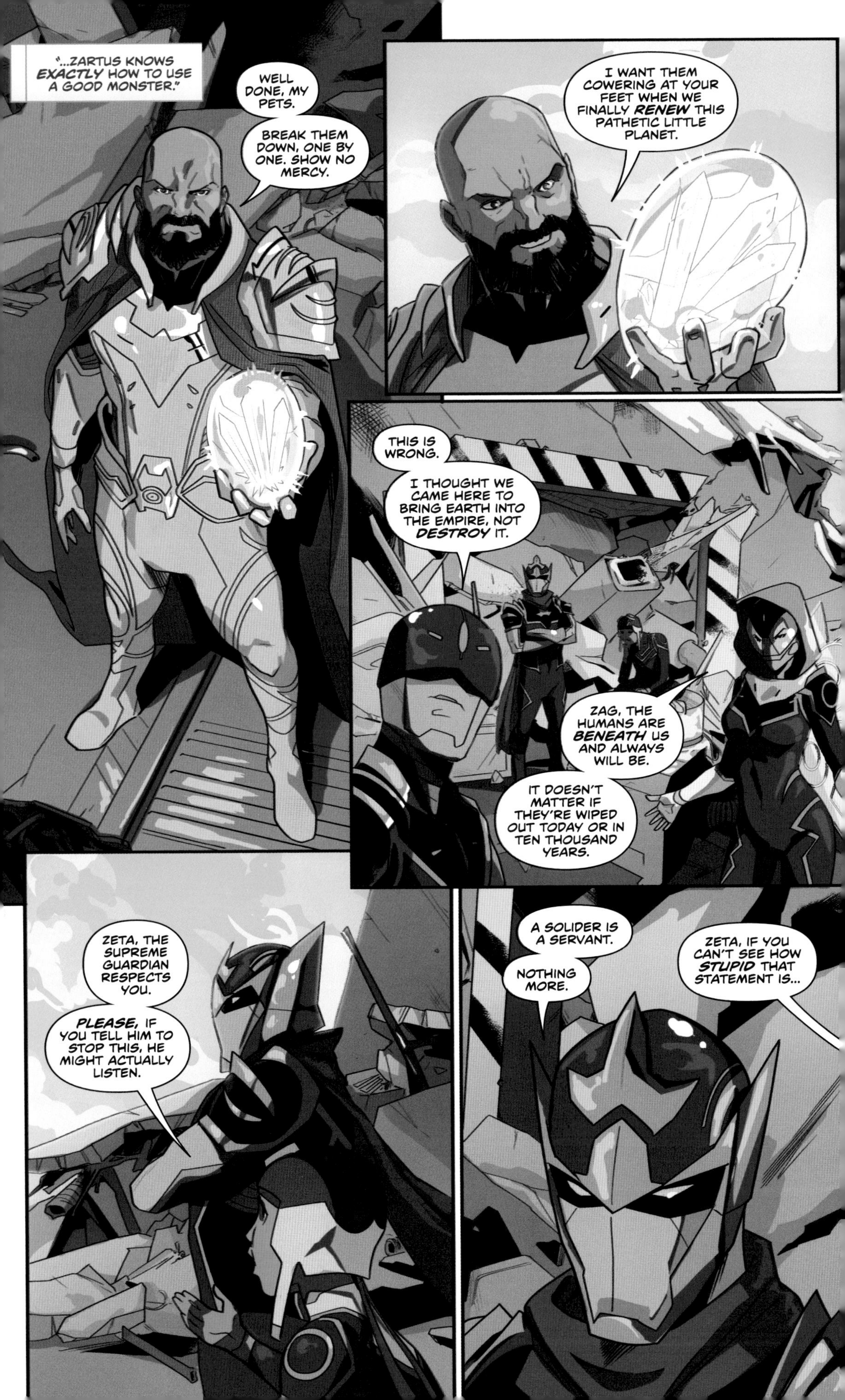
"...ZARTUS KNOWS EXACTLY HOW TO USE A GOOD MONSTER."
WELL DONE, MY PETS.
BREAK THEM DOWN, ONE BY ONE. SHOW NO MERCY.
I WANT THEM COWERING AT YOUR FEET WHEN WE FINALLY RENEW THIS PATHETIC LITTLE PLANET.
THIS IS WRONG.
I THOUGHT WE CAME HERE TO BRING EARTH INTO THE EMPIRE, NOT DESTROY IT.
ZAG, THE HUMANS ARE BENEATH US AND ALWAYS WILL BE.
IT DOESN'T MATTER IF THEY'RE WIPED OUT TODAY OR IN TEN THOUSAND YEARS.
ZETA, THE SUPREME GUARDIAN RESPECTS YOU.
PLEASE, IF YOU TELL HIM TO STOP THIS, HE MIGHT ACTUALLY LISTEN.
A SOLIDER IS A SERVANT.
NOTHING MORE.
ZETA, IF YOU CAN'T SEE HOW STUPID THAT STATEMENT IS...

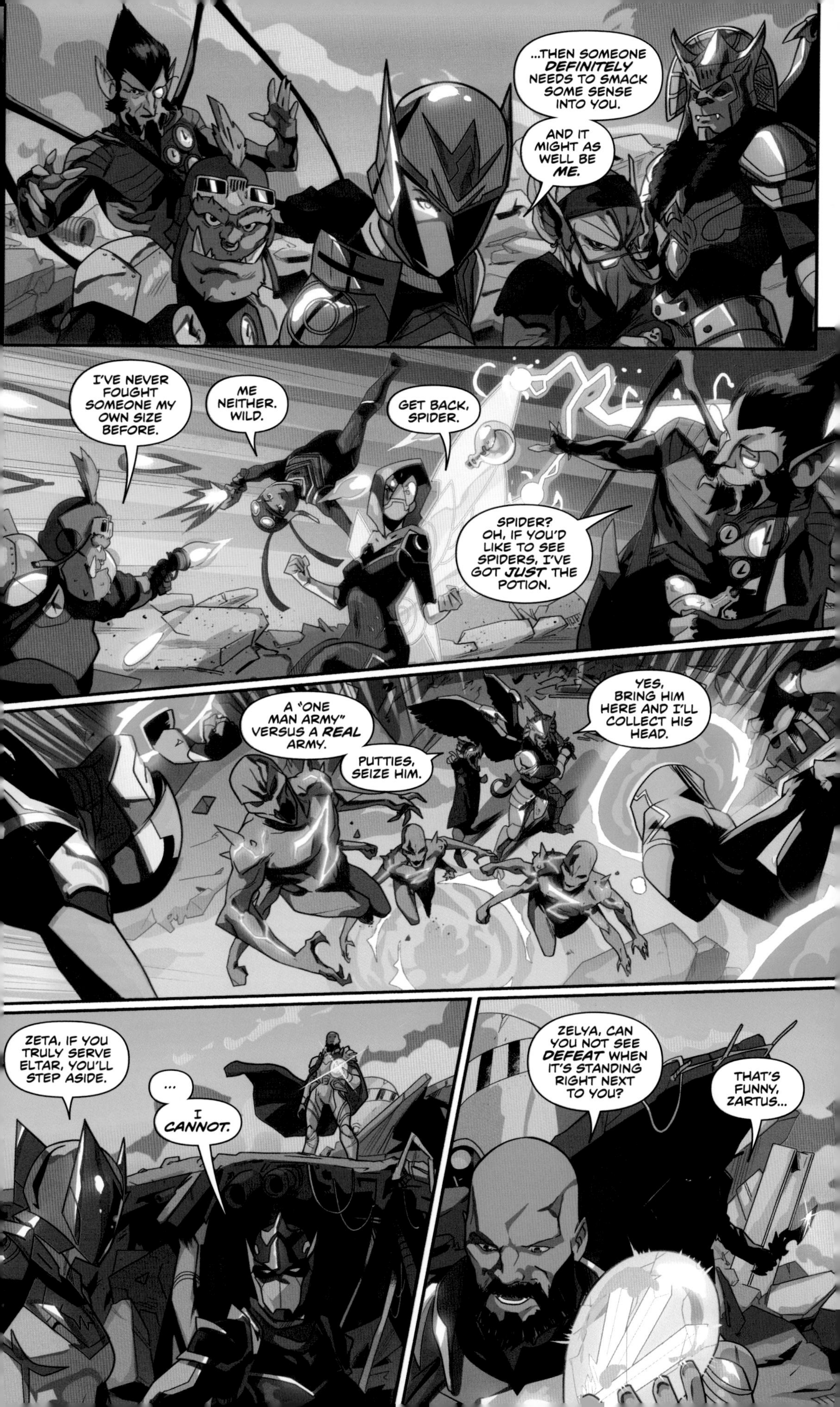
...THEN SOMEONE DEFINITELY NEEDS TO SMACK SOME SENSE INTO YOU.
AND IT MIGHT AS WELL BE ME.
I'VE NEVER FOUGHT SOMEONE MY OWN SIZE BEFORE.
ME NEITHER. WILD.
GET BACK, SPIDER.
SPIDER? OH, IF YOU'D LIKE TO SEE SPIDERS, I'VE GOT JUST THE POTION.
A "ONE MAN ARMY" VERSUS A REAL ARMY.
PUTTIES, SEIZE HIM.
YES, BRING HIM HERE AND I'LL COLLECT HIS HEAD.
ZETA, IF YOU TRULY SERVE ELTAR, YOU'LL STEP ASIDE.
...
I CANNOT.
ZELYA, CAN YOU NOT SEE DEFEAT WHEN IT'S STANDING RIGHT NEXT TO YOU?
THAT'S FUNNY, ZARTUS...

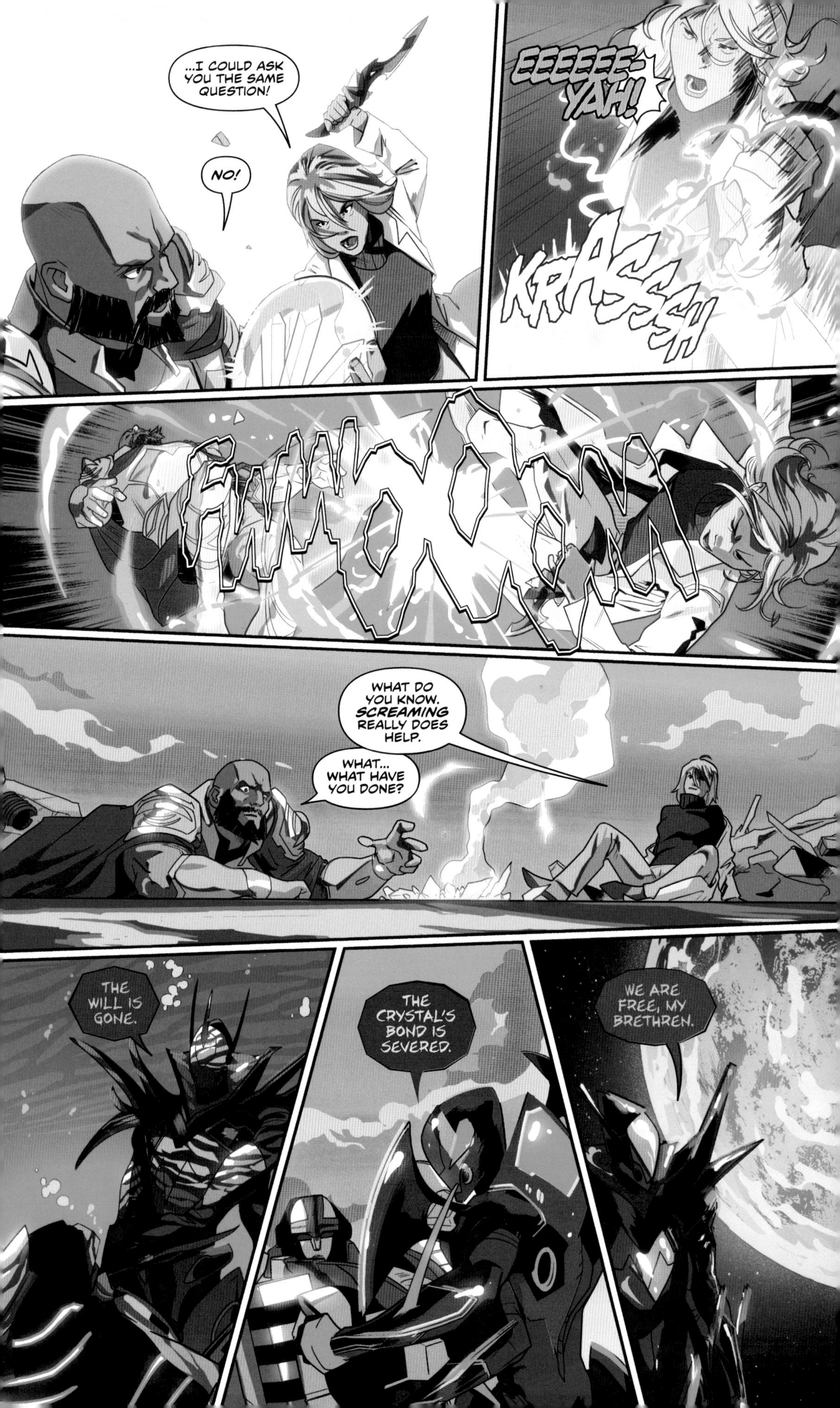

...I COULD ASK YOU THE SAME QUESTION!
NO!
EEEEEE-YAH!
KRASSH
FWOOOM
WHAT DO YOU KNOW. SCREAMING REALLY DOES HELP.
WHAT... WHAT HAVE YOU DONE?
THE WILL IS GONE.
THE CRYSTAL'S BOND IS SEVERED.
WE ARE FREE, MY BRETHREN.

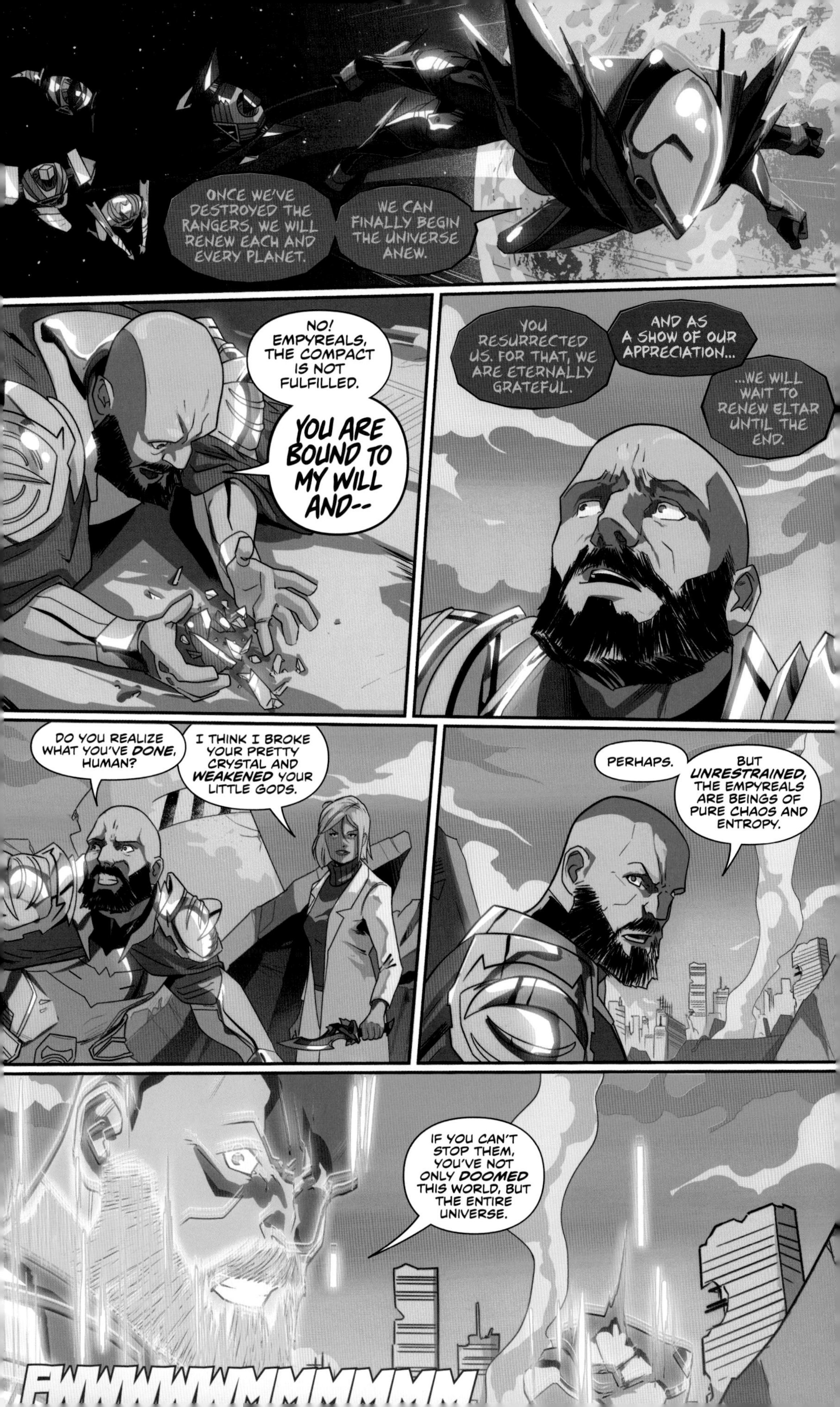
ONCE WE'VE DESTROYED THE RANGERS, WE WILL RENEW EACH AND EVERY PLANET.
WE CAN FINALLY BEGIN THE UNIVERSE ANEW.
NO! EMPYREALS, THE COMPACT IS NOT FULFILLED.
YOU ARE BOUND TO MY WILL AND--
YOU RESURRECTED US. FOR THAT, WE ARE ETERNALLY GRATEFUL.
AND AS A SHOW OF OUR APPRECIATION...
...WE WILL WAIT TO RENEW ELTAR UNTIL THE END.
DO YOU REALIZE WHAT YOU'VE DONE, HUMAN?
I THINK I BROKE YOUR PRETTY CRYSTAL AND WEAKENED YOUR LITTLE GODS.
PERHAPS.
BUT UNRESTRAINED, THE EMPYREALS ARE BEINGS OF PURE CHAOS AND ENTROPY.
IF YOU CAN'T STOP THEM, YOU'VE NOT ONLY DOOMED THIS WORLD, BUT THE ENTIRE UNIVERSE.
FWWWWWMMMMMMM

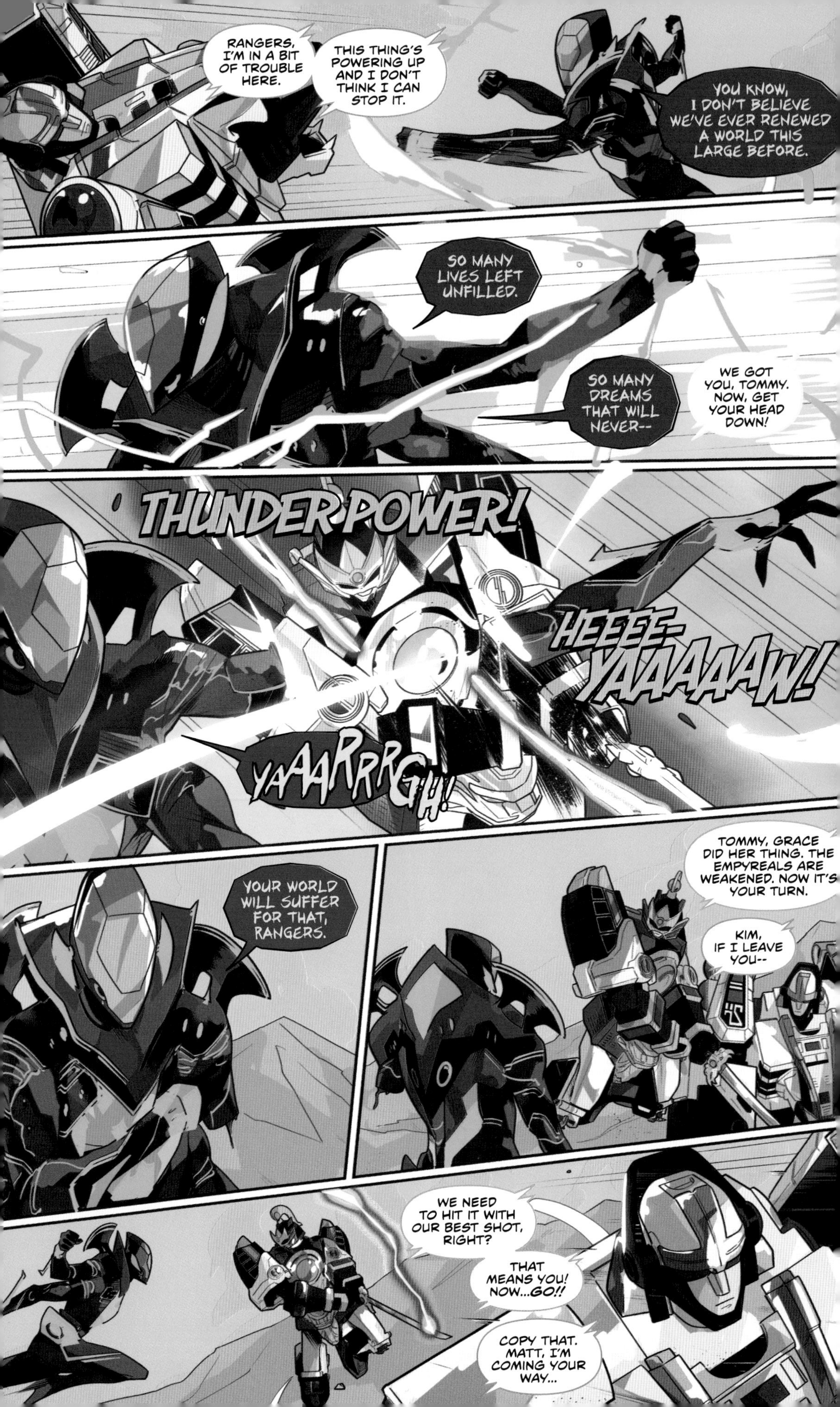

RANGERS, I'M IN A BIT OF TROUBLE HERE.
THIS THING'S POWERING UP AND I DON'T THINK I CAN STOP IT.
YOU KNOW, I DON'T BELIEVE WE'VE EVER RENEWED A WORLD THIS LARGE BEFORE.
SO MANY LIVES LEFT UNFILLED.
SO MANY DREAMS THAT WILL NEVER--
WE GOT YOU, TOMMY. NOW, GET YOUR HEAD DOWN!
THUNDER POWER!
HEEEE-YAAAAAAW!
YAAARRRGH!
YOUR WORLD WILL SUFFER FOR THAT, RANGERS.
TOMMY, GRACE DID HER THING. THE EMPYREALS ARE WEAKENED. NOW IT'S YOUR TURN.
KIM, IF I LEAVE YOU--
WE NEED TO HIT IT WITH OUR BEST SHOT, RIGHT?
THAT MEANS YOU! NOW...GO!!
COPY THAT. MATT, I'M COMING YOUR WAY...

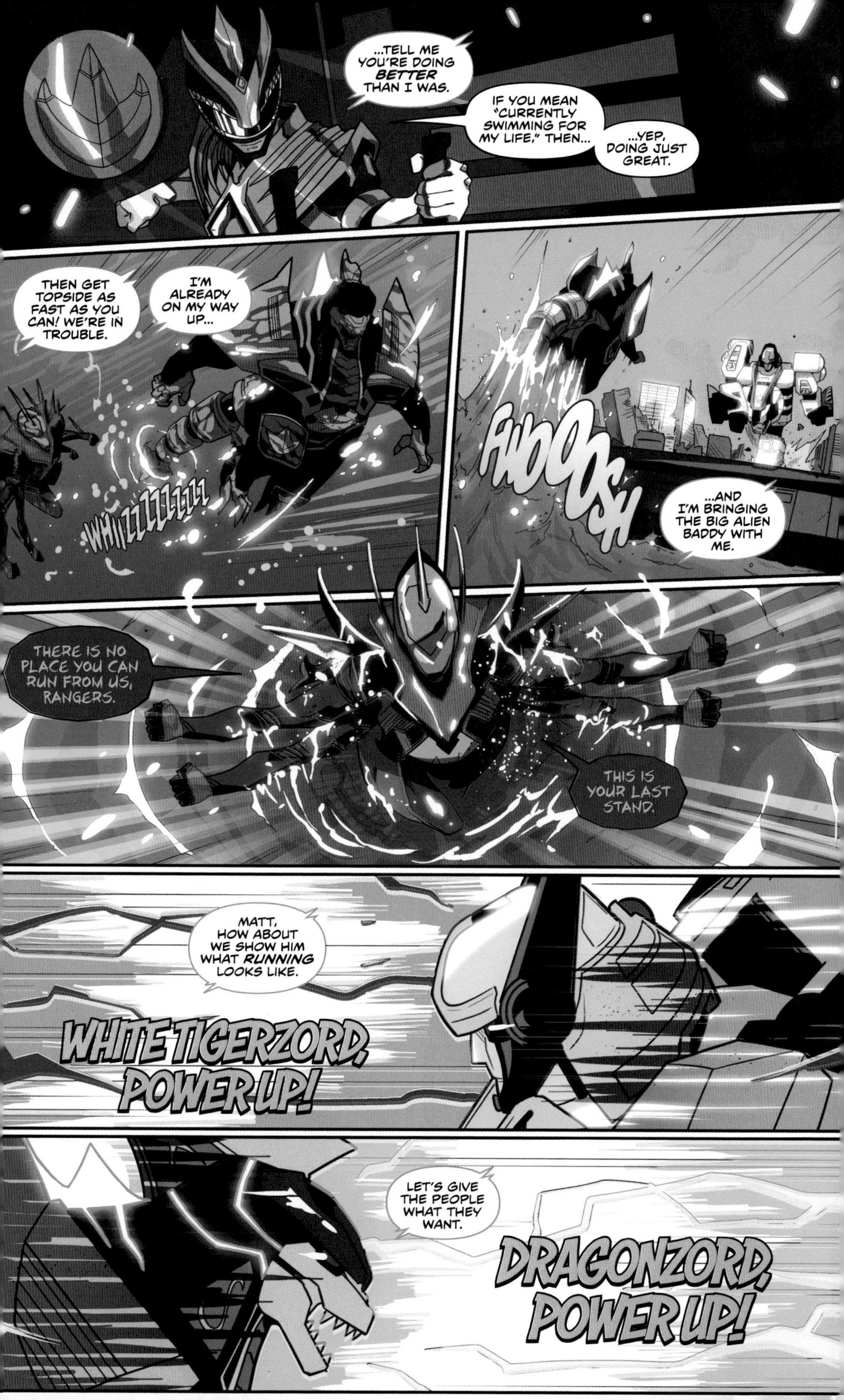
...TELL ME YOU'RE DOING BETTER THAN I WAS.
IF YOU MEAN "CURRENTLY SWIMMING FOR MY LIFE," THEN...
...YEP, DOING JUST GREAT.
THEN GET TOPSIDE AS FAST AS YOU CAN! WE'RE IN TROUBLE.
I'M ALREADY ON MY WAY UP...
WHIIZZZZZZZZ
FWOOOOSH
...AND I'M BRINGING THE BIG ALIEN BADDY WITH ME.
THERE IS NO PLACE YOU CAN RUN FROM US, RANGERS.
THIS IS YOUR LAST STAND.
MATT, HOW ABOUT WE SHOW HIM WHAT RUNNING LOOKS LIKE.
WHITE TIGERZORD, POWER UP!
LET'S GIVE THE PEOPLE WHAT THEY WANT.
DRAGONZORD, POWER UP!

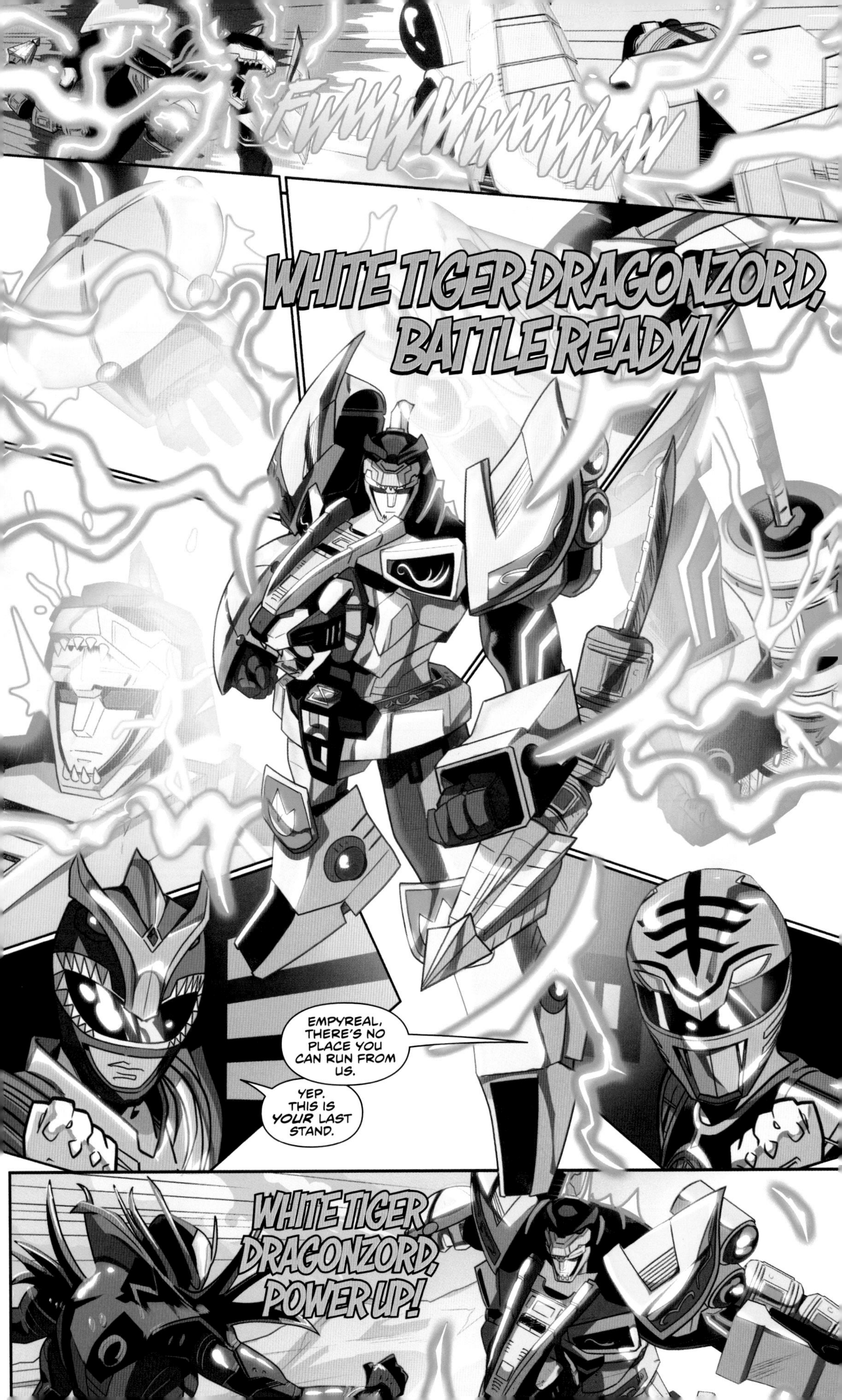
FWMMWWWWWWW
WHITE TIGER DRAGONZORD, BATTLE READY!
EMPYREAL, THERE'S NO PLACE YOU CAN RUN FROM US.
YEP. THIS IS *YOUR* LAST STAND.
WHITE TIGER DRAGONZORD, POWER UP!

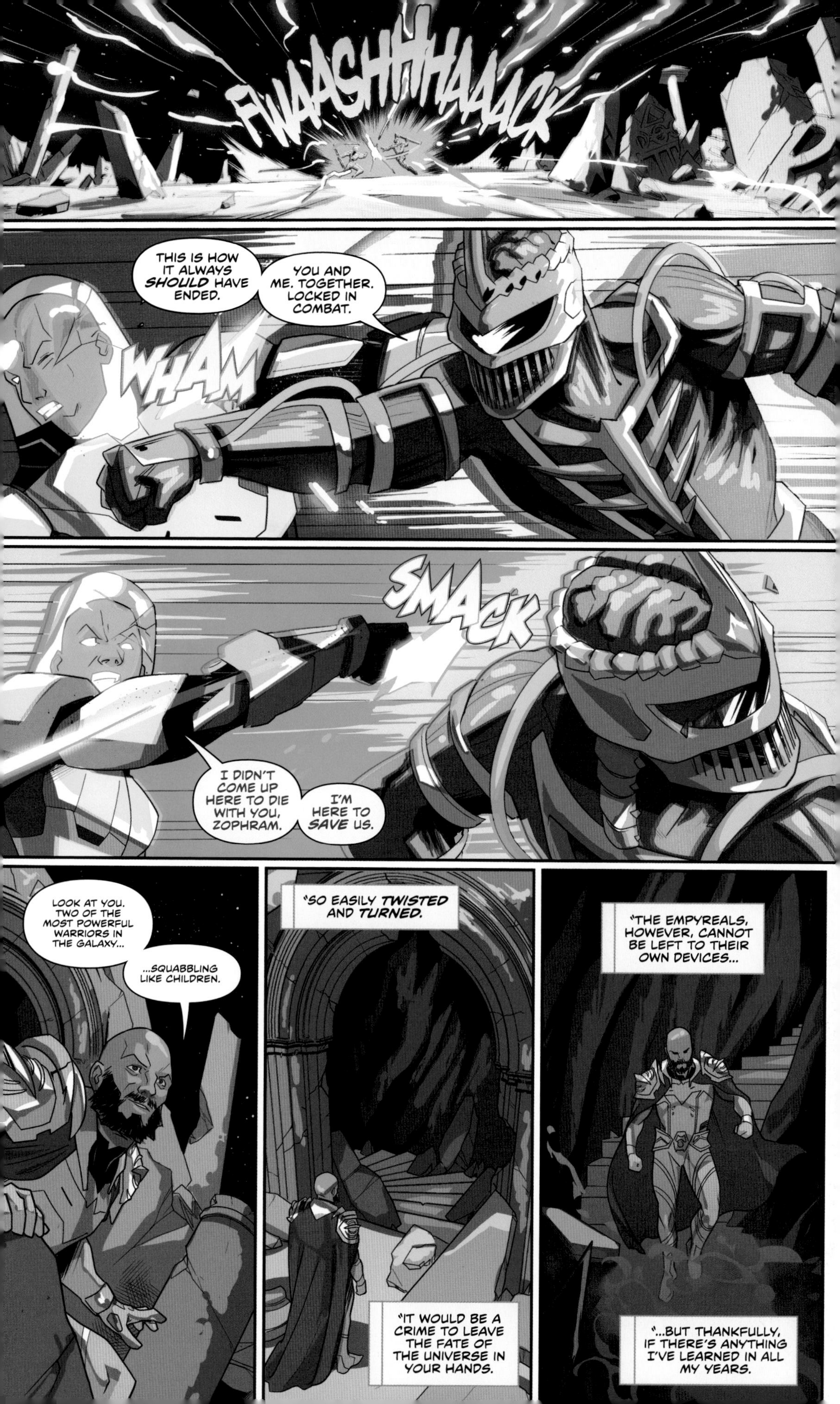
FWAASHHHAAACK
THIS IS HOW IT ALWAYS SHOULD HAVE ENDED.
YOU AND ME. TOGETHER. LOCKED IN COMBAT.
WHAM
SMACK
I DIDN'T COME UP HERE TO DIE WITH YOU, ZOPHRAM.
I'M HERE TO SAVE US.
LOOK AT YOU. TWO OF THE MOST POWERFUL WARRIORS IN THE GALAXY...
...SQUABBLING LIKE CHILDREN.
"SO EASILY TWISTED AND TURNED.
"IT WOULD BE A CRIME TO LEAVE THE FATE OF THE UNIVERSE IN YOUR HANDS.
"THE EMPYREALS, HOWEVER, CANNOT BE LEFT TO THEIR OWN DEVICES...
"...BUT THANKFULLY, IF THERE'S ANYTHING I'VE LEARNED IN ALL MY YEARS.

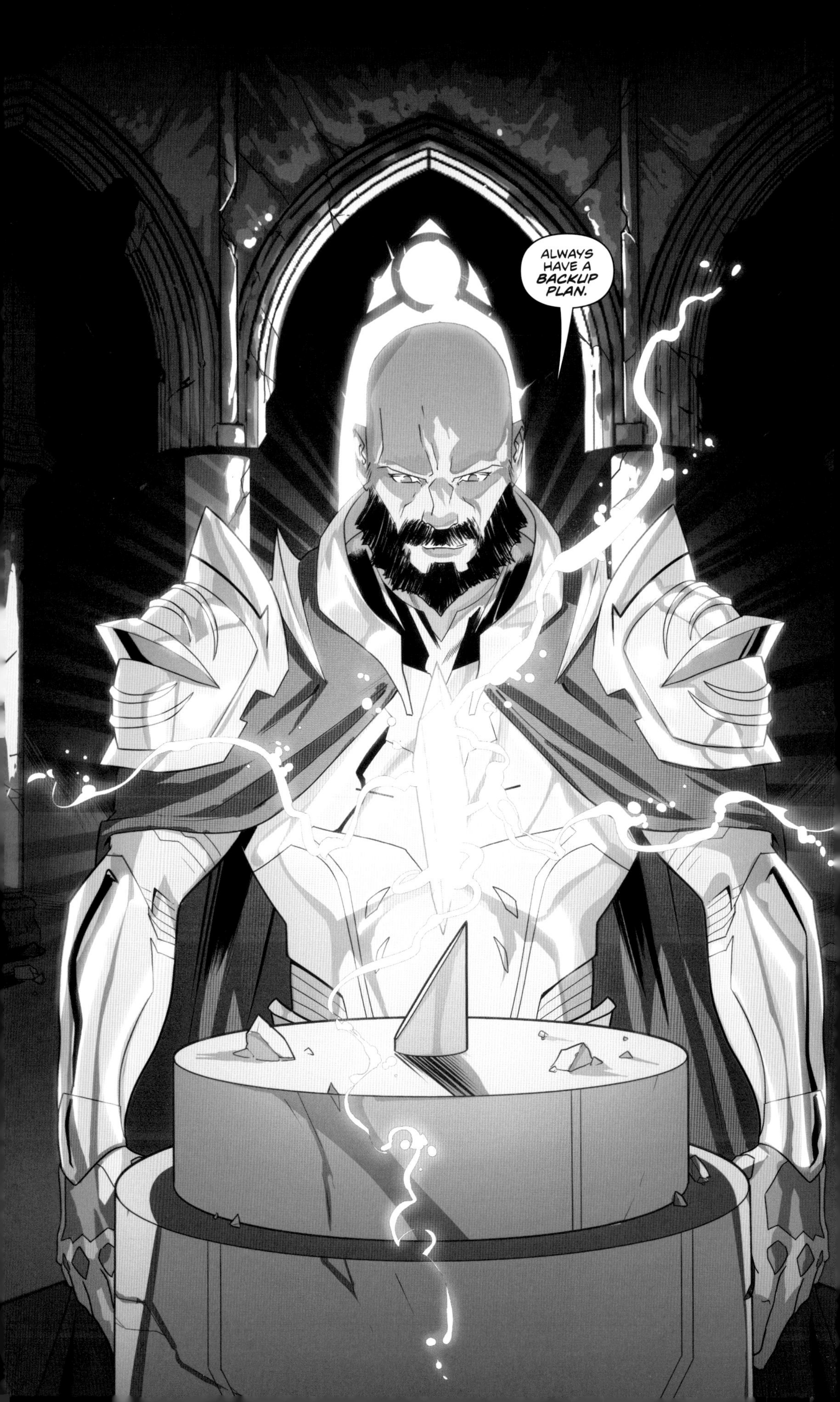
ALWAYS HAVE A BACKUP PLAN.

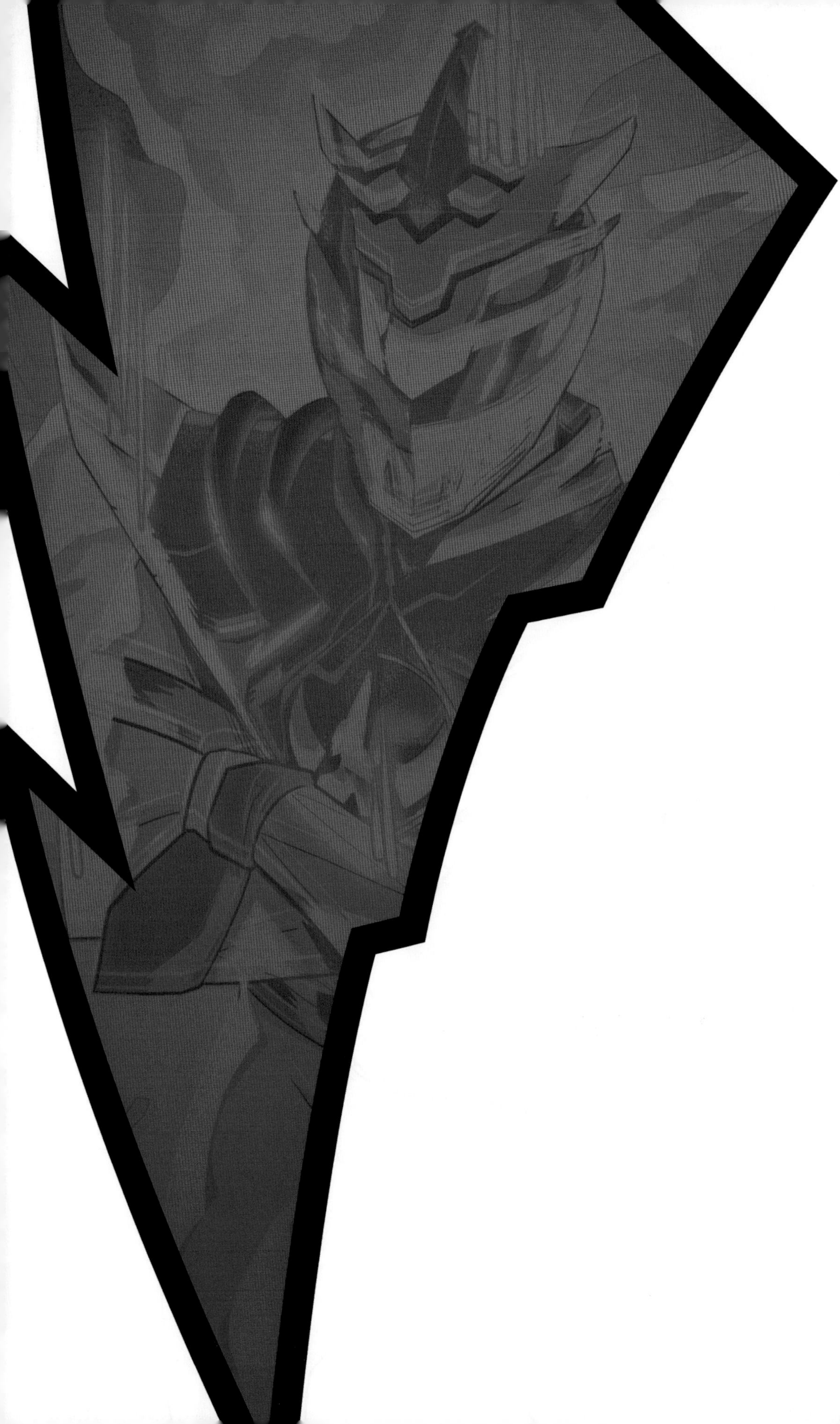

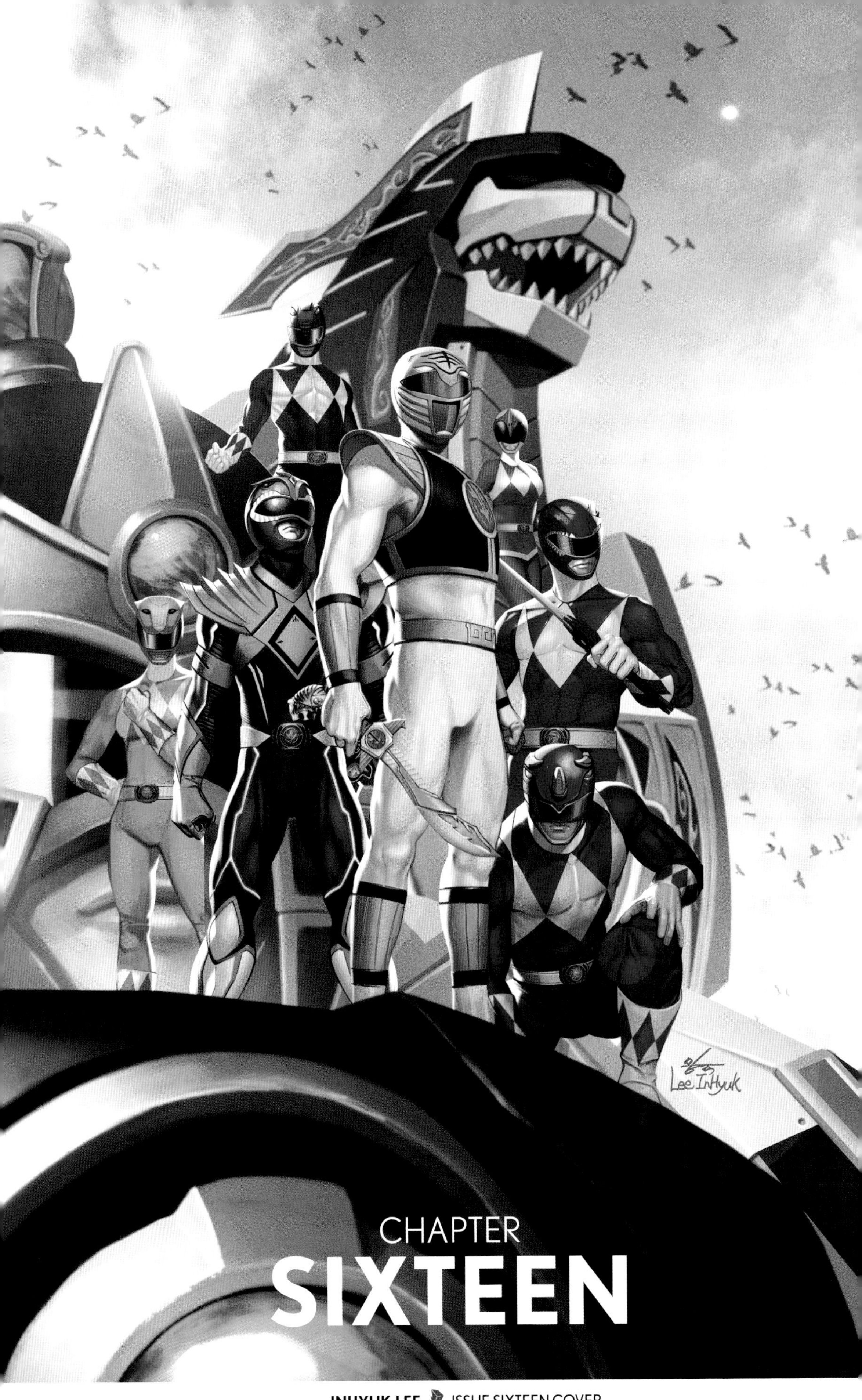
Lee InHyuk

CHAPTER SIXTEEN

INHYUK LEE | ISSUE SIXTEEN COVER

YOU'RE *REPLACING* ME?

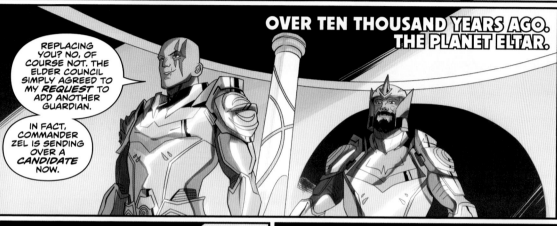

OVER TEN THOUSAND YEARS AGO. THE PLANET ELTAR.

REPLACING YOU? NO, OF COURSE NOT. THE ELDER COUNCIL SIMPLY AGREED TO MY *REQUEST* TO ADD ANOTHER GUARDIAN.

IN FACT, COMMANDER ZEL IS SENDING OVER A *CANDIDATE* NOW.

THE GOOD COMMANDER SAYS HE'S THE *BEST WARRIOR* IN BRONZE COMPANY.

HE'S YOUNG AND INEXPERIENCED, BUT AT LEAST HE HASN'T DEVELOPED ANY *BAD HABITS.*

YOU AND I HAVE BEEN DOING JUST *FINE* ON OUR OWN.

HAVEN'T I ALWAYS WATCHED YOUR BACK?

YOU HAVE, ZARTUS... WHICH IS WHY WE NEED TO FIND SOMEONE TO WATCH *YOURS.*

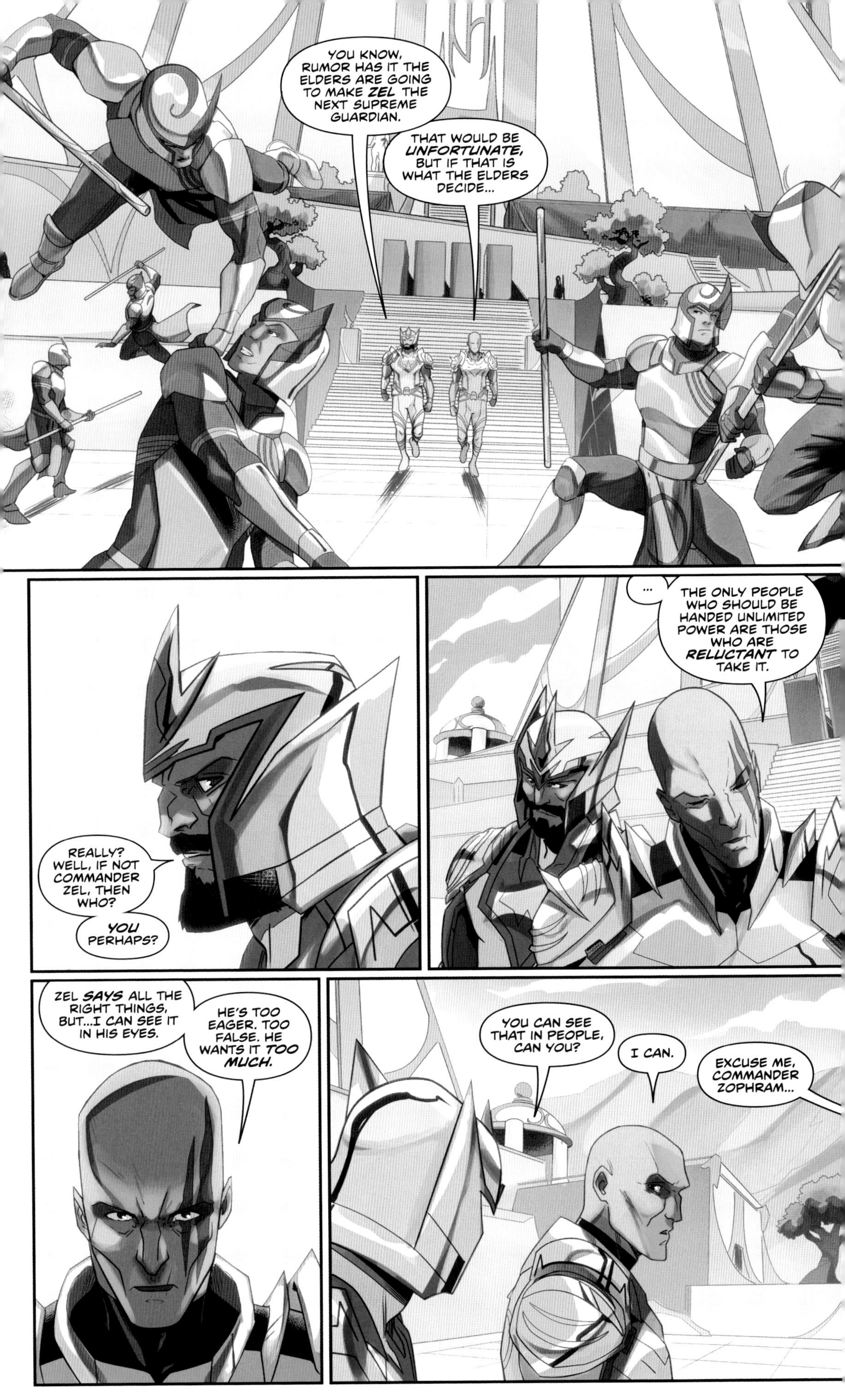
YOU KNOW, RUMOR HAS IT THE ELDERS ARE GOING TO MAKE ZEL THE NEXT SUPREME GUARDIAN.
THAT WOULD BE UNFORTUNATE, BUT IF THAT IS WHAT THE ELDERS DECIDE...
REALLY? WELL, IF NOT COMMANDER ZEL, THEN WHO?
YOU PERHAPS?
...
THE ONLY PEOPLE WHO SHOULD BE HANDED UNLIMITED POWER ARE THOSE WHO ARE RELUCTANT TO TAKE IT.
ZEL SAYS ALL THE RIGHT THINGS, BUT...I CAN SEE IT IN HIS EYES.
HE'S TOO EAGER. TOO FALSE. HE WANTS IT TOO MUCH.
YOU CAN SEE THAT IN PEOPLE, CAN YOU?
I CAN.
EXCUSE ME, COMMANDER ZOPHRAM...

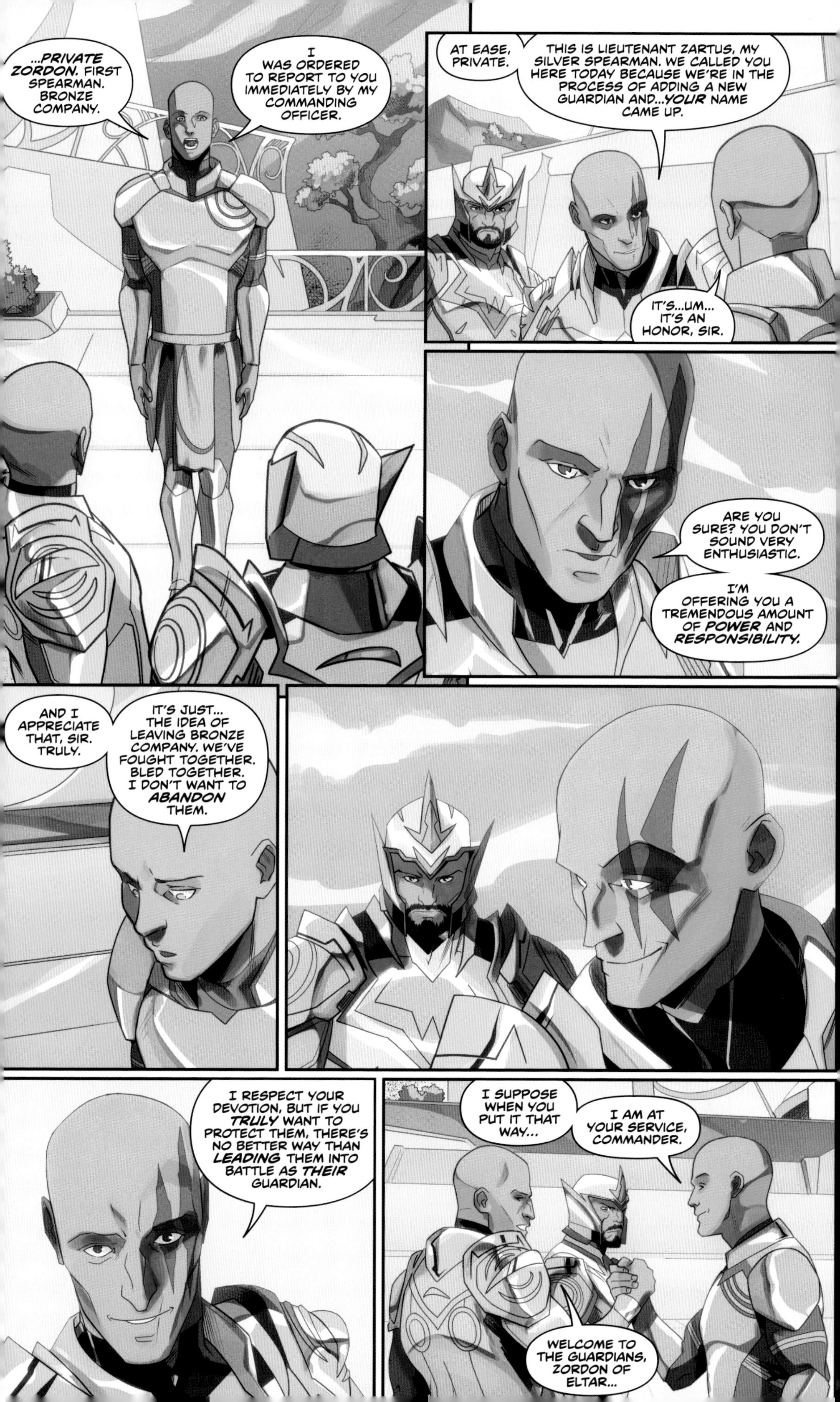

...PRIVATE ZORDON. FIRST SPEARMAN. BRONZE COMPANY.
I WAS ORDERED TO REPORT TO YOU IMMEDIATELY BY MY COMMANDING OFFICER.
AT EASE, PRIVATE.
THIS IS LIEUTENANT ZARTUS, MY SILVER SPEARMAN. WE CALLED YOU HERE TODAY BECAUSE WE'RE IN THE PROCESS OF ADDING A NEW GUARDIAN AND...YOUR NAME CAME UP.
IT'S...UM... IT'S AN HONOR, SIR.
ARE YOU SURE? YOU DON'T SOUND VERY ENTHUSIASTIC.
I'M OFFERING YOU A TREMENDOUS AMOUNT OF POWER AND RESPONSIBILITY.
AND I APPRECIATE THAT, SIR. TRULY.
IT'S JUST... THE IDEA OF LEAVING BRONZE COMPANY. WE'VE FOUGHT TOGETHER. BLED TOGETHER. I DON'T WANT TO ABANDON THEM.
I RESPECT YOUR DEVOTION, BUT IF YOU TRULY WANT TO PROTECT THEM, THERE'S NO BETTER WAY THAN LEADING THEM INTO BATTLE AS THEIR GUARDIAN.
I SUPPOSE WHEN YOU PUT IT THAT WAY...
I AM AT YOUR SERVICE, COMMANDER.
WELCOME TO THE GUARDIANS, ZORDON OF ELTAR...

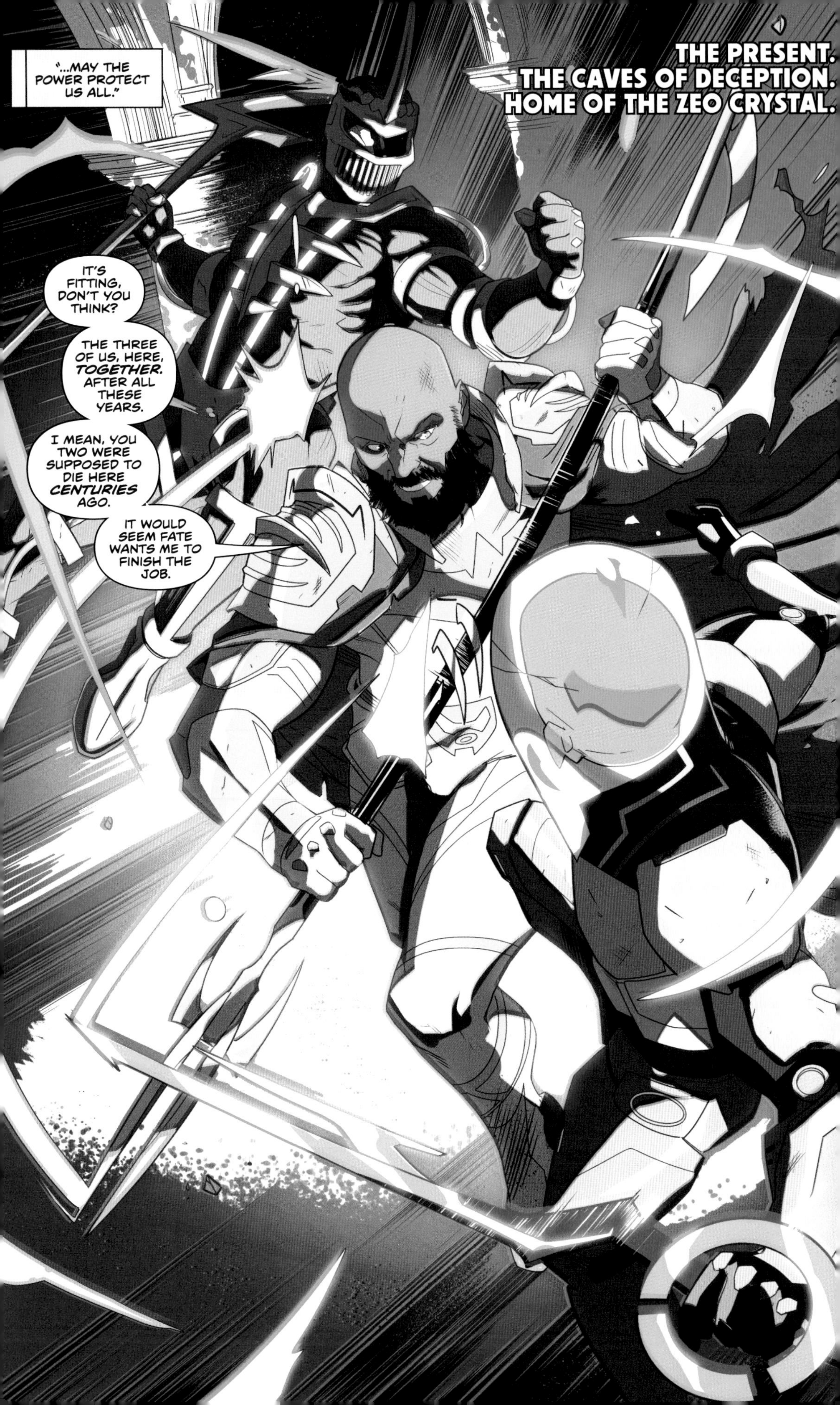

"...MAY THE POWER PROTECT US ALL."
THE PRESENT. THE CAVES OF DECEPTION. HOME OF THE ZEO CRYSTAL.
IT'S FITTING, DON'T YOU THINK?
THE THREE OF US, HERE, *TOGETHER.* AFTER ALL THESE YEARS.
I MEAN, YOU TWO WERE SUPPOSED TO DIE HERE *CENTURIES* AGO.
IT WOULD SEEM FATE WANTS ME TO FINISH THE JOB.

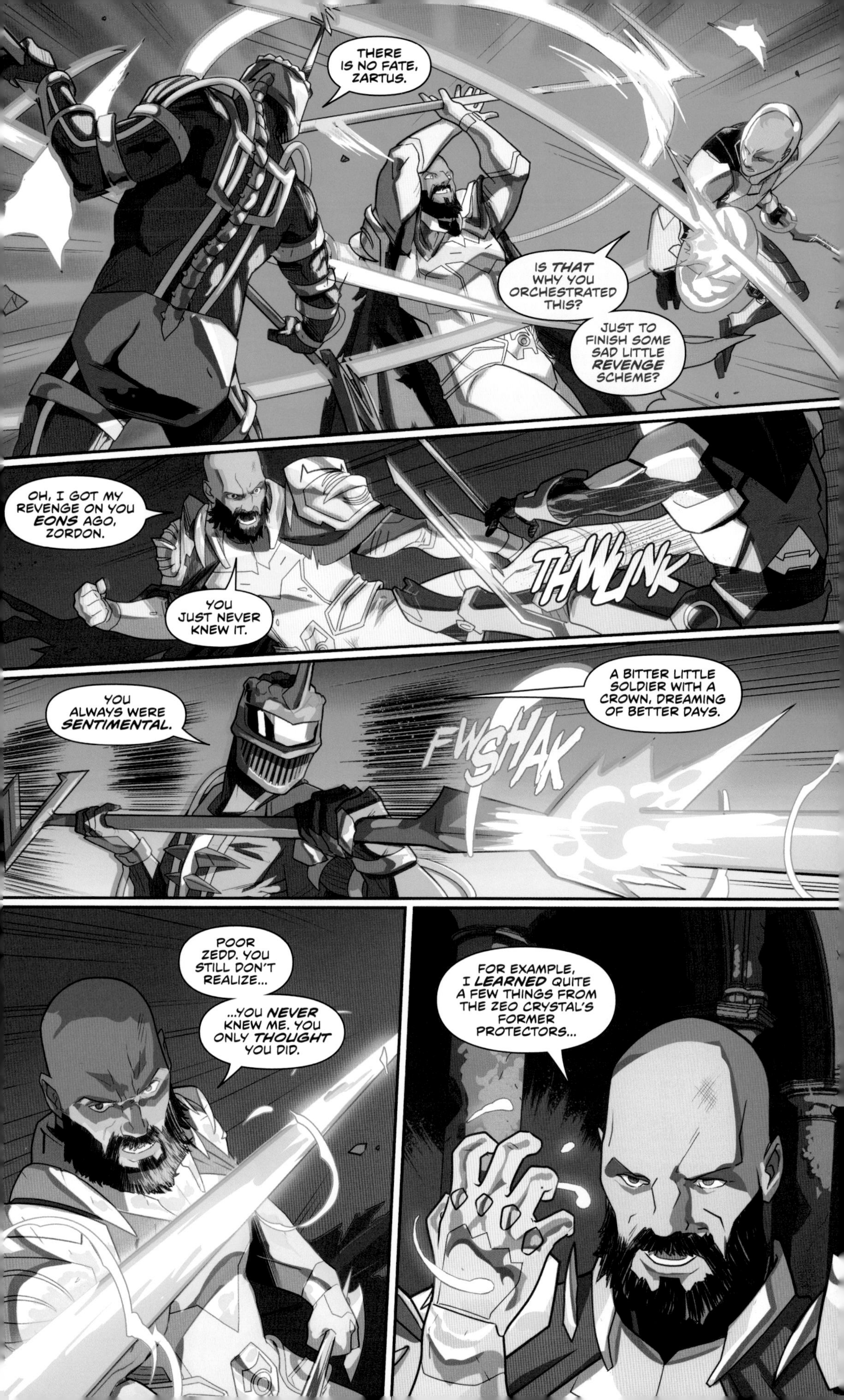
THERE IS NO FATE, ZARTUS.
IS THAT WHY YOU ORCHESTRATED THIS?
JUST TO FINISH SOME SAD LITTLE REVENGE SCHEME?
OH, I GOT MY REVENGE ON YOU EONS AGO, ZORDON.
YOU JUST NEVER KNEW IT.
THMUNK
YOU ALWAYS WERE SENTIMENTAL.
A BITTER LITTLE SOLDIER WITH A CROWN, DREAMING OF BETTER DAYS.
FWSHAK
POOR ZEDD. YOU STILL DON'T REALIZE...
...YOU NEVER KNEW ME. YOU ONLY THOUGHT YOU DID.
FOR EXAMPLE, I LEARNED QUITE A FEW THINGS FROM THE ZEO CRYSTAL'S FORMER PROTECTORS...

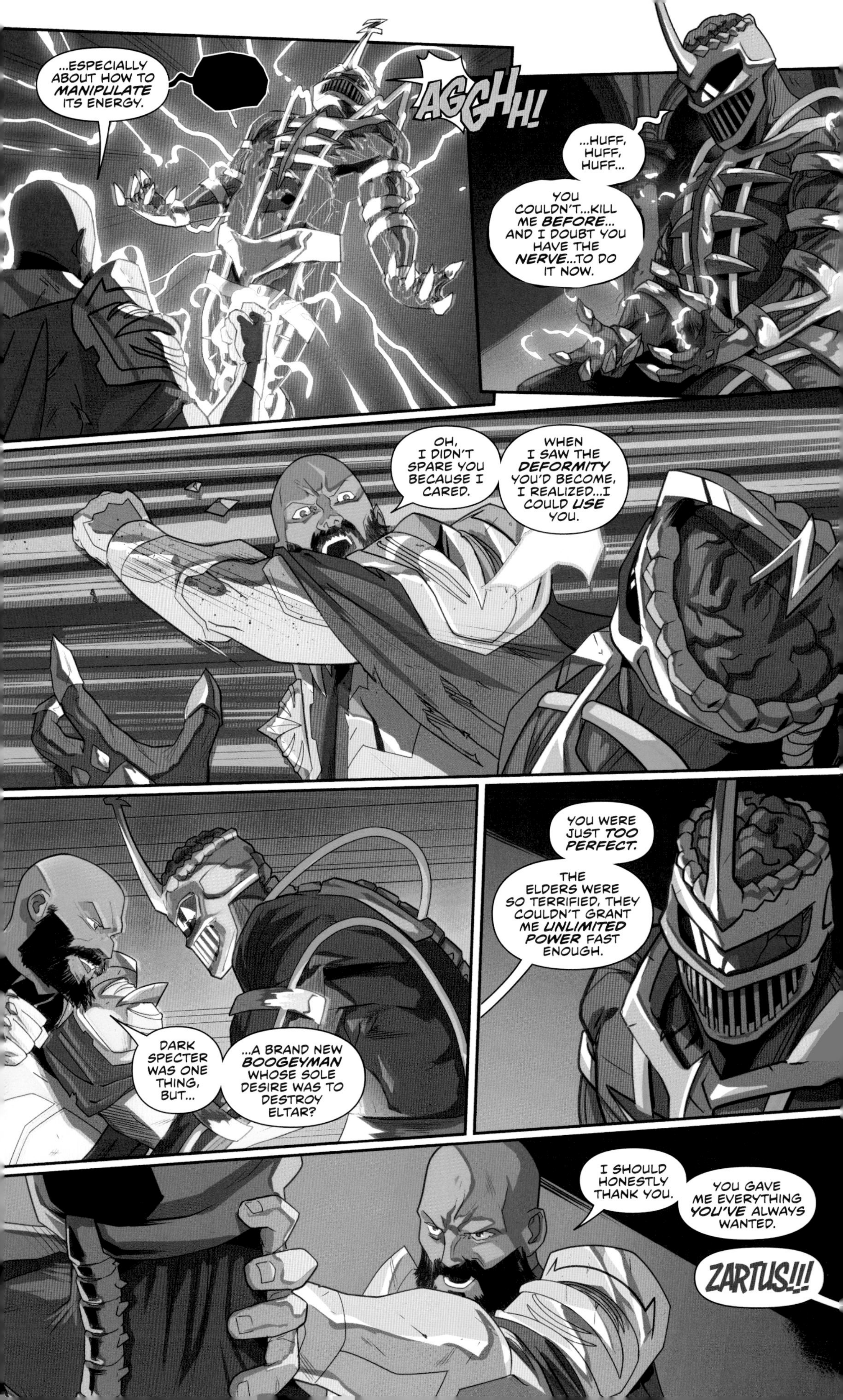
...ESPECIALLY ABOUT HOW TO *MANIPULATE* ITS ENERGY.
AGGHH!
...HUFF, HUFF, HUFF...
YOU COULDN'T...KILL ME *BEFORE*... AND I DOUBT YOU HAVE THE *NERVE*...TO DO IT NOW.
OH, I DIDN'T SPARE YOU BECAUSE I CARED.
WHEN I SAW THE *DEFORMITY* YOU'D BECOME, I REALIZED...I COULD *USE* YOU.
DARK SPECTER WAS ONE THING, BUT...
...A BRAND NEW *BOOGEYMAN* WHOSE SOLE DESIRE WAS TO DESTROY ELTAR?
YOU WERE JUST *TOO PERFECT.*
THE ELDERS WERE SO TERRIFIED, THEY COULDN'T GRANT ME *UNLIMITED POWER* FAST ENOUGH.
I SHOULD HONESTLY THANK YOU.
YOU GAVE ME EVERYTHING *YOU'VE* ALWAYS WANTED.
ZARTUS!!!

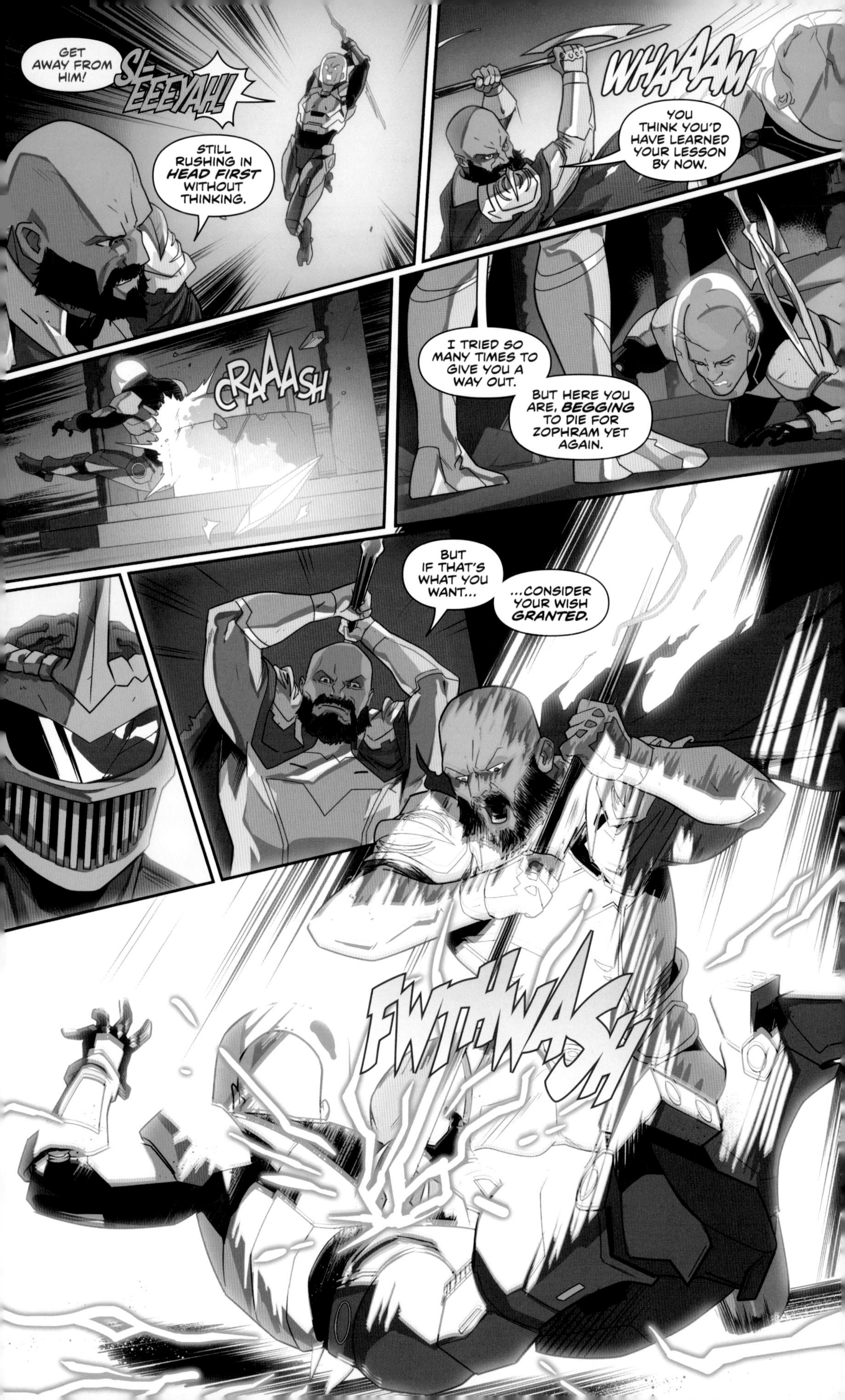
GET AWAY FROM HIM!
SI-EEEYAH!
STILL RUSHING IN HEAD FIRST WITHOUT THINKING.
WHAAAM
YOU THINK YOU'D HAVE LEARNED YOUR LESSON BY NOW.
CRAAASH
I TRIED SO MANY TIMES TO GIVE YOU A WAY OUT.
BUT HERE YOU ARE, BEGGING TO DIE FOR ZOPHRAM YET AGAIN.
BUT IF THAT'S WHAT YOU WANT...
...CONSIDER YOUR WISH GRANTED.
FWTHWASH

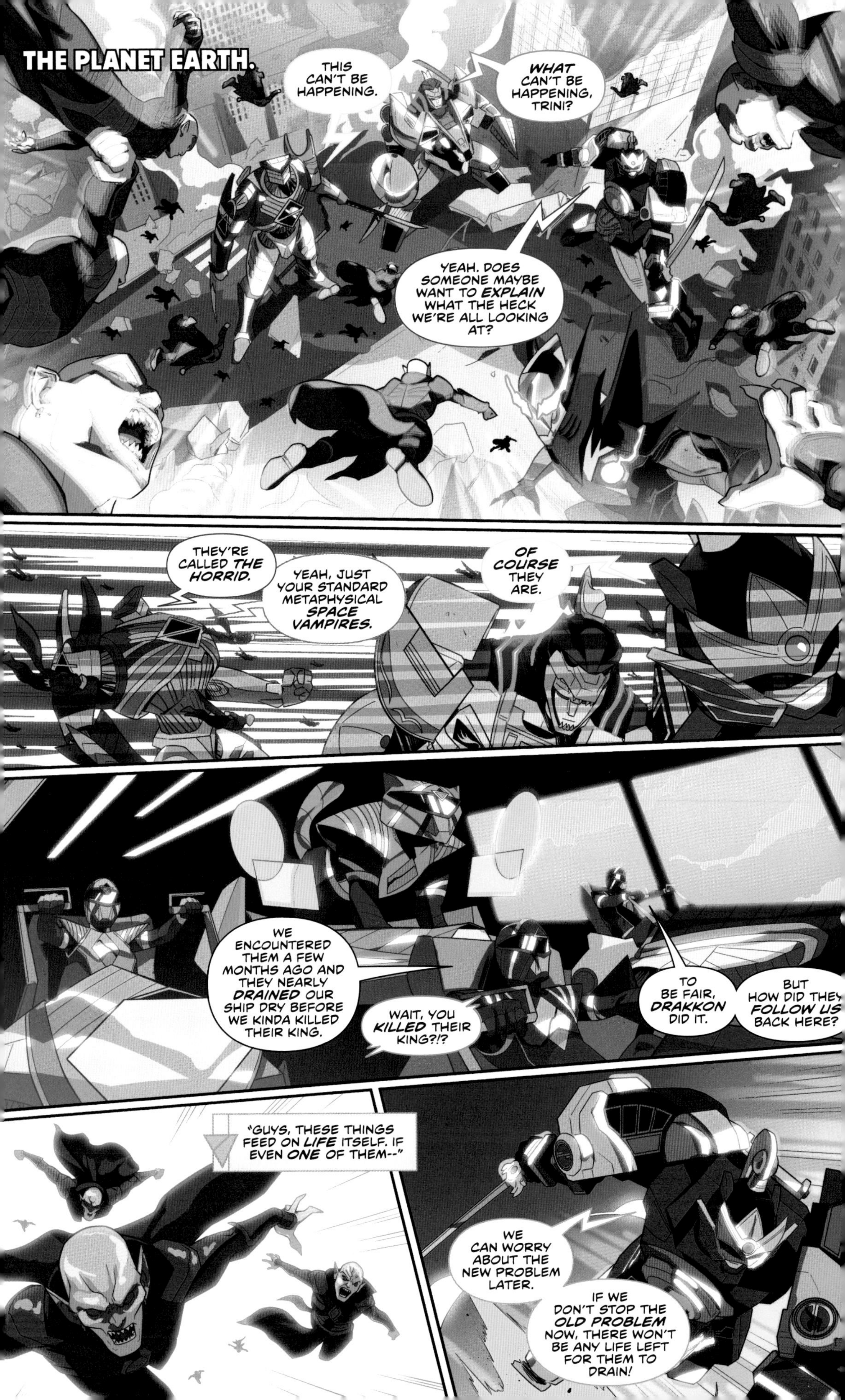
THE PLANET EARTH.
THIS CAN'T BE HAPPENING.
WHAT CAN'T BE HAPPENING, TRINI?
YEAH. DOES SOMEONE MAYBE WANT TO EXPLAIN WHAT THE HECK WE'RE ALL LOOKING AT?
THEY'RE CALLED THE HORRID.
YEAH, JUST YOUR STANDARD METAPHYSICAL SPACE VAMPIRES.
OF COURSE THEY ARE.
WE ENCOUNTERED THEM A FEW MONTHS AGO AND THEY NEARLY DRAINED OUR SHIP DRY BEFORE WE KINDA KILLED THEIR KING.
WAIT, YOU KILLED THEIR KING?!?
TO BE FAIR, DRAKKON DID IT.
BUT HOW DID THEY FOLLOW US BACK HERE?
"GUYS, THESE THINGS FEED ON LIFE ITSELF. IF EVEN ONE OF THEM--"
WE CAN WORRY ABOUT THE NEW PROBLEM LATER.
IF WE DON'T STOP THE OLD PROBLEM NOW, THERE WON'T BE ANY LIFE LEFT FOR THEM TO DRAIN!

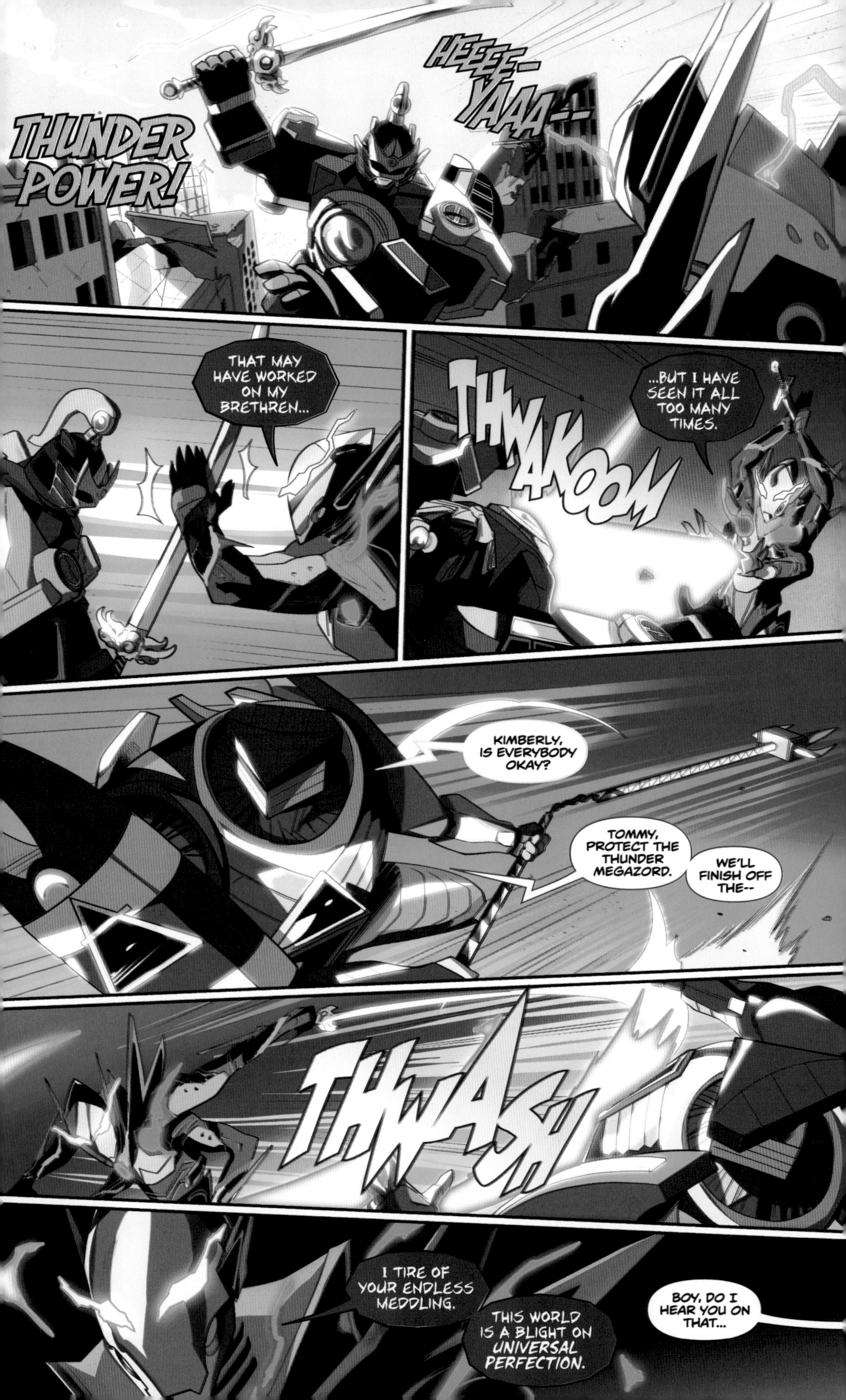
THUNDER POWER!
HEEEE-YAAA--!
THAT MAY HAVE WORKED ON MY BRETHREN...
THWAKOOM
...BUT I HAVE SEEN IT ALL TOO MANY TIMES.
KIMBERLY, IS EVERYBODY OKAY?
TOMMY, PROTECT THE THUNDER MEGAZORD.
WE'LL FINISH OFF THE--
THWASH
I TIRE OF YOUR ENDLESS MEDDLING.
THIS WORLD IS A BLIGHT ON UNIVERSAL PERFECTION.
BOY, DO I HEAR YOU ON THAT...

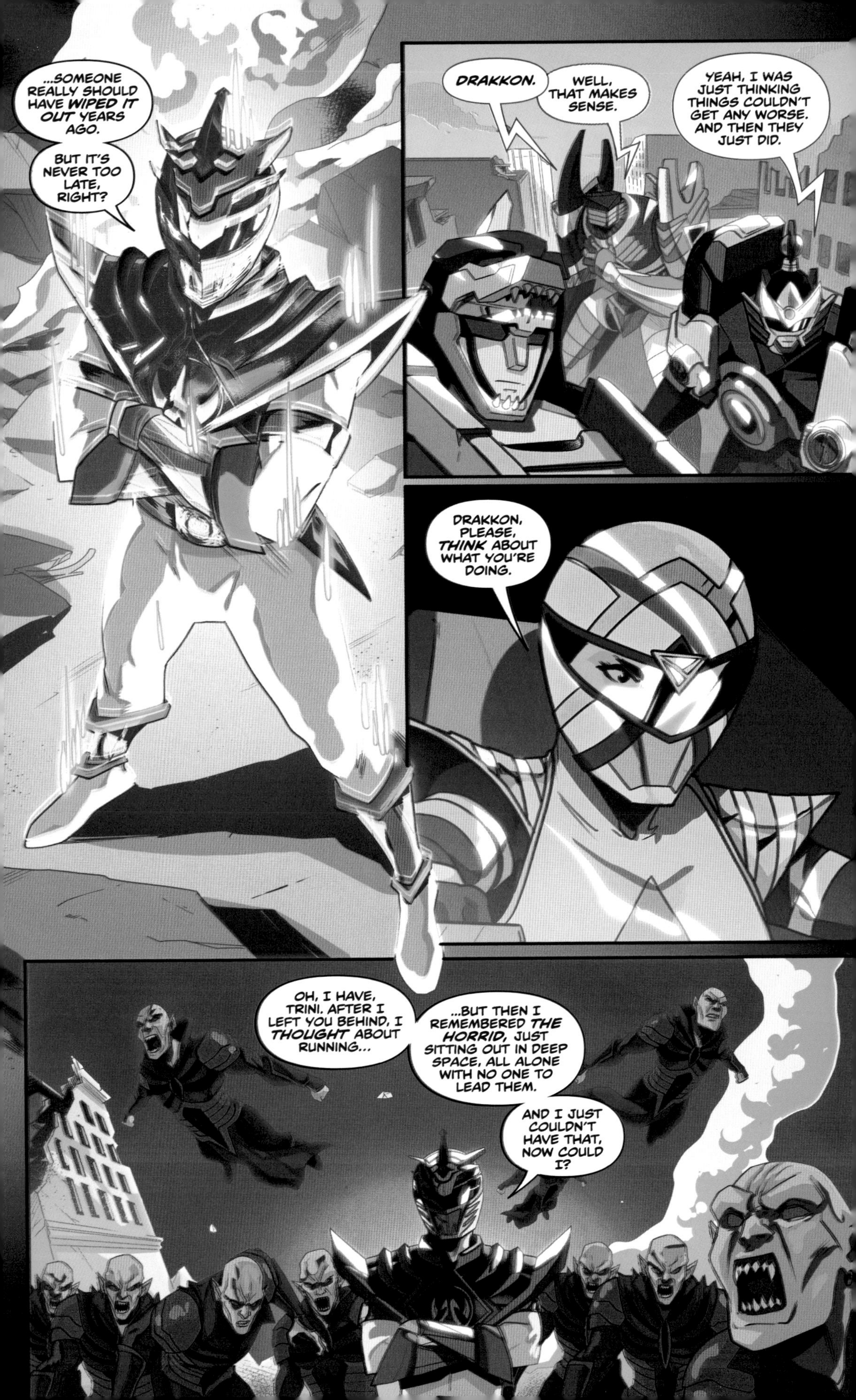
...SOMEONE REALLY SHOULD HAVE WIPED IT OUT YEARS AGO.
BUT IT'S NEVER TOO LATE, RIGHT?
DRAKKON.
WELL, THAT MAKES SENSE.
YEAH, I WAS JUST THINKING THINGS COULDN'T GET ANY WORSE. AND THEN THEY JUST DID.
DRAKKON, PLEASE, THINK ABOUT WHAT YOU'RE DOING.
OH, I HAVE, TRINI. AFTER I LEFT YOU BEHIND, I THOUGHT ABOUT RUNNING...
...BUT THEN I REMEMBERED THE HORRID, JUST SITTING OUT IN DEEP SPACE, ALL ALONE WITH NO ONE TO LEAD THEM.
AND I JUST COULDN'T HAVE THAT, NOW COULD I?

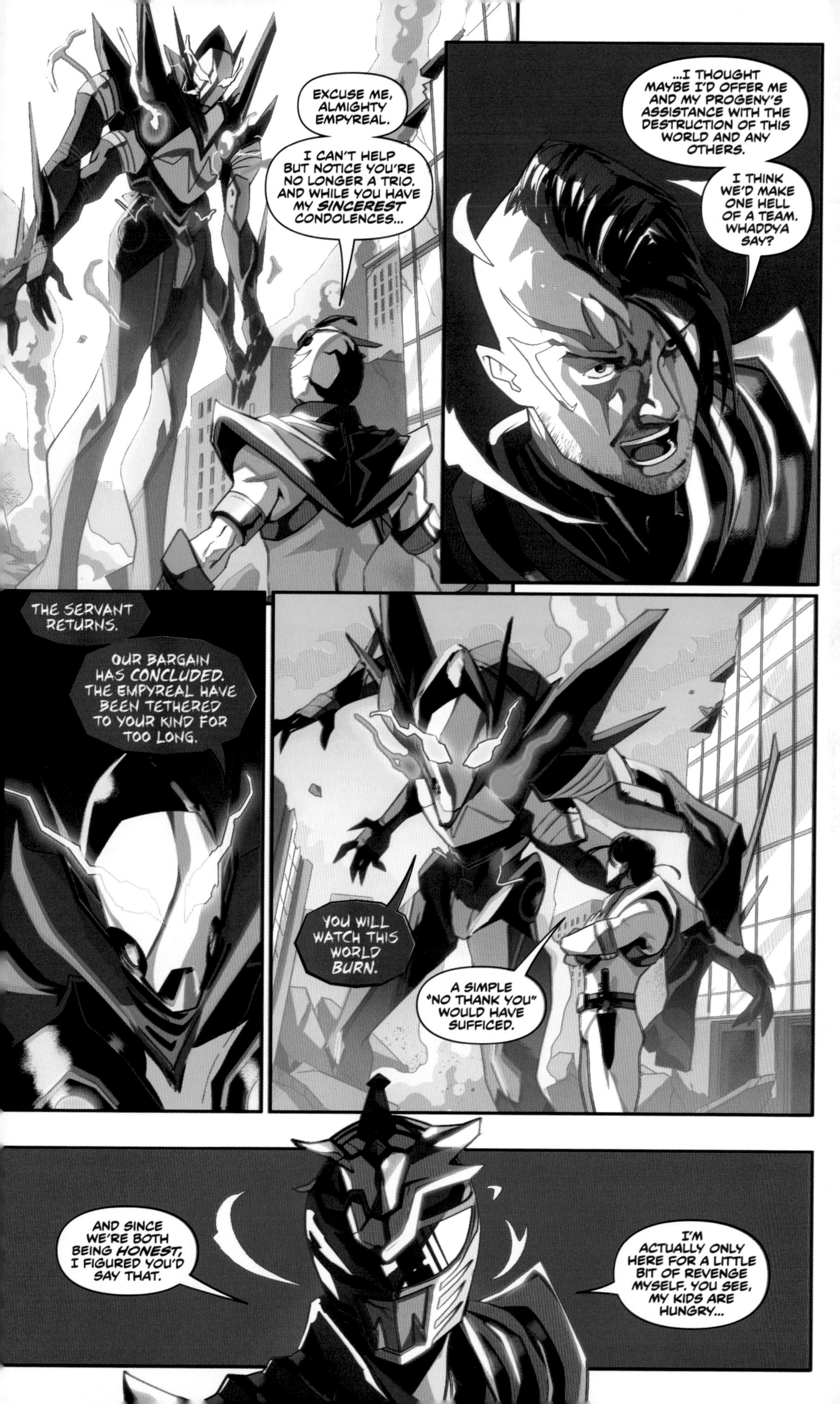
EXCUSE ME, ALMIGHTY EMPYREAL.
I CAN'T HELP BUT NOTICE YOU'RE NO LONGER A TRIO. AND WHILE YOU HAVE MY SINCEREST CONDOLENCES...
...I THOUGHT MAYBE I'D OFFER ME AND MY PROGENY'S ASSISTANCE WITH THE DESTRUCTION OF THIS WORLD AND ANY OTHERS.
I THINK WE'D MAKE ONE HELL OF A TEAM. WHADDYA SAY?
THE SERVANT RETURNS.
OUR BARGAIN HAS CONCLUDED. THE EMPYREAL HAVE BEEN TETHERED TO YOUR KIND FOR TOO LONG.
YOU WILL WATCH THIS WORLD BURN.
A SIMPLE "NO THANK YOU" WOULD HAVE SUFFICED.
AND SINCE WE'RE BOTH BEING HONEST, I FIGURED YOU'D SAY THAT.
I'M ACTUALLY ONLY HERE FOR A LITTLE BIT OF REVENGE MYSELF. YOU SEE, MY KIDS ARE HUNGRY...

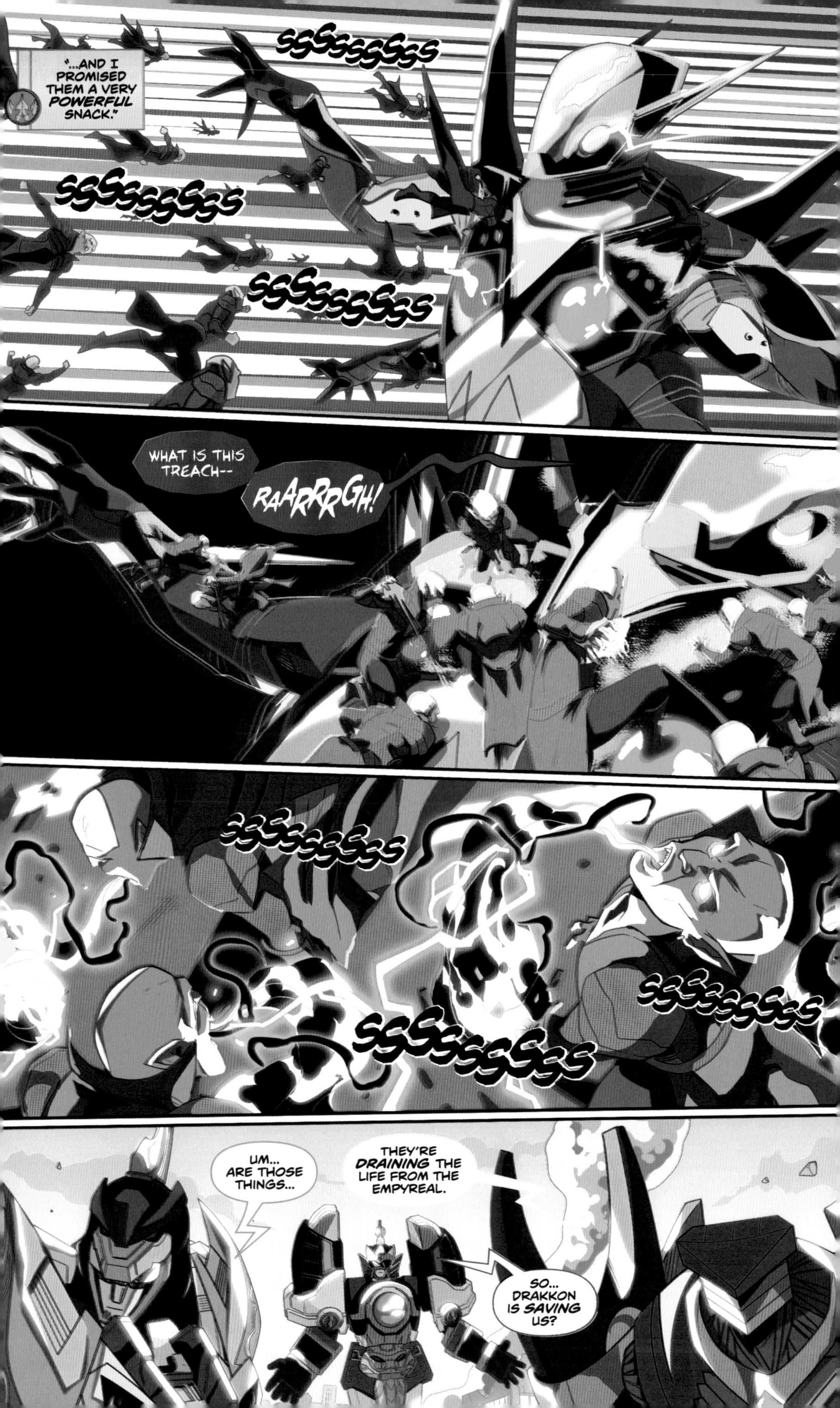
"...AND I PROMISED THEM A VERY POWERFUL SNACK."
SSSSSSSSSS
SSSSSSSSSS
SSSSSSSSSS
WHAT IS THIS TREACH--
RAARRRGH!
SSSSSSSSSS
SSSSSSSSSS
SSSSSSSSSS
UM... ARE THOSE THINGS...
THEY'RE DRAINING THE LIFE FROM THE EMPYREAL.
SO... DRAKKON IS SAVING US?

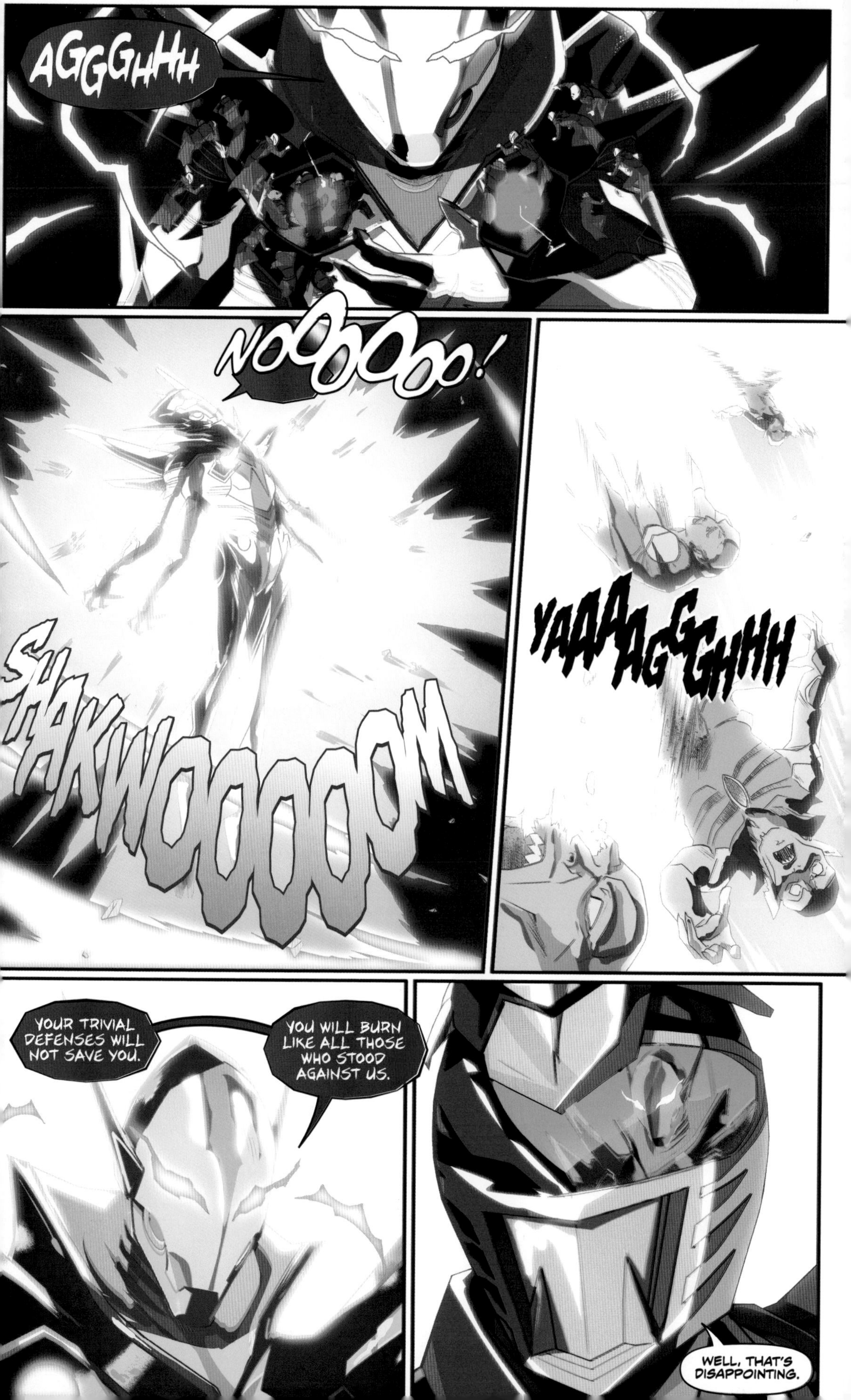
AGGGHHH
NOOOOOO!
SHAKWOOOOOOM
YAAAAGGGHHH
YOUR TRIVIAL DEFENSES WILL NOT SAVE YOU.
YOU WILL BURN LIKE ALL THOSE WHO STOOD AGAINST US.
WELL, THAT'S DISAPPOINTING.

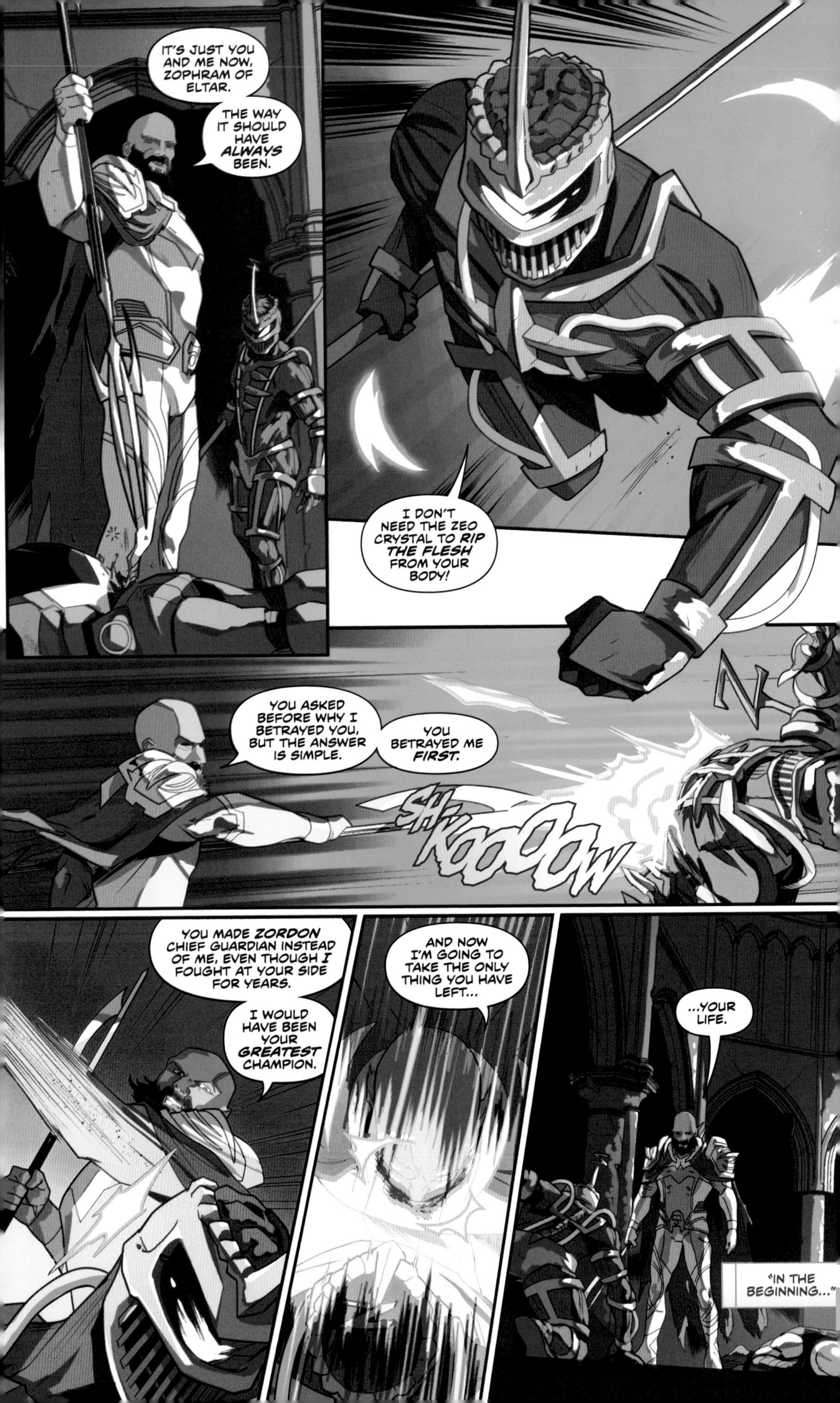
IT'S JUST YOU AND ME NOW, ZOPHRAM OF ELTAR.
THE WAY IT SHOULD HAVE *ALWAYS* BEEN.
I DON'T NEED THE ZEO CRYSTAL TO *RIP THE FLESH* FROM YOUR BODY!
YOU ASKED BEFORE WHY I BETRAYED YOU, BUT THE ANSWER IS SIMPLE.
YOU BETRAYED ME *FIRST.*
SH-KOOOOOW
YOU MADE *ZORDON* CHIEF GUARDIAN INSTEAD OF ME, EVEN THOUGH *I* FOUGHT AT YOUR SIDE FOR YEARS.
I WOULD HAVE BEEN YOUR *GREATEST* CHAMPION.
AND NOW I'M GOING TO TAKE THE ONLY THING YOU HAVE LEFT...
...YOUR LIFE.
"IN THE BEGINNING..."

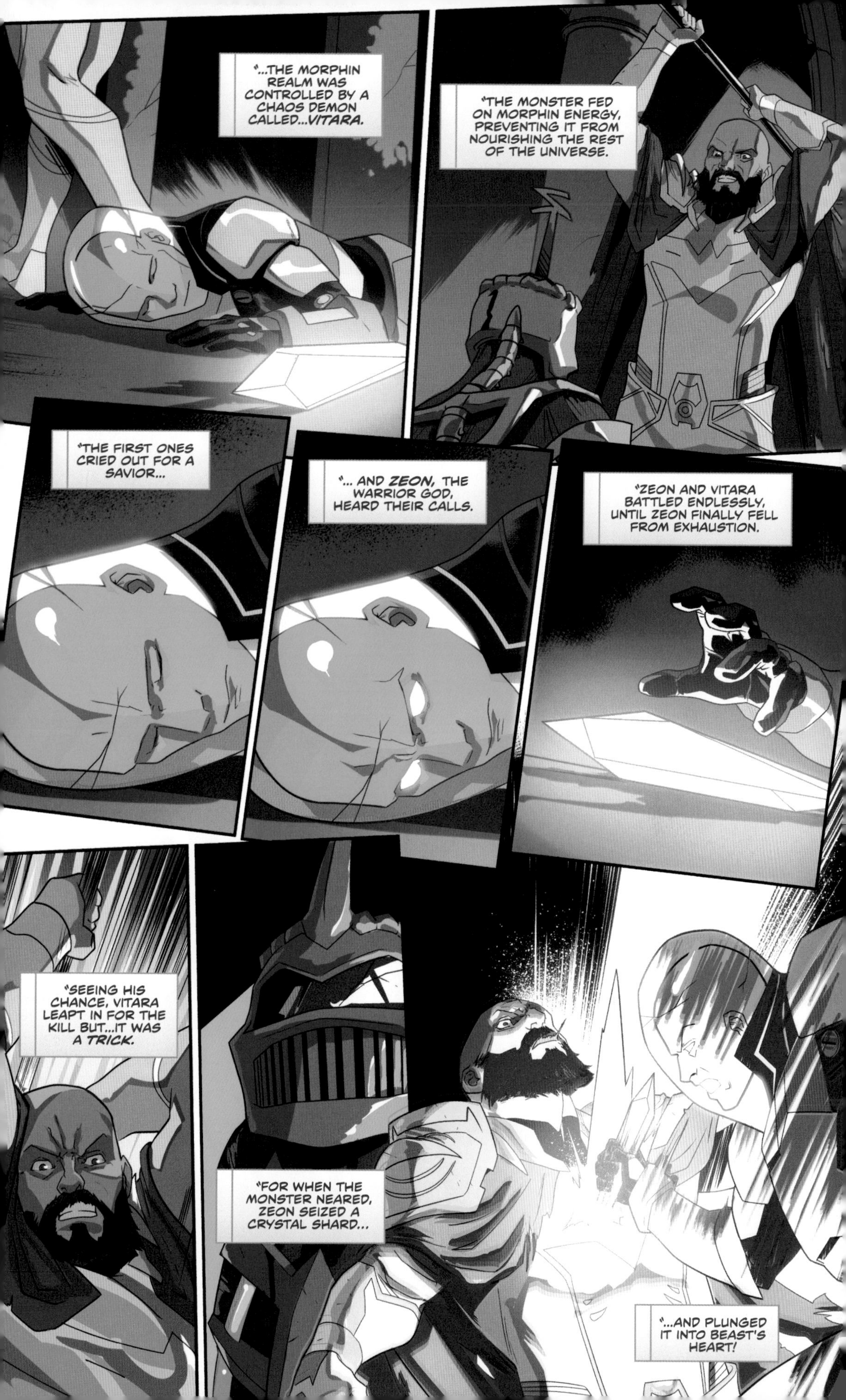
"...THE MORPHIN REALM WAS CONTROLLED BY A CHAOS DEMON CALLED...*VITARA*.
"THE MONSTER FED ON MORPHIN ENERGY, PREVENTING IT FROM NOURISHING THE REST OF THE UNIVERSE.
"THE FIRST ONES CRIED OUT FOR A SAVIOR...
"... AND *ZEON*, THE WARRIOR GOD, HEARD THEIR CALLS.
"ZEON AND VITARA BATTLED ENDLESSLY, UNTIL ZEON FINALLY FELL FROM EXHAUSTION.
"SEEING HIS CHANCE, VITARA LEAPT IN FOR THE KILL BUT...IT WAS A *TRICK*.
"FOR WHEN THE MONSTER NEARED, ZEON SEIZED A CRYSTAL SHARD...
"...AND PLUNGED IT INTO BEAST'S HEART!

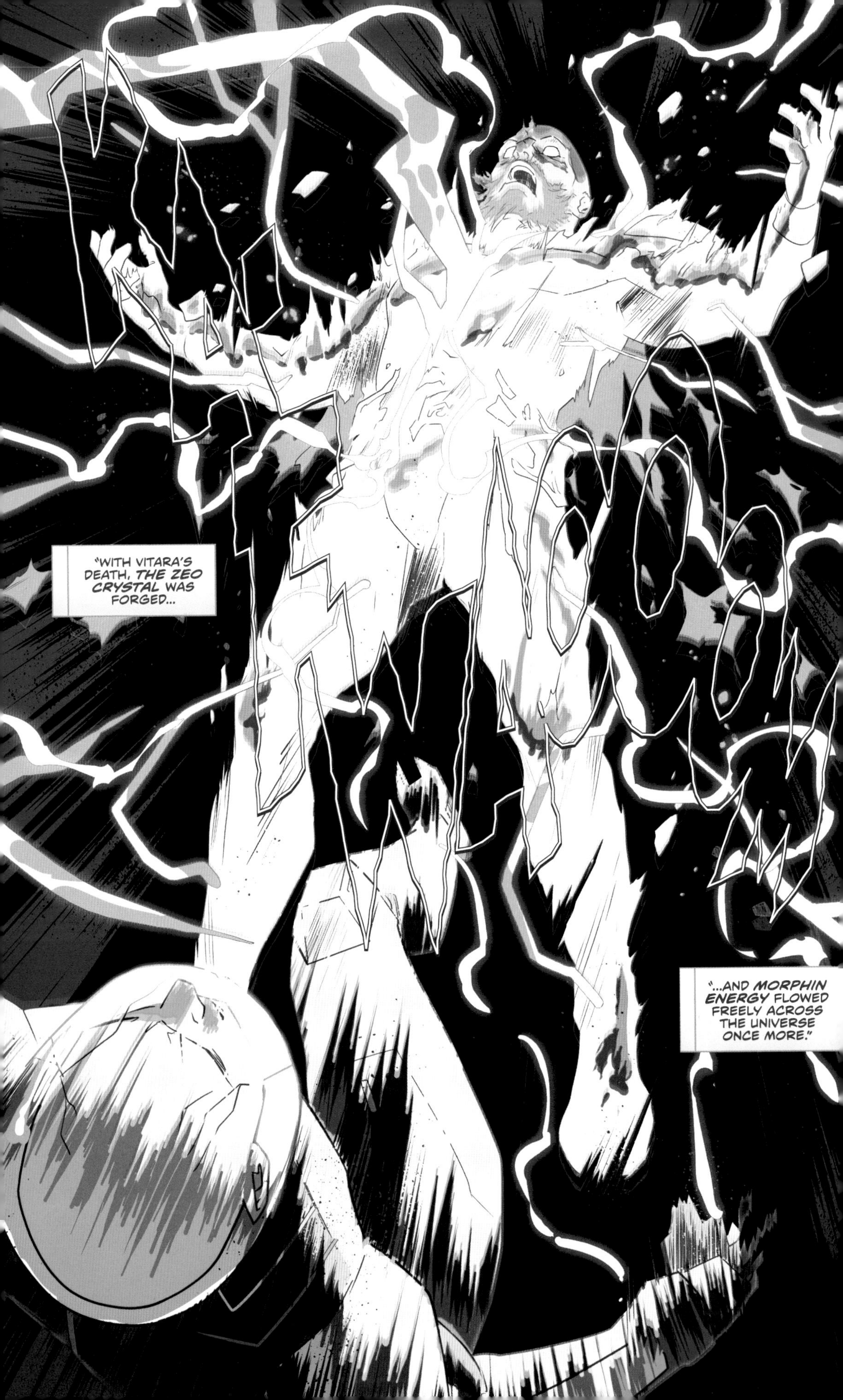
"WITH VITARA'S DEATH, *THE ZEO CRYSTAL* WAS FORGED...
"...AND *MORPHIN ENERGY* FLOWED FREELY ACROSS THE UNIVERSE ONCE MORE."

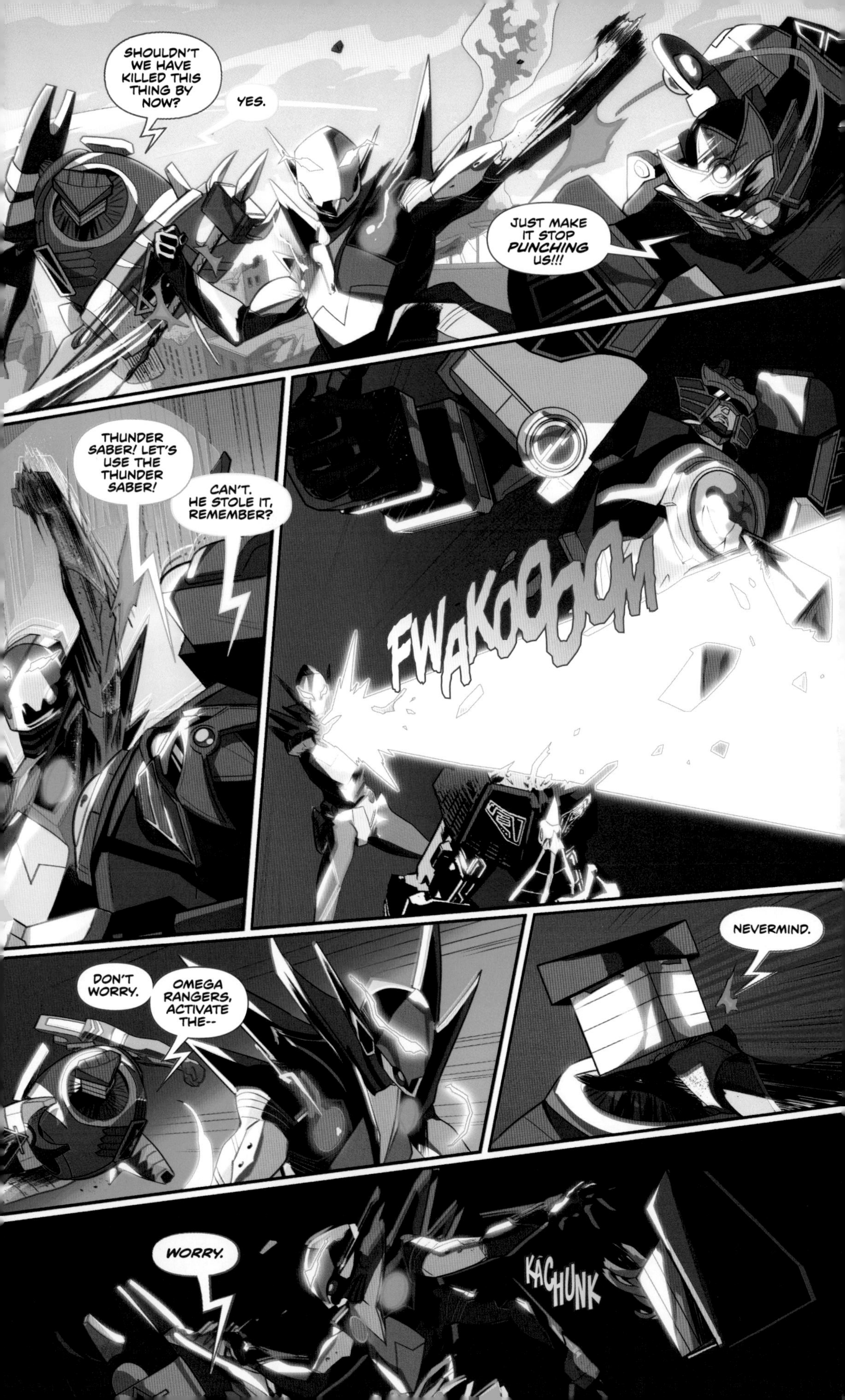
SHOULDN'T WE HAVE KILLED THIS THING BY NOW?
YES.
JUST MAKE IT STOP PUNCHING US!!!
THUNDER SABER! LET'S USE THE THUNDER SABER!
CAN'T. HE STOLE IT, REMEMBER?
FWAKOOOOM
DON'T WORRY.
OMEGA RANGERS, ACTIVATE THE--
NEVERMIND.
WORRY.
KACHUNK

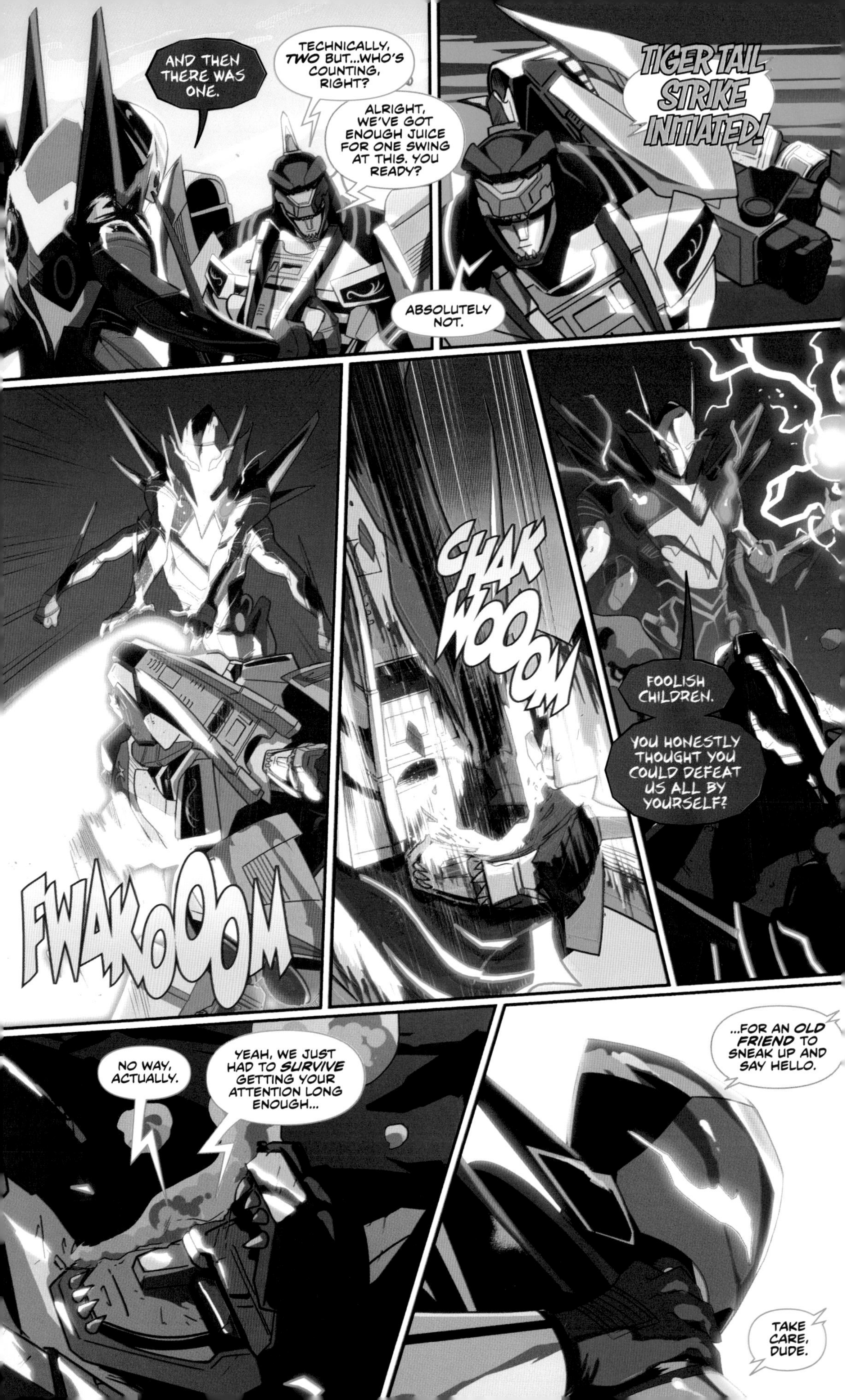

AND THEN THERE WAS ONE.
TECHNICALLY, TWO BUT...WHO'S COUNTING, RIGHT?
ALRIGHT, WE'VE GOT ENOUGH JUICE FOR ONE SWING AT THIS. YOU READY?
ABSOLUTELY NOT.
TIGER TAIL STRIKE INITIATED!
FWAKOOOM
CHAK WOOOOM
FOOLISH CHILDREN.
YOU HONESTLY THOUGHT YOU COULD DEFEAT US ALL BY YOURSELF?
NO WAY, ACTUALLY.
YEAH, WE JUST HAD TO SURVIVE GETTING YOUR ATTENTION LONG ENOUGH...
...FOR AN OLD FRIEND TO SNEAK UP AND SAY HELLO.
TAKE CARE, DUDE.

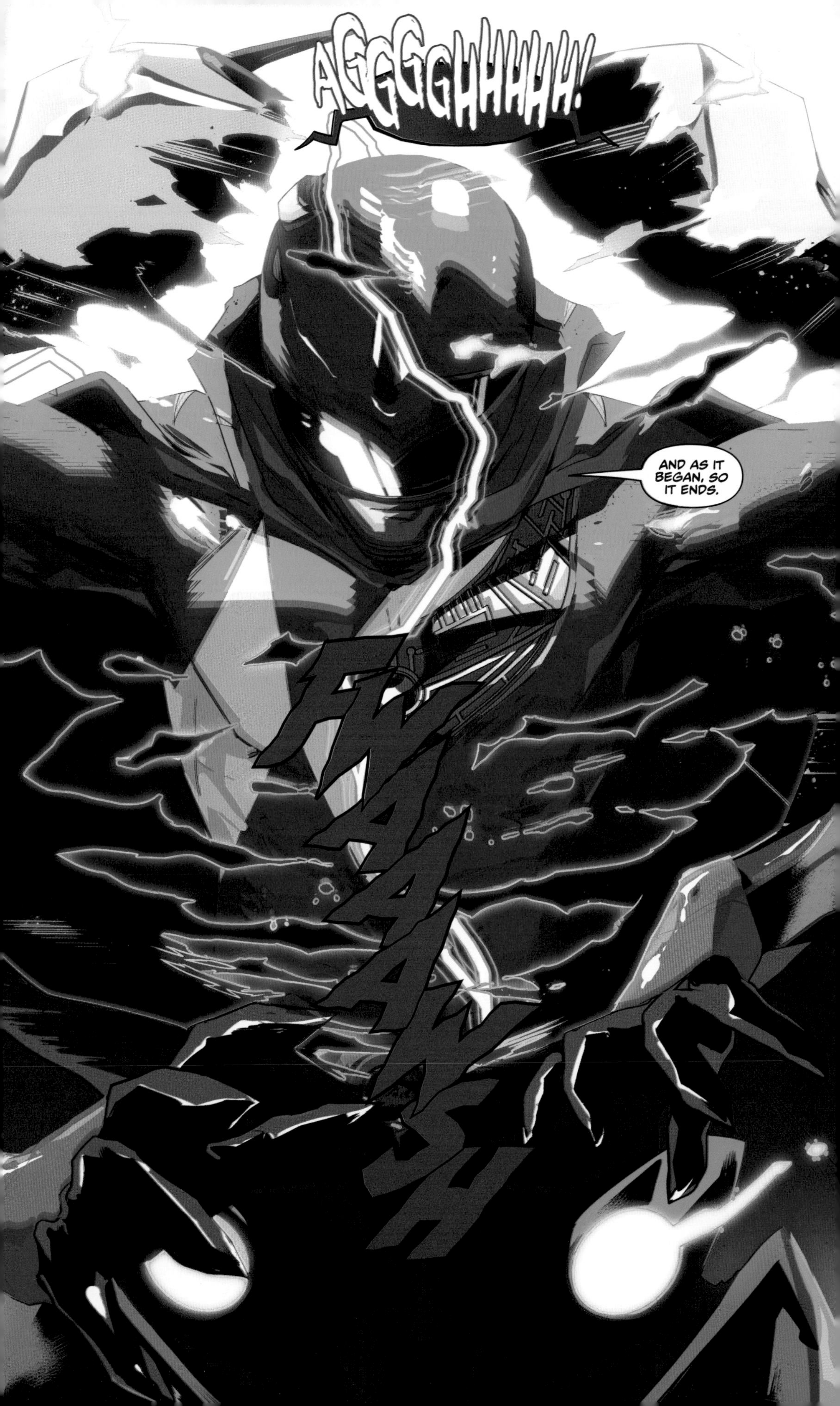
AGGGGHHHHH!
AND AS IT BEGAN, SO IT ENDS.
FWAAAASHH

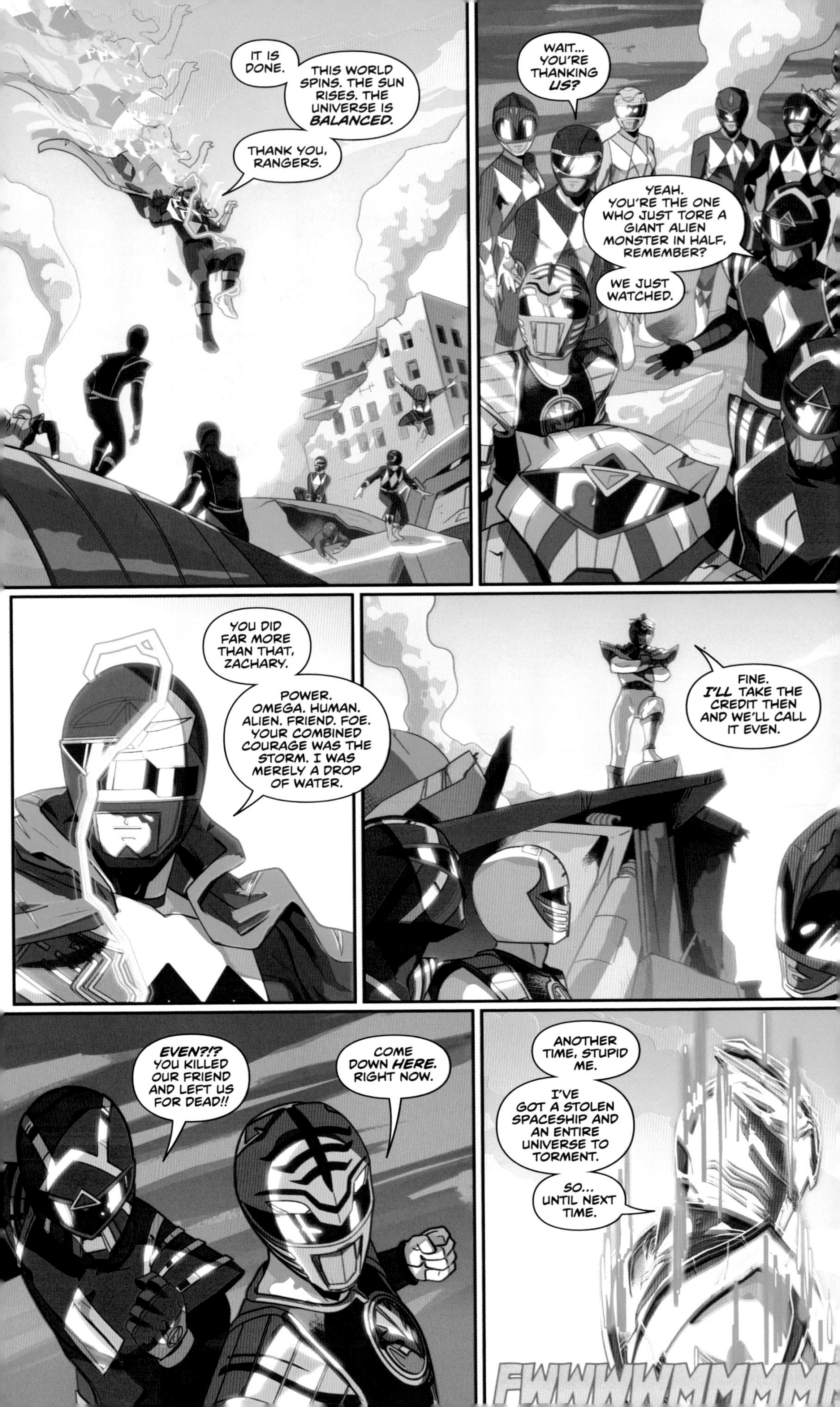
IT IS DONE.
THIS WORLD SPINS. THE SUN RISES. THE UNIVERSE IS BALANCED.
THANK YOU, RANGERS.
WAIT... YOU'RE THANKING US?
YEAH. YOU'RE THE ONE WHO JUST TORE A GIANT ALIEN MONSTER IN HALF, REMEMBER?
WE JUST WATCHED.
YOU DID FAR MORE THAN THAT, ZACHARY.
POWER. OMEGA. HUMAN. ALIEN. FRIEND. FOE. YOUR COMBINED COURAGE WAS THE STORM. I WAS MERELY A DROP OF WATER.
FINE. I'LL TAKE THE CREDIT THEN AND WE'LL CALL IT EVEN.
EVEN?!? YOU KILLED OUR FRIEND AND LEFT US FOR DEAD!!
COME DOWN HERE. RIGHT NOW.
ANOTHER TIME, STUPID ME.
I'VE GOT A STOLEN SPACESHIP AND AN ENTIRE UNIVERSE TO TORMENT.
SO... UNTIL NEXT TIME.
FWWWWMMMMM

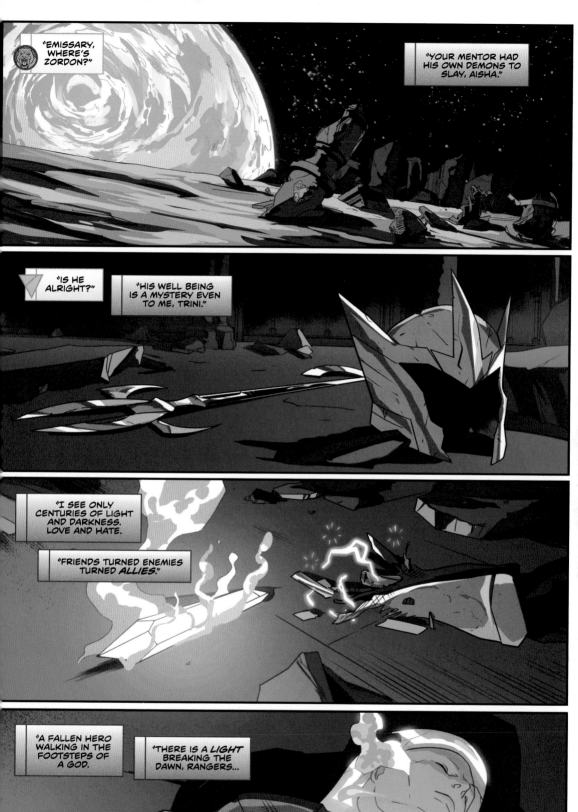

"EMISSARY, WHERE'S ZORDON?"

"YOUR MENTOR HAD HIS OWN DEMONS TO SLAY, AISHA."

"IS HE ALRIGHT?"

"HIS WELL BEING IS A MYSTERY EVEN TO ME, TRINI."

"I SEE ONLY CENTURIES OF LIGHT AND DARKNESS. LOVE AND HATE.

"FRIENDS TURNED ENEMIES TURNED ALLIES."

"A FALLEN HERO WALKING IN THE FOOTSTEPS OF A GOD.

"THERE IS A LIGHT BREAKING THE DAWN, RANGERS...

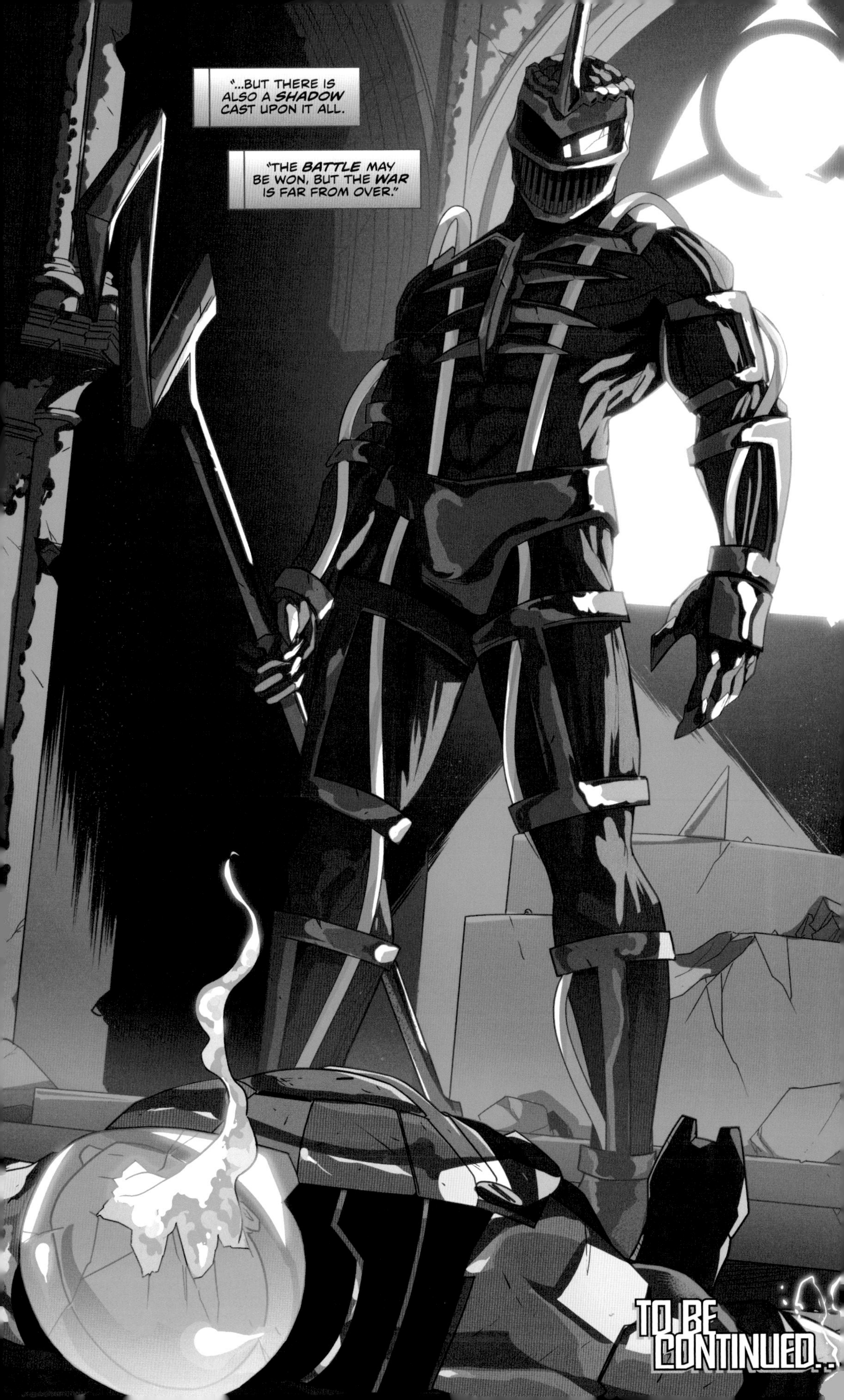
"...BUT THERE IS ALSO A SHADOW CAST UPON IT ALL.
"THE BATTLE MAY BE WON, BUT THE WAR IS FAR FROM OVER."
TO BE CONTINUED...

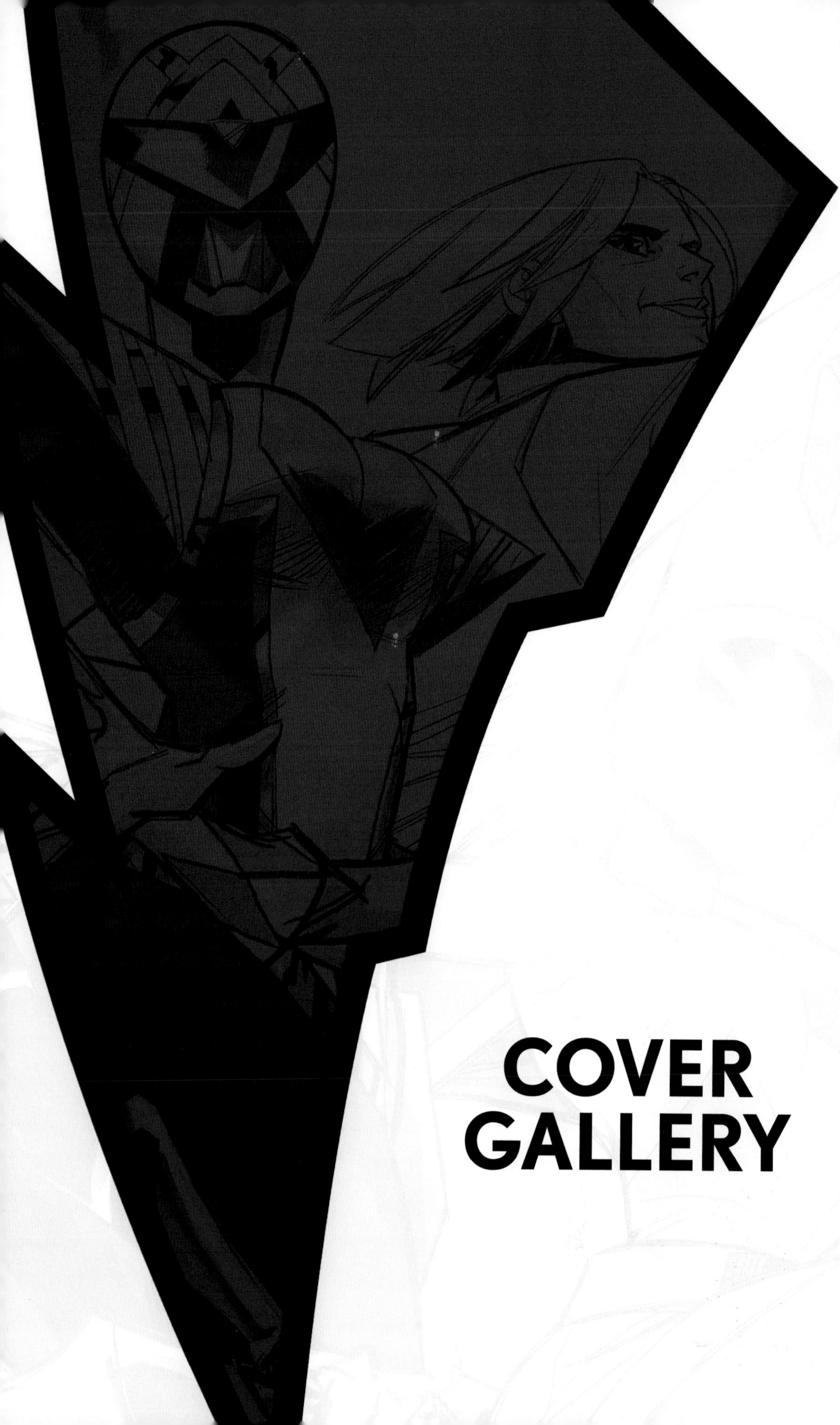

COVER GALLERY

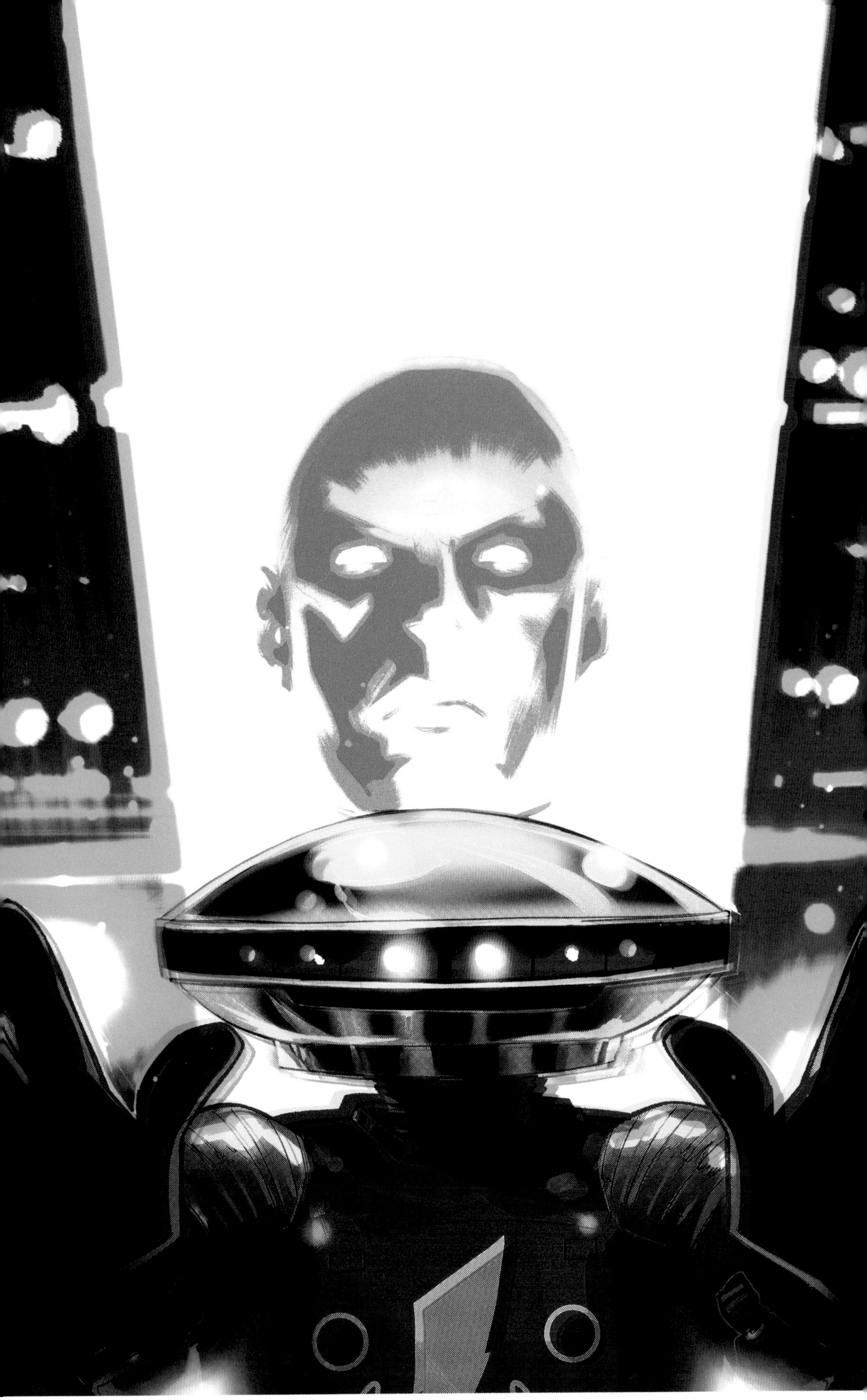

ELEONORA CARLINI MIGHTY MORPHIN #13 VARIANT COVER

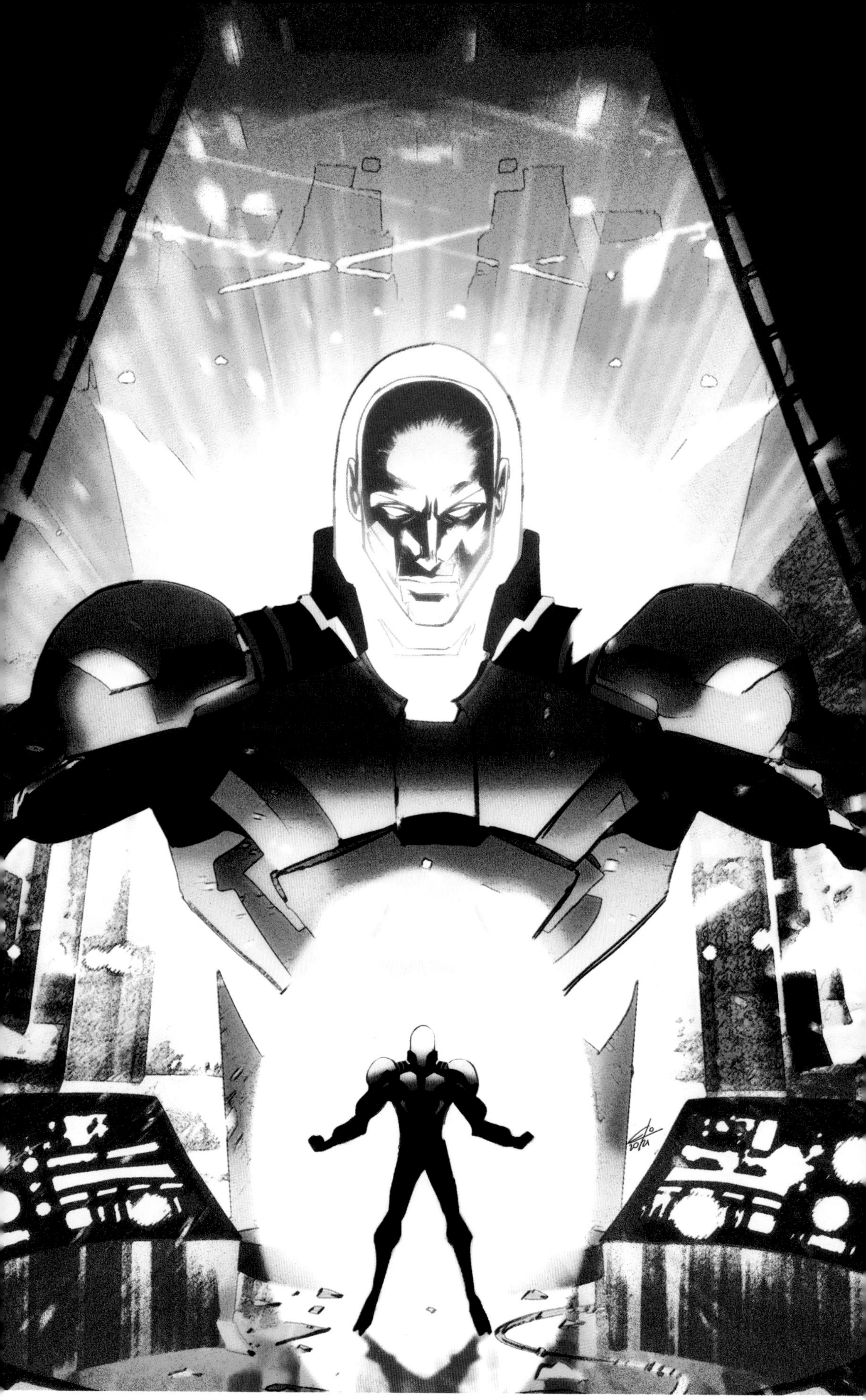

ELEONORA CARLINI MIGHTY MORPHIN #14 VARIANT COVER

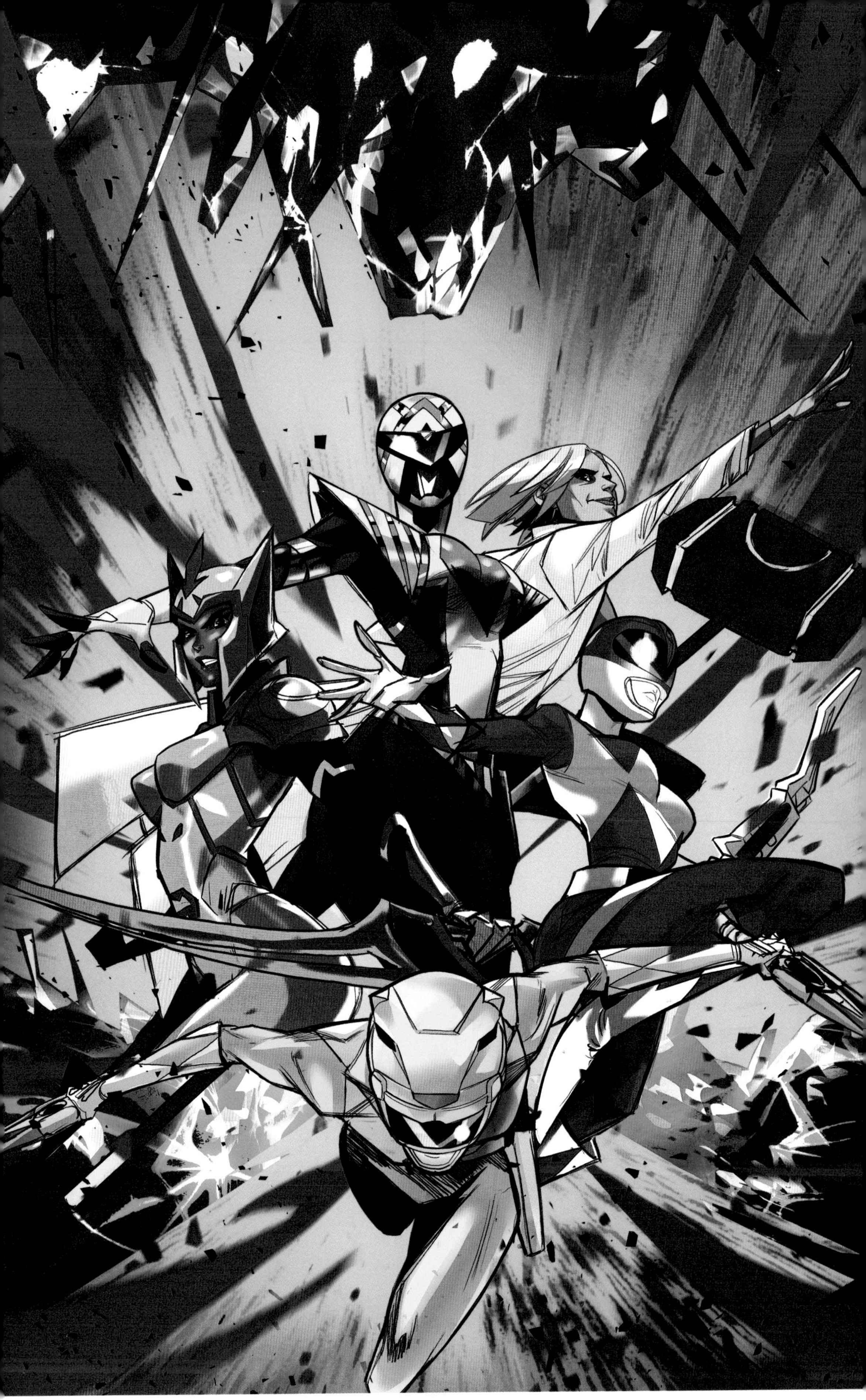

ELEONORA CARLINI MIGHTY MORPHIN #15 VARIANT COVER

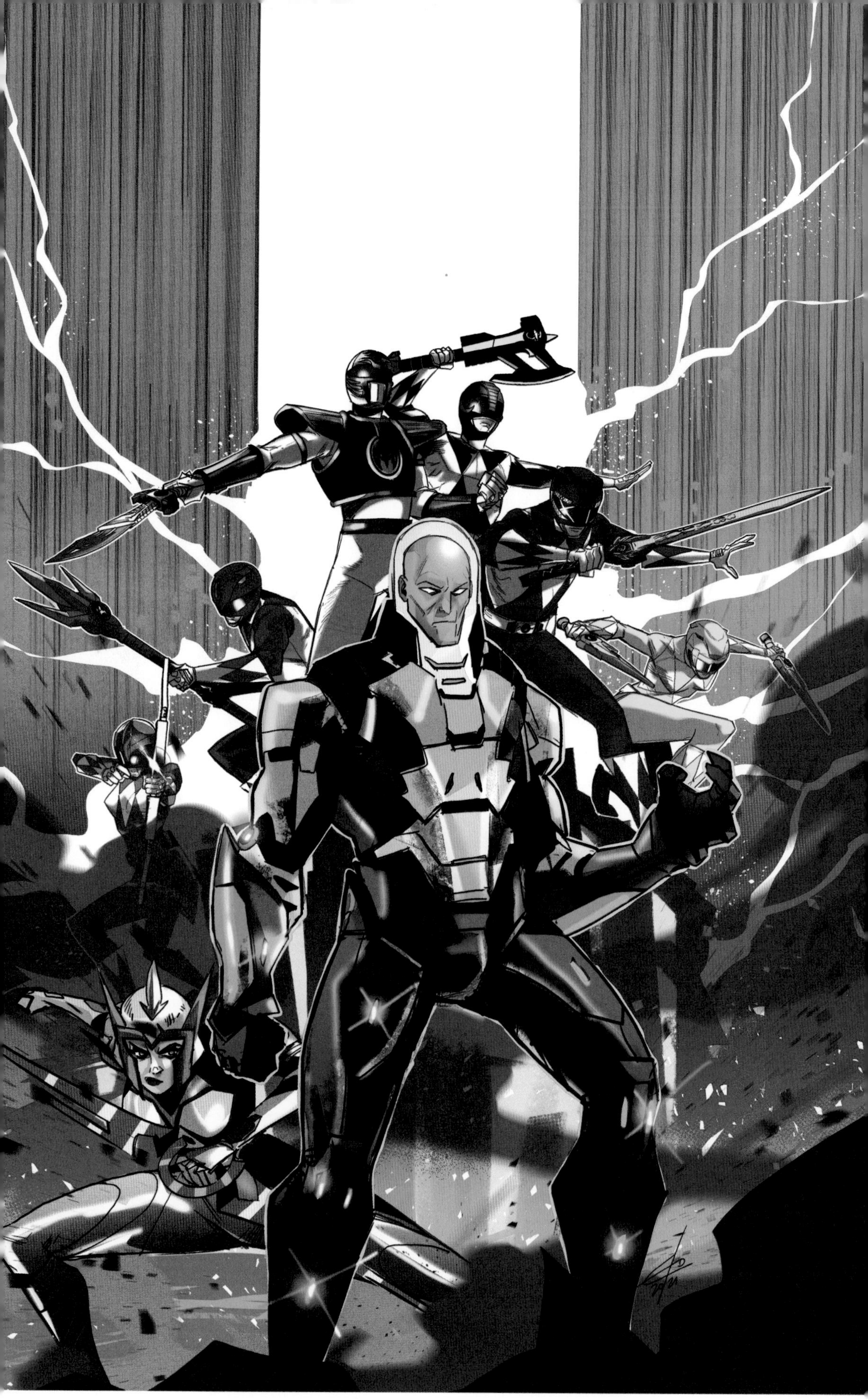

ELEONORA CARLINI MIGHTY MORPHIN #16VARIANT COVER

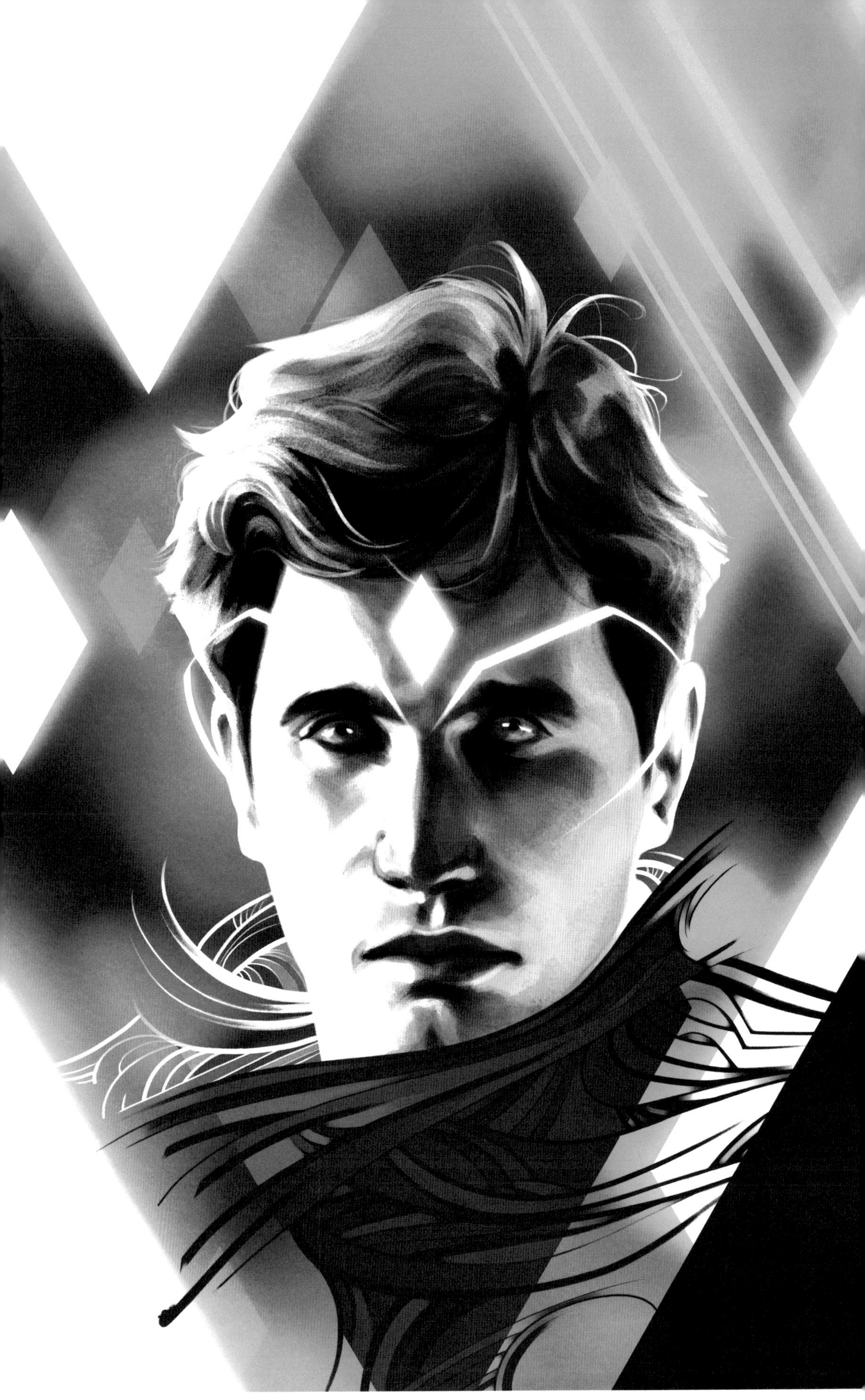

GOÑI MONTES MIGHTY MORPHIN #13 VARIANT COVER

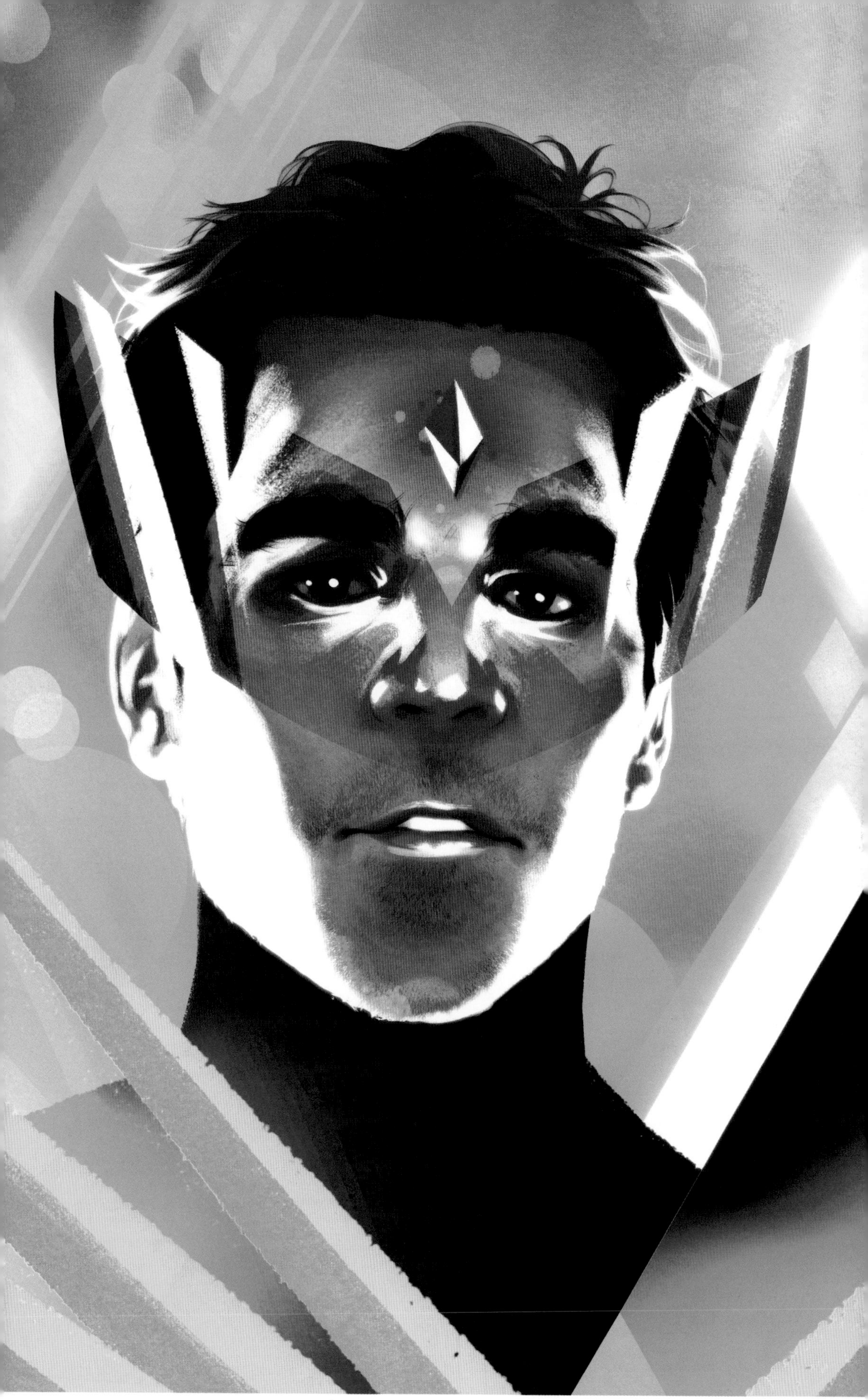

GOÑI MONTES MIGHTY MORPHIN #15 VARIANT COVER

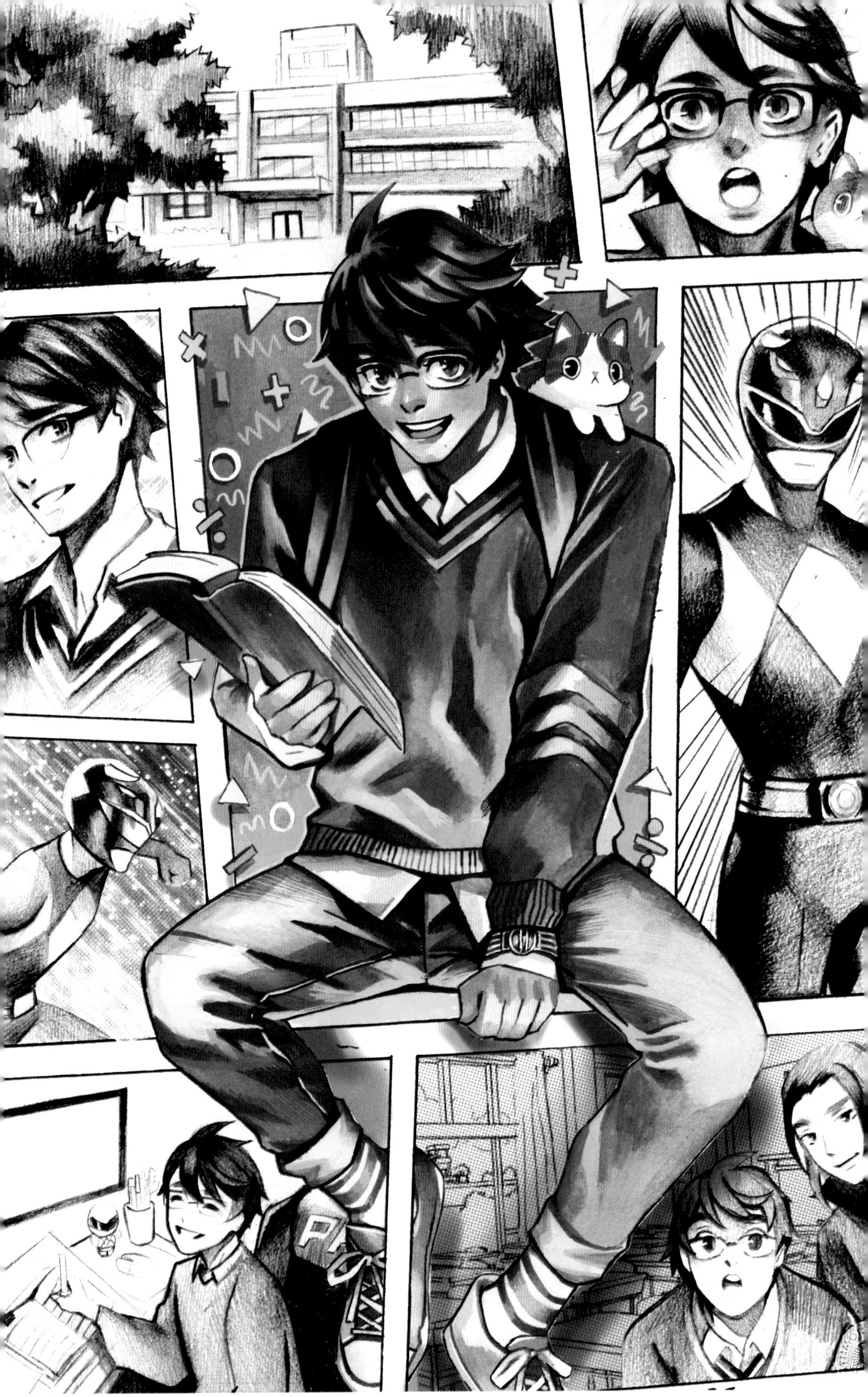

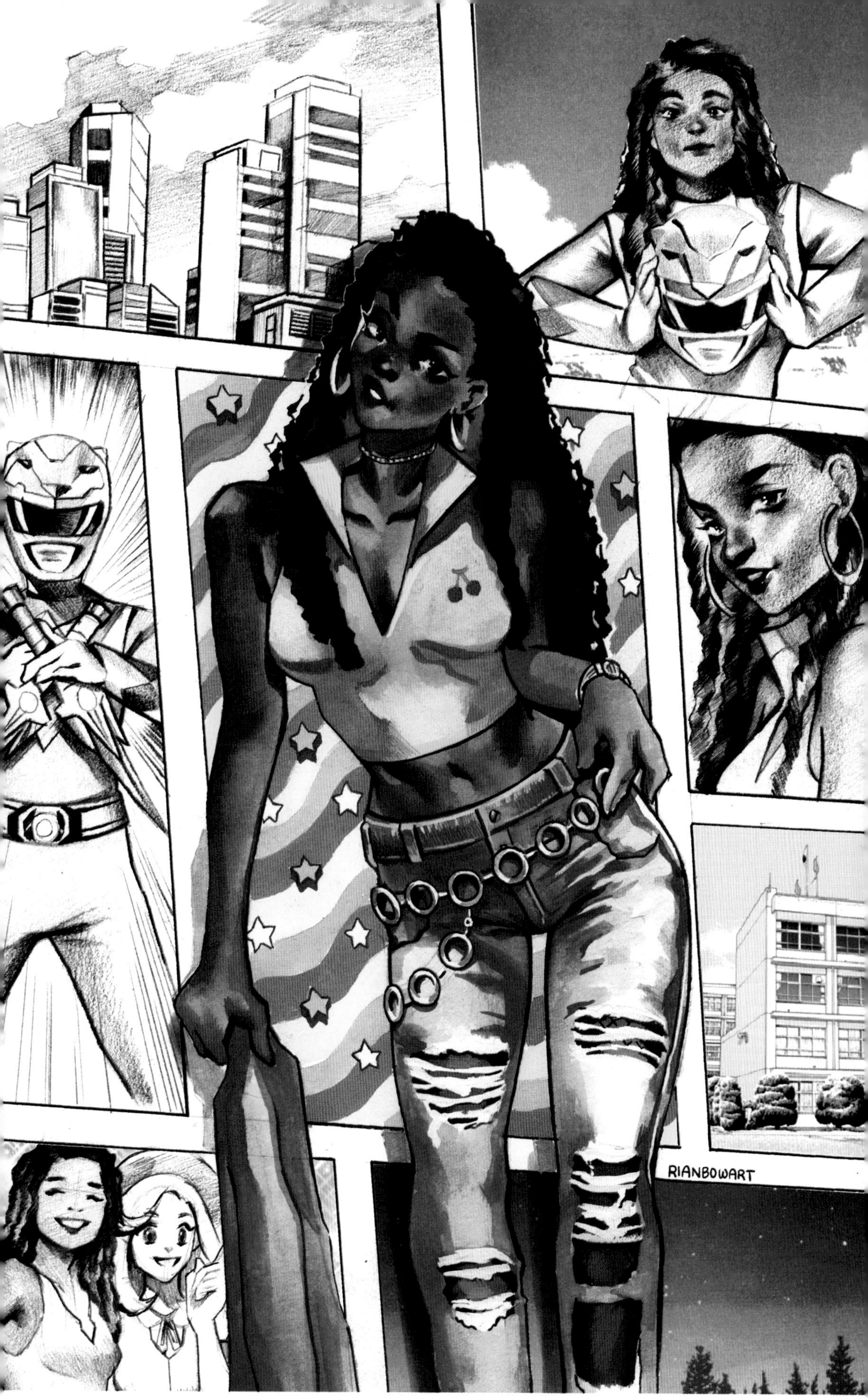
RIANBOWART

RIAN GONZALES MIGHTY MORPHIN #16 VARIANT COVER

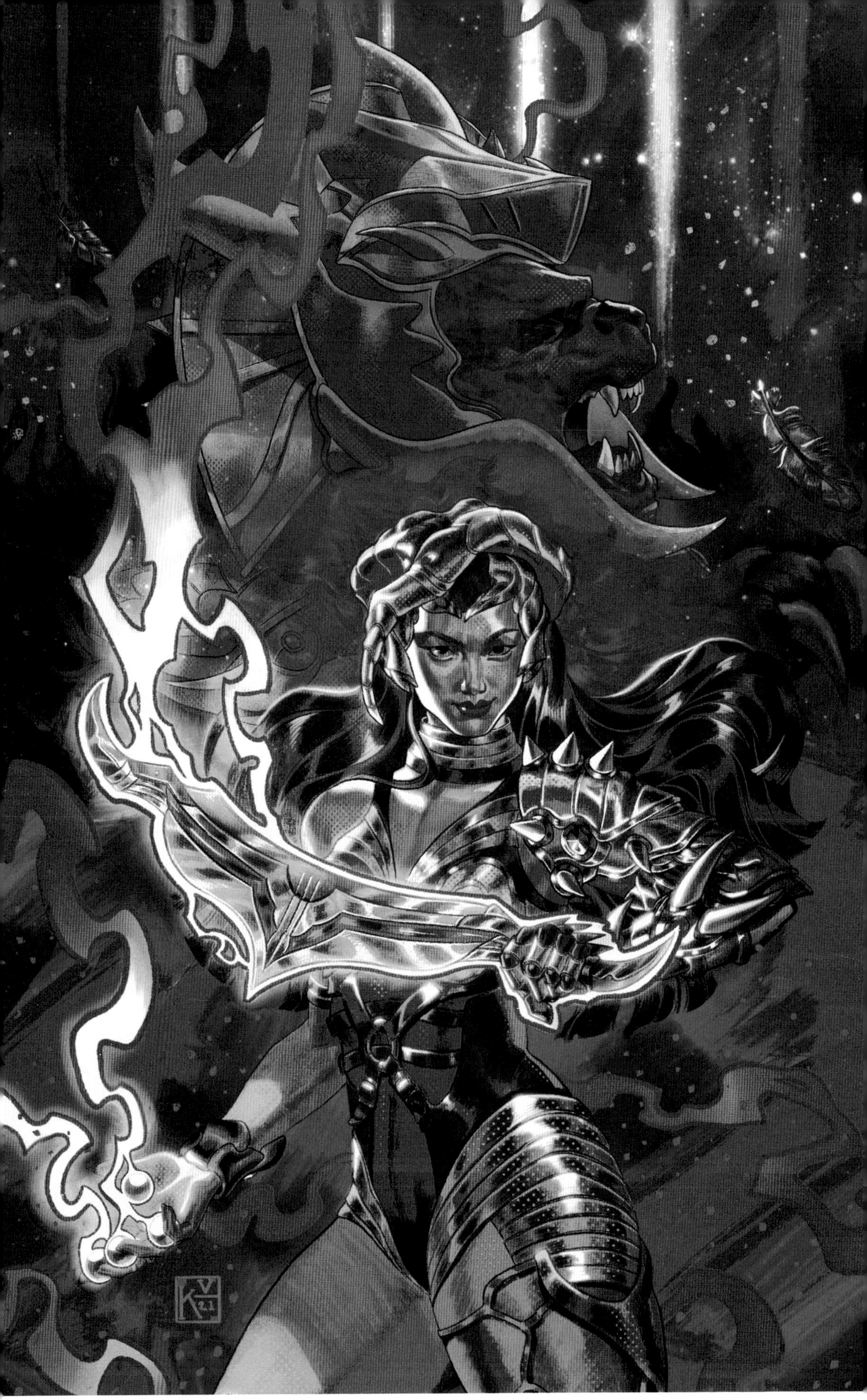
KV
21

KEYLA VALERIO MIGHTY MORPHIN #14 VARIANT COVER

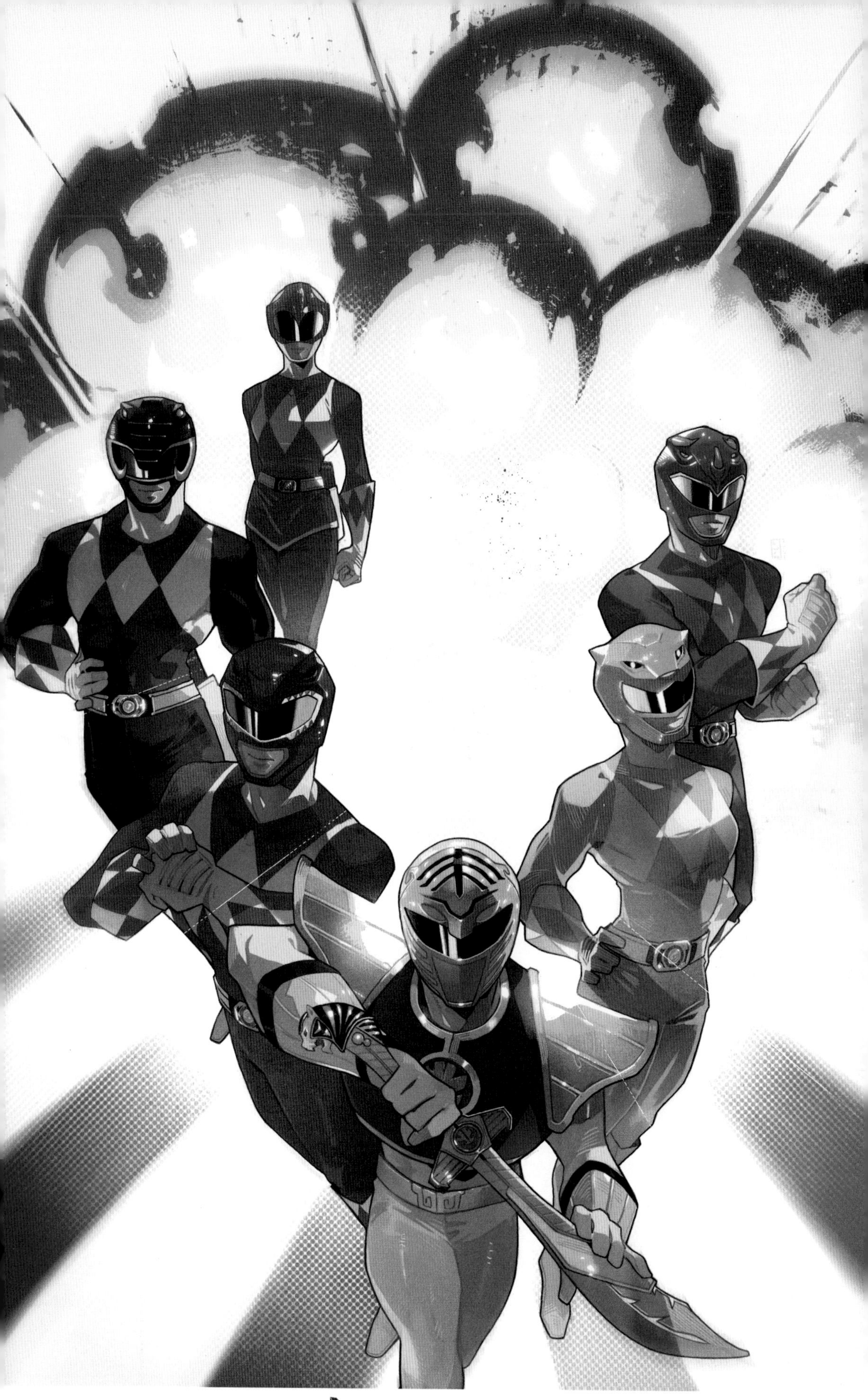

JO MI-GYEONG MIGHTY MORPHIN #16 VARIANT COVER

DISCOVER
MORE POWER RANGERS!

HIGGINS • PRASETYA • HERMS
ORLANDO • HOWELL • LAWSON
MIGHTY MORPHIN
POWER RANGERS
VOLUME ONE
INTRODUCTION BY POWER RANGERS EXECUTIVE PRODUCER JUDD "CHIP" LYNN

HIGGINS • PRASETYA
SILAS • HERMS
VALENZA • ORLANDO
HOWELL • LAWSON
MIGHTY MORPHIN
POWER RANGERS
VOLUME TWO

FLETCHER
THOMPSON
HOWARD
DI NICUOLO
STERN
MIGHTY MORPHIN
POWER RANGERS
PINK
INTRODUCTION BY AMY JO JOHNSON KIMBERLY HART, THE ORIGINAL PINK RANGER

POWER RANGERS
RYAN PARROTT LUCAS WERNECK JOANA LAFUENTE

MIGHTY MORPHIN
POWER RANGERS
POSTER BOOK
FEATURING 20 REMOVABLE POSTERS

PARROTT • MORA • ANGULO
SABAN'S
GO GO POWER RANGERS
VOLUME ONE

Mighty Morphin Power Rangers
Kyle Higgins, Hendry Prasetya, Matt Herms
Volume 1
ISBN: 978-1-60886-893-3 | $19.99
Volume 2
ISBN: 978-1-60886-942-8 | $16.99
Volume 3
ISBN: 978-1-60886-977-0 | $16.99
Volume 4
ISBN: 978-1-68415-031-1 | $16.99

Mighty Morphin Power Rangers: Pink
Kelly Thompson, Brenden Fletcher, Tini Howard, Daniele Di Nicuolo
ISBN: 978-1-60886-952-7 | $19.99

Saban's Go Go Power Rangers
Ryan Parrott, Dan Mora
Volume 1
ISBN: 978-1-68415-193-6 | $16.99

Saban's Power Rangers: Aftershock
Ryan Parrott, Lucas Werneck
ISBN: 978-1-60886-937-4 | $14.99

Mighty Morphin Power Rangers Poster Book
Goñi Montes, Jamal Campbell, Joe Quinones
ISBN: 978-1-60886-966-4 | $19.99

Mighty Morphin Power Rangers Adult Coloring Book
Goñi Montes, Jamal Campbell, Hendry Prasetya
ISBN: 978-1-60886-955-8 | $16.99

Mighty Morphin Power Rangers Year One: Deluxe HC
Kyle Higgins, Hendry Prasetya, Steve Orlando
ISBN: 978-1-68415-012-0 | $75.00

BOOM! STUDIOS

AVAILABLE AT YOUR LOCAL COMICS SHOP AND BOOKSTORE
Find a comic shop near you at www.comicshoplocator.com
WWW.**BOOM-STUDIOS**.COM

Licensed by: Hasbro

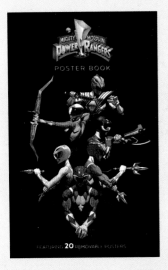